The Encyclopedia of

MISTRESSES

The Encyclopedia of

MISTRESSES

Dawn B. Sova, Ph.D.

Robson Books

This book is dedicated to
my son Rob Gregor

This edition first published in Great Britain in 2001 by Robson Books,
10 Blenheim Court, Brewery Road, London N7 9NY

A member of the Chrysalis Group plc

British Library Cataloguing in Publication Data
A catalogue record for this title is available from the British Library.

ISBN 1 86105 387 8

Typeset in 11/14pt Wiess by FiSH Books, London WC1
Printed by Bell & Bain Ltd., Glasgow

Acknowledgements

Sincere appreciation belongs to my agent, Bert Holtje of James Peters Associates, Inc., for encouraging and supporting my pursuit of this topic. I am equally grateful to Daniel Bial and Chris Steiner, editors at Longmeadow Press, for their patience in extending deadlines and quick responses when just one more mistress story needed to be added. Their skills and talents as editors shaped and molded this book, giving it the form required by the substance.

Invaluable assistance was provided by the numerous library friends whom I have made in the course of researching such a work. To I. Macarthur Nickles, Director of the Garfield (NJ) Library, goes my award for patience and perseverance for his interest and professional skills in helping me to hunt down often impossible-to-find sources. The following individuals have also performed near-miracles in obtaining books, pamphlets, and other materials from libraries all over the United States: Karen Calandriello, Mary Ann Cali, Patricia Gelinski, Linda Jackson and Kathleen Zalenski of the Garfield (NJ)

Acknowledgements

Library; Penny Kaplan, Robert Nedswick, and Gale Zimmer of the Maurice Pine (Fair Lawn, NJ) Library. I would have never received any of these books had not Mrs. Angela Miranda of the Garfield Public Library faithfully called me, sometimes several times daily, when books arrived.

In addition, Mr. Fred Pernell of the Still Pictures Branch of the National Archives, Mr. Jerry Kearns of the Library of Congress, and Ms. Sharon Farrell of the Grover Cleveland Home and Museum offered suggestions and sources to contact for photos and additional information.

Although last in mention, my family is most important in appreciation, for they provided the love and encouragement which kept me sane as the deadlines loomed. My son Rob Gregor has been an irreplaceable assistant in researching, copying, and generally doing the groundwork for this book. My parents, Emil and Violet Sova, provided the safe harbor and quiet place to escape the pressures of writing this book.

Despite their often casual concern for the mistresses of great men, the writers of histories and biographies listed in the bibliography at the end of this book must also be acknowledged. For each biography listed, there may be ten others of the same man which make no mention of the woman or women whose lives influenced the successes and achievements of the man so honored. I hope that this book sheds at least a little light on the many women who have been behind their better-known men.

Introduction

Mistress. The word evokes the image of an expensively dressed, pampered younger woman—the "other woman" whose adoring married lover showers her with gifts and passion in return for unquestioning submission to his every sexual and emotional need. The fantasy mistress is a fully sexually accessible woman who lives only to please her lover, a woman who is nurturing and understanding in contrast to the competitive and critical image of the wife. Fiction such as Fanny Hurst's *Backstreet* popularizes the fantasy of the passive mistress and ignores the diverse women who become mistresses and their multitude of reasons for doing so. Real mistresses are not so uniform—nor so passive. Some women opt to become mistresses because only in that role can they become part of their lovers' lives, while for others the lures are the promises of luxury and ease. Still others find that the role of mistress is an entry level position to power and fame.

Whatever their motivations, and whatever their origins, the

mistresses in this book share the common trait of having become significant to history either through their own or their lovers' lives. They might have begun as prostitutes, courtesans, actresses, or slaves, but they all exert an identifiable positive or negative influence on the lives of the men with whom they are linked. Official royal mistress or unacknowledged wife surrogate, each woman has risked social disapproval, financial uncertainty, or even the loss of her own social or political standing to follow her heart, for whatever her reasons. Reviled or revered, these women have used their talents in the bedroom to wield often heady power in the throne room, the battlefield, the boardroom, and even in the pulpit. Their influences have forged political treaties, solidified or disrupted powerful alliances, changed national boundaries, and created as well as toppled kings.

Beauty, sex, ambition, wit, or friendship—all have been used by women to cross class barriers. For every aristocratic Madame du Chateaubriand or Lady Castlemaine, there is a lower class serving girl or prostitute such as Nell Gwynn or Lola Montez who has managed to leave her imprint on history. Cleopatra, a ruler in her own right, used her influence as mistress to both Mark Antony and Julius Caesar to gain certain advantages that political negotiations could not.

Mistresses have changed history in all countries, in all ages. An insult to Aspasia, mistress of Pericles, the ruler of Greece's Golden Age, is said to have been the cause of the lengthy and costly Peloponnesian Wars. Maria Walewska, a married Polish aristocrat, caused Napoleon Bonaparte more anguish than his losses at the Battle of Waterloo as she saved her beloved Poland. Wallis Warfield Simpson, a plain-looking, twice-divorced American, captured the heart of a king of England who gladly gave up his throne to keep her. The young prostitutes, Mandy Rice-Davies and Christine Keeler, nearly toppled the British government in the John Profumo scandal. Okoi, the mistress of Japanese Prime Minister Katsura, was used by his opponents as their excuse for eventually ousting him from power. American history also includes numerous women who, as mistresses, have influenced such power brokers as Thomas Jefferson, Alexander Hamilton, Warren Harding, Grover Cleveland, Henry Ford, Franklin Delano Roosevelt, John Fitzgerald Kennedy, Wilbur Mills, and others. Would our early government have developed differently had Benjamin Franklin remained in France with his beloved Madame Helvetius? Could slavery have ended decades earlier had Thomas Jefferson acknowledged his love for Sally Hemings and their children? How might our history have differed had Dwight D. Eisenhower left his wife to marry Kay Summersby, thus sabotaging his political career?

Mistresses have also had great impact on the worlds of art and literature. Jean-Jacques Rousseau might have remained the poor apprentice watchmaker from Geneva, had he not attracted the sophisticated. Madame Warens, who nurtured both his mind and his body. James Joyce might never have written his great novels had not Nora Barnacle nurtured his artistic temperament, cleaned up his physical world, and aroused his libido. Pablo Picasso might have omitted a complete stage of his career without the inspiration and loving presence of Françoise Gilot.

Despite their vast influence, throughout most of history the names and the lives of mistresses have been relegated to the shadows of the men with whom they were involved, when they were mentioned at all. To learn even the barest details about the lives of the mistresses, a researcher has had to comb through numerous texts and references to the men in their lives, piecing together significant dates, events, and experiences. Few of the mistresses have attracted interest for their own stories, aside from those born into powerful families or those who have achieved unusual fame or notoriety on their own.

The entries in this *Encyclopedia* acknowledge the famous mistresses who have become a part of history as well as the many forgotten women whose lives were subsumed by their lovers. There are numerous surprise couplings between the famous and the near-famous which defy convention as well as the imagination. Some of the stories have happy endings, while others, although true, seem almost contrived in the lessons which they teach regarding the wages of sin. While some mistresses thrive, becoming upwardly mobile in their relationships, others play the role of wife with greater fidelity and fewer rights than many legally married women of their time. Women are discarded, and they discard men. Even the ways in which the mistresses end their days vary greatly. Some, like Barbara Villiers or Mrs. Fitzherbert, are comfortably pensioned off by a king. Others, like Wallis Simpson, marry their kings or, as in the cases of Fredegond, Tz'u Hsi, and Wu Zi Tian, become rulers themselves. Many more, however, end their days alone, poor, and unloved, having been replaced by their lovers and forgotten. In short, the characters and the circumstances are extremely varied, and therein lies the fascination with the mistress.

A

Abélard, Peter (1079–1142) See Héloïse.

Agrippina the Younger (A.D. 15–59) Although born to nobility during the reign of Augustus Caesar, Agrippina was exiled from Rome when Caligula came to power. Her properties were confiscated, forcing the young noblewoman to raise her son, Nero, in impoverished circumstances. This humiliation, coupled with innate ambition, made Agrippina determined to use Nero to achieve prominence, whatever the price. Her opportunity arose in A.D. 41, when Caligula was assassinated by the Imperial guardsmen and her Uncle Claudius was catapulted into power. Agrippina rejoined the Roman Imperial Family and bided her time as she raised her son.

Using innuendo and evidence presented through intermediaries, Agrippina made certain that Claudius was fully informed of the numerous sexual dalliances of his wife, Messalina. By A.D. 48, Claudius could no longer stand being cuckolded, and Messalina was executed for her infidelities. Even though she was his niece, Agrippina aggressively offered Claudius emotional and sexual solace, tantalizing him so that he ignored the taboo of legal incest. She conquered his heart and his body, besting even Caligula's widow, Lolia, who would have brought him powerful political allies. To further establish her future power and to ease Nero's way to the throne, Agrippina convinced Claudius to marry his daughter Octavia to her son.

Only one obstacle remained to making Nero the next emperor. Claudius' ten-year-old son, Brittanicus, stood next in line for the throne as the only legitimate male heir. Once again, using all her charms and sexual skills, Agrippina convinced Claudius in A.D. 54 to adopt her now-adult son, a move which legally made Nero the eldest son and heir to the throne. Before Claudius could reconsider his move, Agrippina poisoned the unsuspecting man during a celebratory dinner a few days later, and Nero became the emperor.

Nero, as emperor, simply delivered the speeches written for him and performed the official duties while Agrippina wielded the power. He was content to play the role of Emperor and to allow his mother her way until the two clashed over his decision to abandon Octavia and take an ex-slave as his mistress. Fueled by his new-found desire, Nero refuted his mother's warning that public disapproval of his actions would cost him power. At first he banished her from court, then he became paranoid that she was plotting against him. His mistress, Poppaea Sabina, urged him to murder his mother.

Nero invited Agrippina to court, then sent her home in a poorly constructed ship designed to sink, but Agrippina cheated death by swimming to shore. Soldiers sent by Nero, however, awaited her on shore, and stabbed her to death. Thus, Agrippina's success in gaining political power for her son and herself ended in her death—and a rocky time for Rome under the eccentric tyrannies of Nero.

Alba, Duchess of (1762–1802) Heiress and successor to both the substantial fortune and the highly respected name of the Spanish house of Alba, the duchess was popularly addressed as Maria Teresa Cayetana despite having been baptized with thirty-one Christian names soon after her birth. Her great beauty seduced the hearts of many men and she might never have even looked in the direction of the deaf, ugly, and generally ill-tempered painter Francisco Goya, had he not become a social prize over whom even the Queen of Spain and other noble ladies wrangled.

An independent woman with no formal education but a good amount of common sense, the Duchess of Alba first married at the age of thirteen but kept control of most of her huge inheritance, thereby guaranteeing her continued independence. She dabbled eagerly in court politics and made Queen Maria Luisa furious by stealing one of the queen's young lovers. Adding insult to injury, the young duchess then had copies of the queen's latest French gowns made, dressed her household maids in them, and paraded them through the park near the royal palace.

The true conquest, however, was to steal the loyalty of the prominent painter Francisco Goya from the court, and the duchess went about capturing her prize in her typically unique way. Rather than ask him to paint her portrait, as many women before had, the duchess began their relationship by asking him to apply her makeup. Thus, she had him make her into the masterpiece, instead of a painted copy.

After that, the Duchess of Alba became a favorite subject of Goya, who painted her in a range of poses, both sensual and beatified. In turn, he received gold and silver platters filled with delicacies from the kitchens of the Alba household. After the Duke of Alba died in 1796, the thirty-four-year-old duchess retired to her home in official mourning, but it seems that Goya joined her, for he disappeared for six months during this period, and sketches dated from this time are all of the Alba household.

The affair appears to have ended after only these few months, but Goya and the duchess retained a patron-patroness relationship for several years after, and biographers suggest that they may also have remained casual lovers. In 1802, when the Duchess of Alba died amid rumors that she may have been poisoned by her archrival, Queen Maria Luisa, Goya sketched plans for her mausoleum. The drawing remained in his collection, but the monument was never built.

Alexander VI, Pope (1431–1503) See **de Cattanei, Vanozza;** **Farnese, Giulia.**

Alexander I, Tsar (1777–1825) See de Krudner, Baroness Julie.

Alfonso XXIII, King of Spain (1886–1941) See **Otero, Caroline.**

Antony, Marc (83 B.C.–30 B.C.) See **Cleopatra.**

Armand, Inessa (1879–1920) Elizabeth d'Herbenville was born in Paris of a French father and a Scottish mother. When her father died, Elizabeth's French aunt and Scottish grandmother took positions as teachers in the home of a wealthy Moscow textile manufacturer, Eugene Armand, who lived in a mansion surrounded by lush woods overlooking a lake. There, Elizabeth polished her talents, and she acquired the affectionate nickname, "Inessa," from the Armand family. She became an accomplished pianist, and could speak Russian, German, English, and French without discernible accents. She was described as having unruly, dark chestnut hair, great hypnotic eyes, and a wild spirit.

When Inessa was eighteen, she married Alexander Evgenevich, the second son of the family, who was two years her senior. In the next five years, she bore him five children, three boys and two girls, and lived the life of a wealthy matron. Dissatisfaction set in, however, and bored with her wealth and limited society, she became involved in social reform working with prostitutes. In 1904 she left her husband and children to study in Stockholm with feminist leader Ellen Key, but such study paled in contrast to the excitement of revolution which she found in the Russian colony of Stockholm. She was soon converted to Bolshevism and returned to Russia in 1905 to join the revolution. She was arrested and spent nine months in prison. She resumed her revolutionary activities as a courier for the Bolsheviks after her release and was again arrested in 1907, this time on the charge of undermining the armed forces.

Her husband bailed her out, but she continued to work with the Bolsheviks, and at her next arrest was exiled for two years to the far northern prison of Arkhangelsk. She managed to escape before serving the two years and fled to Paris with two of her children, son Andrey and daughter Ina. She was welcomed with open arms by the Russian colony now headed by Vladimir Ilich Lenin. Her exploits made thirty-year-old

Inessa a true revolutionary and he found her an apartment next to his. Lenin's wife, Olga Krupskaya, took an immediate liking to Inessa and her children, and later in life offered to leave Lenin in order to free him so that he could marry Inessa. He refused the offer.

In 1911 Inessa joined Lenin in starting a school to train underground workers at Longjumeau, outside of Paris. Students were boarded with the village families, and villagers were told that the school was to give "refresher" courses to Russian schoolteachers, while in reality, these "students" were training to be revolutionaries. Inessa taught seminars on political science and she created a communal kitchen in her dining room.

In 1912 Inessa was sent to tour the Bolshevik cells in Russia, where she was again jailed but released at her husband's insistence. When she joined Lenin and his wife in Cracow, she was suffering from tuberculosis. She entered a sanatorium for treatment at Les Avants in 1914, then rejoined the revolutionary group in Berne.

Inessa became the soothing influence in Lenin's life, and she often played Beethoven's sonata, the "Appassionata," to calm him. Beyond making life easier for Lenin, Inessa took an active role in the revolution. She appeared as Lenin's representative at the International Socialist Bureau Conference in Zimmerwald in 1914 and 1915, and she served as a delegate to the 1916 conference. She returned to Russia in 1917 with Lenin and Olga.

Inessa died of typhus in the Caucasus in 1920, and her body was brought back to Moscow. Lenin was overwhelmed by grief and appeared pale and shaken at her funeral. Although he depended upon his wife for stability, Inessa had been his source of joy and the woman whom he had loved fiercely and unrelentingly. In the difficult months preceding her death, she had buoyed his spirits by sharing his daydreams of the plenty that Communism would bring to everyone.

Aspasia (?475 B.C.–?) Aspasia began her career by managing a brothel in Megara and then moved to Athens, where she opened a school in the teaching of elocution and philosophy for young women. Well-known philosophers and playwrights of the day, such as Socrates, Anaxagoras, and Euripides, also attended her classes and the dictator of the Golden Age of Athens, Pericles, soon joined them.

Aspasia (BROWN BROTHERS)

Once the already-married, forty-year-old leader met Aspasia, he decided to make her his mistress. Within months, she was pregnant with his child and had moved into his house, while his wife was hurriedly moved out and married to someone else. Aspasia was not a citizen of Athens, so Pericles couldn't marry her, but he willed all of his belongings to their son, Pericles II.

Aspasia occupied most of Pericles' time, and his political career suffered. Political enemies used their hatred of Aspasia to undermine her lover's power and she was placed on trial and charged with impiety toward the gods and with procuring young girls from good families for sexual orgies with Pericles. Further, Pericles' political enemies charged that the Peloponnesian War was fought because of a slight which the town of Megara had given to Aspasia, and which Pericles felt honor-bound to avenge. She was eventually acquitted of the charges. At her behest, Pericles convinced the legislature to legitimize her son, Pericles II. She mourned only briefly when Pericles died a short while later. Nothing more is known of her life after Pericles' death, except that she became the mistress of a wealthy sheep dealer soon after and faded into obscurity.

Astor, Mary (1906–1987) One of America's "silver screen sweethearts," she was born Lucille Vasconcellos Loughanke. Her large, seemingly innocent eyes peered out at admiring audiences to project an air of virginal young womanhood. The discovery and publication in 1936 of her personal diary revealed quite another – more interesting – side of her personality.

Beautiful and poised, Mary had been pushed into a screen career early by her father who thought that his lovely young daughter had the potential to be a star. Although she failed her initial screen test for D.W. Griffith, in 1921 she soon found work as a bit player in several silent movies which started what would become a long, if tempestuous, career. By 1924 John Barrymore used his influence to make Mary his leading lady in *Beau Brummel*, and she reciprocated by briefly becoming his leading lady in bed. Throughout the 1920s, Mary appeared in numerous movies, but her career began to wane as the silent screen gave way to talking pictures. Mary landed few movie parts until she tried her hand at a stage show which gave her the publicity that drew the attention of the studios.

While her three-year marriage to Dr. Franklyn Thorpe was deteriorating, she openly began to attend parties, theater reviews, and other public functions with playwright, critic, and director, George S. Kaufman, who was also married. In her diary, which was excerpted with relish by many of the nation's tabloids and newspapers, Mary gushed about Kaufman's "remarkable staying power" and the joys of his body against hers, pushing her to heights of "thrilling ecstasy." While the public hungrily devoured these sensational tidbits of the torrid romance, they also wondered why the lovely, delicate, and beautiful Mary raved about the unattractive Kaufman, whose thick glasses, large nose, and awkward appearance hardly seemed designed to titillate and elicit cries of rapture such as, "he is perfect," as Mary wrote in the diary after one remarkable evening.

By 1936, the time the scandal broke, her two-year relationship with Kaufman had already ended. She had just begun to strengthen her career when the diary was leaked to the newspapers. Though the trial judge refused to admit the entries as evidence in court, the press had a field day with the contents, which they somehow managed to obtain. Unlike previous stars, Mary actually benefitted from the revelations that she was a passionate, sensual woman underneath her virginal veneer. The highly publicized trial for custody of her daughter put Mary's name on the front page of every major American newspaper for weeks, and the movie industry was quick to capitalize on it. She made a string of films after this, including the one for which she is best known, *The Maltese Falcon.*

Although later films followed, her career was all but over in 1949, when she began a fight against alcoholism. She died in 1987 of complications due to pulmonary emphysema.

B

Baker, Josephine (1906–1975) Husbands, lovers, and admirers filled her life, and she was a star of the *Folies Bergères* and darling of the Jazz Age, but the woman, whom Picasso called the "Nefertiti of now," began her life in severe poverty. Josephine Baker was born in St. Louis, the illegitimate daughter of domestic worker, Carrie McDonald, and flamboyant brothel drummer, Eddie Carson. Her father drifted in and out of her life while her mother struggled to feed Josephine with whom she lived in a vacant boxcar. Josephine often scavenged for food and began work as a domestic in exchange for room and board at the age of eight. Her employer overworked Josephine and made her sleep in the cellar with the dog in a large box.

Lively and passionate, Josephine always attracted men, and she married twice before making her name on the Parisian stage. Her first marriage, at the age of thirteen, ended in divorce a year later, and she remarried at sixteen but waited years to divorce this husband, who inconveniently re-entered her life when she was about to marry Italian Count Pepito de Abatino in 1927. Her fourth husband was

French orchestra leader Jo Bouillon, with whom she entered into a marriage of convenience in 1947, as she turned forty-one and began to fear aging. Throughout her life, Joseplline had numerous brief affairs, often simultaneously, with men with whom she worked or met in her travels. Three of her more famous lovers of some duration were ragtime musician, Eubie Blake; French novelist, George Sims; and the future King of Sweden, Crown Prince Gustav VI, whom she never stopped loving and whose death in 1973 caused her anguish.

Josephine was sixteen years old and part of the road company of *Shuffle Me*, the first all-black musical to make it to Broadway, when Eubie Blake, then in his thirties and half of the successful writer-and composer team of Sissle and Blake, heard about her talent and sent a veteran dancer to review her. She had auditioned for the Broadway production a year earlier, but the producers had been unwilling to violate New York laws which prohibited the use of chorus girls under the age of sixteen. The scout from the Sissle and Blake office returned with enthusiastic praise for Josephine, who was taken out of the road company and put on Broadway. Blake became her confidant and protector, and the two remained together for three years until Josephine was recruited for "La Revue Negre" at the *Folies Bergères*. In those years, she also appeared in *Chocolate Dandies*, another Sissle and Blake hit musical. In later years, Blake said that he had fallen under her spell and that, at least with him, she had been "a one-man-at-a time girl."

After only a year in the *Folies*, Josephine was the toast of Paris and the recipient of numerous gifts of precious jewelry, money, and even a lavish apartment on the Champs-Elysées. She hired a 23-year-old journalist named George Sims to act as secretary, to clip and file her press clippings and to answer her piled-up correspondence. Sims had just begun to publish mystery stories under the pseudonym of George Simenon; he later went on to write over five hundred books. His professional relationship with Josephine soon became personal as he found it difficult to retain his composure and answer letters while a nude Josephine walked around the apartment office. He was tall, broad-shouldered, and handsome, and Josephine soon made her own interest in Sims clear. Both were sexually voracious and uninhibited, but Sims enjoyed the adventure while Josephine wanted love. When he quit his job, leaving her as well, Josephine became deeply depressed, then plunged recklessly into a series of affairs to help erase her feelings of rejection. She married Abatino the following year.

When Josephine reached Copenhagen on her first world tour in 1928, she was welcomed by the Danes as a work of art. Already the Black American had acquired fame for her scandalous dancing in the *Folies Bergères*, wearing a string of bananas in the famous "banana dance" and only a "G-string" in "The Dance of the Savages." In Stockholm, she met with the royal family of Sweden including Gustav, the Crown Prince. Blond and blue-eyed, the prince was the stereotype of Nordic manhood. He was also married to an English woman named Louise Mountbatten. After attending five performances of her show, the prince decided to go backstage to meet Josephine.

In her dressing room La Baker was surrounded by her menagerie of Mildred the cheetah, Ethel the chimp, as well as assorted birds, cats, and dogs. Josephine was an impressive specimen of womanhood in her barely-there gray satin dress, bare midsection, and a genuine unset diamond glued into her navel.

The prince and Josephine sped away the next morning on the Imperial train through Sweden and spent one glorious month of love in his summer palace in the deepest of winter. With only three servants, the two lovers temporarily escaped their responsibilities by reveling in the snow, enjoying roaring fires, and sinking into the luxurious beds.

After a month, the affair came to an end and the future King of Sweden returned to his official role, while Josephine returned to the stage. For a time, the "poor little girl from East St. Louis" had been a princess and her life had been illuminated by the intense love of a prince. When she spoke of Gustav later, she often said that she "had been his coffee and he her cream."

Josephine lived forty-seven years longer, during which she aimed to create a world brotherhood by adopting twelve children of different races and nationalities and raising them together as her "Rainbow Tribe." She appeared at civil rights rallies, called and sent telegrams to world leaders, and attempted to influence the course of the world. On 14 April 1975, in Paris, five days after a lavish gala celebrating her fifty years in show business, Josephine, after suffering a cerebral hemorrhage, died while in a coma.

Balanchine, George (1904–1983) See **Danilova, Alexandra.**

Balletti, Manon (1740–1776) The legendary lover Casanova met Manon when she was only ten years old. She was the young sister of his closest friend—and the daughter of an actress, Silvia Balletti, who was also briefly Casanova's lover.

The two fell in love when Casanova was thirty-two years old and Manon was seventeen, a virgin yet worldly because she was surrounded by actors in her mother's house. Despite his passion for her, Casanova couldn't remain faithful and their three years together were filled with numerous tearful scenes and stories of Manon waiting dejectedly at the house in the Rue du Petit-Lion-St.-Sauveur for her unfaithful lover's return.

Casanova had asked Manon to break off her engagement with her clavichord teacher and the two became affianced. In his memoirs, he expressed regret for his unfaithfulness—usually after having seduced other women. Yet, Manon remained faithful. When Casanova landed in prison after being sued by creditors in Paris, it was Manon Balletti who sent her diamond earrings so that he could buy himself out.

When Manon finally and sadly broke off their engagement, returning his portrait and letters, Casanova was devastated. Despite his escapades, he sincerely believed that he would one day return to Manon and settle down. She married a few years later, but her life and happiness were short. Manon died at the age of thirty-six, and Casanova records in the story of his life that he firmly believed that his behavior had shortened her life.

Barnacle, Nora (1884–1951) Nora Barnacle was muse to the writings of the Irish novelist and poet, James Joyce, one of the giants of twentieth century literature, yet could not have been less suited for the part. A poorly educated chambermaid from Dublin, Nora met the religiously trained Joyce on June 16, 1904. She supposedly shocked him by having sex with him that night—and she remained his mistress

Manon Balleti (NATIONAL PORTRAIT GALLERY)

for twenty-seven years. He immortalized her in the highly controversial novel, *Ulysses*, in the character of Molly Bloom, and he set the happenings of the novel on the day they had met.

The earthy Nora found life with Joyce amusing. He was shy and professorial, and he begged her to dominate him. While he projected a physical image of meek piety, he wrote her letters graphically describing those sexual activities which he enjoyed most. At Joyce's request, she often packed a pair of her soiled, worn underwear into his suitcase for him to fondle when they were apart.

Nora played the role of dominatrix to the fetish-prone Joyce who persistently pleaded for her abuse. She provided mothering to this volatile Irish writer. To appease him, she insulted him, calling him "simple-minded Jim." While the literary world heaped praise on his work, Nora told friends that she hardly understood what others saw in his writing.

Clearly they loved each other, for she stuck by him while they and their two children lived in Trieste, Italy, Zurich, Switzerland, and Paris, subsisting mainly on gifts and Joyce's meager earnings as a language instructor. When the family finally became financially comfortable late in his writing career, she stayed with him, tending to his increasing drinking problem, until he died.

Barry, Joan (1919–) Red-haired, vivacious twenty-two-year-old Joan Barry caught the attention of fifty-two-year-old Charlie Chaplin in 1941 when she went to his studio for a screen test. She must have impressed him, for he not only made her his mistress but he also paid for the acting and singing lessons necessary to groom her for the role of leading lady in his films.

Their relationship was satisfying for about a year, until Chaplin's eyes began to wander and he asked Joan to leave just before Christmas, 1942. She left for a time, then returned one evening with a gun and forced her way into his house. She broke windows, threatened suicide, and was arrested. When she left jail, thirty days later, Joan told Hollywood columnist Hedda Hopper that she was pregnant with Chaplin's child. His marriage to Oona O'Neill was placed on hold, and he ordered his lawyers to deal with Joan's paternity suit.

The court proceedings which followed resembled a circus, and the news media used the paternity suit as a means of stirring up public opinion against Chaplin, who had already angered the nation because of his left-wing views and for refusing to become an American citizen. After blood tests proved that Chaplin was not the baby's father, the court acquitted him but he was still ordered to pay child support despite other evidence which showed that Barry had enjoyed other lovers at the same time that she was Chaplin's mistress. After the trial, Chaplin suffered attacks by the press for his political views and the public turned against him. He left the country in 1952 with his new wife and settled in Switzerland.

What happened to Joan Barry afterward is a mystery. She was committed to a state mental institution in California in 1953, and nothing more has been heard of her.

Barrymore, John (1882–1942) See **Astor, Mary.**

Becu, Marie Jeanne, Comtesse du Barry (1743–1793) Marie Jeanne Becu was born in Vaucouleurs, the illegitimate daughter of a seamstress and a tax collector. After a brief convent education, she was apprenticed to a Paris milliner at the age of fifteen. She was dazzlingly beautiful, with abundant blonde hair and a well-developed bosom which she emphasized by wearing deeply *décolleté* dresses.

At twenty-one, Marie became the mistress of chevalier Jean du Barry, who ran a Paris gambling house and who occasionally lent Marie out to important clients to increase his favor with high-ranking nobles. Du Barry arranged for Marie to meet King Louis XV of France who immediately made plans to designate her his official mistress. Protocol had to be followed, which required that Marie marry a noble before presentation at court. Her former lover's brother, the impoverished Comte Guillaume du Barry, agreed to the marriage for a substantial payment. Legitimately married, the new Madame du Barry was presented at court and became the *maitresse declarée* in 1768.

Marie loved luxury and diamonds, and her great bedroom talents convinced Louis XV to provide her with both. She received a large annual income of 1,200,000 francs, and she could draw on the Royal treasury for all household expenses. She spent extravagantly, filling her closets with dresses and overrunning her annual allowance. One dress, which cost 450,000 francs, had a bodice covered in diamonds shaped into flowers, bows, and ribbons.

She remained Louis XV's official mistress until his death from smallpox in 1777, after which she retired to her château of Louveciennes, near Versailles. During and after her time as mistress, Marie was celebrated for her beauty and her wit, and she was a generous patron of both artists and writers. She went to England in 1792, after the outbreak of the French Revolution, but returned to recover jewelry which had been stolen. Representatives of the new French government jailed her and pressed charges of conspiracy against the new regime. Madame du Barry was convicted and died by the guillotine.

Beecher, Henry Ward (1813–1887) See **Tilton, Elizabeth Richards.**

Belgiojoso, Princess Cristina (1808–1871) Born to Italian aristocracy and married while in her teens to a philandering prince, Princess Cristina was a great beauty whose gleaming black hair and coal-black eyes contrasted sharply with the unique pallor of her complexion. Admirers compared her with the Mona Lisa and the classic serenity of a Raphael Madonna.

Described by some as a cold, immobile apparition, Cristina's cold exterior masked a passion and a powerful personality which drew the leading figures of the Romantic era to her salon. At the age of twenty, she left her husband and ran away to Paris. She soon found herself in the center of an admiring circle of men, which included Franz Liszt and the septuagenarian Marquis Lafayette, when she was only twenty-three years old. A gifted advocate of causes and revolutionary politics, she pleaded the Italian cause to heads of state and kings while she carried on an active love life.

Considered eccentric by many and immoral by others for her continually changing male admirers and her refusal to be tied down to one man, Cristina raised her illegitimate child Marie alone while she wrote volumes on politics, history, and theology.

A great part of Cristina's notoriety lies in the stories which circulated regarding her handling of the death in 1844 of her lover,

Gaetano Stelzi, a young man whom she had hired to tutor her daughter Marie. The sickly young man suffered from tuberculosis, and Cristina with Marie's governess, Mrs. Parker, nursed him until he died. Refusing to give up her lover, Cristina, along with Mrs. Parker, embalmed the body, which they then dressed in a tail coat and placed in a closet to keep near Cristina. A tree trunk was then placed in the coffin to be buried while Stelzi's body remained in the closet until found by Austrian troops searching the house. Rumors of necrophilia were given credence by Cristina's pallid complexion and her cold, deathlike presence, but nothing was ever proven.

Bell, Laura (1829–1894) Called "the Queen of Whoredom" at the height of her notoriety in London in the 1850s, Laura Bell was born the daughter of a bailiff in Ireland and started her career as a shopgirl in Belfast, Ireland. She soon acquired a select clientele in Dublin as a lady of pleasure, and she would ride around the city in her magnificent coach drawn by a pair of white horses. The plenitude of prostitutes in London during that period resulted in serious competition, and Laura deliberately created an image which placed her at the forefront of the profession.

She took London by storm at the time of the Great Exhibition where she could often be found in Hyde Park, surrounded by large numbers of fashionably dressed, wealthy young men. Her most distinguished and memorable lover was the Nepalese Ambassador whose devotion to her extended long after he had left London and her arms. He presented Laura with a priceless ring, which he told her to send back to him if she ever needed help. Laura is reputed to have taken him up on that promise in 1857, when the Indian Mutiny broke out. In collaboration with the India Office, she sent the ring back to India with her request that the Nepalese government either join the British or remain neutral in the mutiny. The Nepal Ghurka regiments sided with the British and Nepal did not join the mutiny, a fact attributed to Laura's sacrifice of the ring.

In later life in the 1860s, Laura converted from whoring to preaching, and she became a social missionary. People flocked to hear the former sinner who had been saved through her faith in God, among them England's Prime Minister William Gladstone and his wife. Many listeners were as dazzled by her oratory as they were by the large diamond rings which sparkled on her fingers as she lifted her hands in praise. Laura continued her social missionary work until her death in 1894 as a respected and respectable voice of salvation.

Bellanger, Marguerite (1840–1886) Like most courtesans, Marguerite Bellanger, the last mistress of French Emperor Napoleon III, invented for herself a past which disguised her peasant origins and which changed her mundane name of Julie Leboeuf to something more glamorous. Despite her success in attracting wealthy and well-placed suitors, Marguerite retained the thick ankles and the rustic manners of a woman of the fields for all of her life.

Her tomboyishness and candor appealed to the Emperor who had sent three members of the imperial household to dine with and scrutinize her. At the cosy dinner, Marguerite thought that she was meant to become the lover of one of her dining companions who were, instead, reviewing her qualifications as mistress to the Emperor. Shortly after, Marguerite and Napoleon III became lovers in his little Saint-Cloud hunting lodge, and she became the last of his official mistresses.

For two years, Marguerite followed her cher seigneur and his court from one residence to another. In Saint-Cloud, her home adjoined the wall which surrounded the Emperor's private park. Napoleon would pass through a hidden door in the wall to meet with Marguerite.

The Empress discovered the affair after a year had passed and became so distraught that she was forced to go to a popular resort to rest and to recoup her strength. In the meantime, Marguerite became totally immersed in her role, viewing herself as more of a wife than a mistress to the Emperor. Less than a year later, however, when Napoleon suffered a physical collapse, his wife decided that the affair had to end. Accompanied by the brother of her husband's secretary, she confronted Marguerite and bluntly told her that the affair was killing Napoleon III. Marguerite was ordered to give him up, and by the middle of 1865, the Emperor no longer spoke of his mistress.

A child was born at Marguerite's house in February 1864, and the

Marguerite Bellanger (BIBLIOTHEQUE NATIONALE)

birth of the boy was registered as "father and mother unknown," although he was given the name of Charles Leboeuf. Later, Marguerite was acknowledged as the child's mother; Napoleon III was likely the father since, after the child was farmed out to be raised by a Parisian jeweler, the emperor gave him an estate in Oise.

Toward the end of her life, Malguerite returned to looking after cows, sheep, and hens, but this time on her own estate. While strolling over her lands one winter day, Marguerite caught a cold, then developed acute peritonitis. She died alone because a jealous servant had shut the door against both the family and the village priest who had come to give last rites.

Bellisle, Marguerite Pauline (1778–1869) Nickname "La Bellilotte," Marguerite was the illegitimate daughter of a gentleman and a cook whose adventures might have remained buried in history, had she not attracted the attention of Napoleon Bonaparte.

As the new bride of a lieutenant in Napoleon's twenty-second infantry of the line, the petite and blonde Marguerite disguised herself as a soldier and shipped out with him on the troopshlp which carried his unit to Egypt in 1798. Once in Cairo, the attractive young woman joined other wives in setting up a home. She soon came to the attention of Napoleon, who was still married to Josephine. He decided upon meeting her that she would become his.

The minor impediment of Marguerite's husband was easily removed. Napoleon arranged to have Marguerite invited to a dinner pary from which Lieutenant Foures was excluded. Napoleon's top aide "accidentally" spilled coffee over Mme. Foures' gown, and the gallant commander-in-chief took the lady into another room to clean off the dress. Guests did not see the pair for several hours.

Napoleon subsequently designed a false mission to get her husband out of the way. He was captured by the British – but news of Napoleon's wild new mistress had already been picked up by their military intelligence. They sent the young husband back to Giro to embarrass Napoleon. The lieutenant soon learned of his wife's indiscretions and he demanded an immediate divorce. Once free, Marguerite flaunted even more openly her affair with Napoleon, and the troops would call out "Vive Clioupatre! Vive la Petite Generale!"

as she rode through the streets of Cairo. Napoleon was obsessed with producing a legitimate heir and fearful that the lack of children was his own fault and not that of his wife Josephine, who had two children from her previous marriage. Napoleon wanted the openly sensual Marguerite to become pregnant. When weeks passed and she showed no signs of pregnancy, he became annoyed with her, despite her very best efforts to oblige, and claimed that "The little stupid one doesn't know how to have one!"

When she returned to Paris sometime after Napoleon, "La Bellilotte" found that she had become a nonentity to both Napoleon and his officers who had formerly protected her, although her former lover did arrange for her marriage to a wealthy nobleman as well as send a generous gift.

In the remainder of her life, Marguerite married a third time, published several novels, and displayed numerous paintings. She lived to the age of ninety, surrounded by her menagerie of canaries and monkeys.

Bergman, Ingrid (1915–1982) Ingrid Bergman's fresh, natural beauty had won the Swedish actress an enthusiastic following when she was first brought to Hollywood in the 1930s to star in a string of box office successes like *Intermezzo*, *For Whom the Bell Tolls*, *Casablanca*, *Gaslight*, *Notorious*, and other, now classic, films.

She seemed content in her long-distance marriage to Swedish physician Peter Lindstrom, with whom she had a daughter, Pia. The virtuous image, projected in her movie roles and perpetuated through the authorized studio publicity releases, did not prepare her public for the shock of learning in 1949 that the married Bergman had become the mistress of the married Italian film director Roberto Rossellini and that she was carrying his child, Robertino.

Close observers weren't surprised by Ingrid's actions. For years, her numerous affairs with directors and actors had been ignored by her patient husband and covered up carefully by the profit-minded studio. She carried on simultaneous affairs with Victor Fleming and Spencer Tracy during the filming of *Dr. Jekyll and Mr. Hyde* (1941), then resumed her relationship with Fleming during the filming of *Joan of Arc* in 1947. She became so close to Gary Cooper during the filming of *For Whom the Bell Tolls* (1942), that his wife, Rocky, commented acidly in the company of other actors that Cooper and Ingrid couldn't stand to be separated, so they were planning more movies together. When the two next filmed *Saratoga Trunk* (1943), cast and crew alike watched their openly flirtatious behavior and listened as Cooper called Ingrid "Frenchie," while she teasingly called him "Texas." In 1945 she began an affair with photographer Robert Capa, with whom she contemplated running away in 1947, but decided that the damage to her career would be too great.

Roberto Rossellini was worth greater risks. He first contacted her in 1948 with the aim of placing her in his next picture. Goldwyn Studios paid his expenses at first, but they stopped paying his bills when he produced no viable script for their star. Ingrid then invited Rossellini to move into the guesthouse on her estate. He escorted her everywhere, leeched off the patient Dr. Lindstrom, and even purchased expensive gifts for her daughter, Pia, and charged them to Lindstrom's account at the toy store. He also borrowed money from Lindstrom, as well as from Ingrid's insurance agent and accountant.

Soon after Rossellini left for Italy, Ingrid followed with the surface intention of making a film with him on the island of Stromboli, but Lindstrom realized the truth when he found that she had taken her furs, most of her dresses, her jewelry, and her clipping books. Despite their intentions to divorce their respective spouses and to marry each other, Ingrid Bergman found that America couldn't accept that the pure and wholesome nun of *The Bells of St. Mary's* or that the pious and virtuous heroine of *Joan of Arc* had dared to defy current morality.

Their first film, *Stromboli* (1949), was a failure because audiences were not receptive to Rossellini's neorealistic technique. Soon after the film was finished, Ingrid gave birth to their son Robertino, whom she had seriously contemplated aborting during the early months of the pregnancy because divorce proceedings were so slow. Her hurried Mexican divorce came through too late for the child to be declared legitimate, despite the equally hurriedly arranged proxy Mexican marriage.

Rossellini jealously refused to allow her to work with any other directors, and in the next five years he directed four more neorealistic films in which Ingrid starred. She became pregnant during work on their second film, *Europa '51*, and gave birth to fraternal twins, Isabella and Isotta, soon after. All five films were financial failures, and Ingrid began to regret her move to Italy. When her Hollywood agent Kay Brown visited her in Rome with the possibility of a film with Twentieth Century Fox, Ingrid jumped at the chance. She left her children with Rossellini's sister, and began in 1956 to film *Anastasia*, for which she later won an Academy Award. The popularity of this movie and the two which followed, *Indiscreet* and *The Inn of the Sixth Happiness*, slowly won her public back.

Rossellini arranged an annulment of their marriage in 1958, but Ingrid had already begun the slow task of winning back her fans by doing her best work on film. She had been discussed eight years earlier in the United States Senate and denounced as the "apostle of degradation," but Ingrid Bergman quietly used her talent to recapture the adoration and support of moviegoers. In 1974 she won the Oscar for Best Supporting Actress for her role in *Murder on the Orient Express* and was nominated in 1978 for an Oscar for Best Actress in her last movie, *Autumn Sonata*. Ingrid Bergman died of cancer in 1982, mourned by millions of fans throughout the world.

Bernhardt, Sarah (1844–1923) She was dubbed the "Divine Sarah" by an adoring public who idolized the woman whose every move made news and whose personal tragedies added further richness to her stage presence. Sarah Bernhardt was the most famous stage actress of her time, and she achieved fame with roles ranging over melodrama, romantic tragedy, and classical tragedy. Playwrights Alexandre Dumas *fils*, Victorien Sardou, and Edmond Rostand wrote plays specifically for her, and she placed her indelible stamp on such classic tragic roles as Phaedre, Lady Macbeth, and Hamlet. She later owned various theaters, the largest being the Théâtre de Nation, which she renamed the Théâtre de Sarah Bernhardt. In addition, she also painted and sculpted works which earned honest artistic praise.

Adored by her public, Sarah Bernhardt claimed to have had over one thousand lovers, many of them rich and powerful men who showered her with expensive gifts. Among them were her leading men as well as many of the most famous writers, politicians, and

Sarah Bernhardt (LIBRARY OF CONGRESS)

statesmen of her time. There were just as many little-known men, whose physical attractiveness made them irresistible to the famous actress. None seemed bothered by the satin-lined, rosewood coffin in her boudoir, bought for the sickly teenaged Sarah, in which she occasionally slept and was photographed several times. Nor were her admirers disturbed by her passionate outbursts, outrageous mood swings, and extensive menagerie of animals, sometimes including a cheetah and a panther, with which she traveled. She was followed by rumor. People gossiped about the polished skull inscribed by Victor Hugo, a skeleton placed facing a mirror, rumored witches' Sabbaths, and other fantastic goings-on which liberally mixed fact with fantasy.

Sarah Bernhardt's early life was a marked contrast to the later fame and adulation which inspired her to take *Quand même* (roughly "even though") as her personal motto. Born Rosine Sarah Bernhard (the "t" was added later) in Paris, she was the daughter of a Jewish Dutch woman named Judith Van Horn, a milliner, and Edouard Bernhard, a law student who later made a successful career in Havre. Her parents never married, but her father settled a dowry of 100,000 francs on Sarah and supported Judith for a year. Judith wanted more and she found her calling as a courtesan in an era when high-priced women of easy virtue were the rage. Sarah was placed with a wet nurse for four years while Judith and her sister, Sarah's aunt Rosine, built up their clientele and made only occasional courtesy calls to the child. When the widowed nurse decided to remarry, she tried to return Sarah to her mother but found that both Judith and Rosine had moved, leaving no forwarding addresses. Thus, Sarah joined the household of the impoverished newlyweds, sharing their damp, unheated single room. While her mother was supported in luxury by lovers, young Sarah slept on an ironing board covered with a quilt and developed a hacking cough during her three months in the filthy and cold surroundings.

Sarah was reluctantly rescued one day when her aunt's elegant coach broke down near where she played in the street, and the child recognized her and begged to be taken home. Unwilling to dirty her coach nor to impose her foul-smelling niece on her beau of the moment, Rosine pushed Sarah away and ordered the coachman to complete repairs and leave quickly. Sarah's caretakers dragged her into the house, refusing to believe her claim that the luxuriously clothed woman was her aunt. Watching from her small second-story window, Sarah desperately climbed out of the window and threw herself onto the cobblestone pavement as the coach drew away, dislocating her shoulder, causing a concussion, and shattering her kneecap. Persistence won, and Sarah was taken by Tante Rosine to the unwilling mother who now called herself Judith Bernhardt.

Three years later, eight-year-old Sarah was sent to a convent school for both an education and discipline to learn control over her terrible temper tantrums. She was baptized a Roman Catholic, and throughout her life she would say, "I'm a Roman Catholic, and a member of the great Jewish race." The mysteries of the religion appealed strongly to her dramatic nature, and teenaged Sarah seriously considered becoming a nun while her mother hoped to train her to become a courtesan. After removing Sarah from the convent, she retained doctors to heal the hacking cough and to stop the occasional spitting up of blood. Frequently wracked with fever and cough, fifteen-year-old Sarah became obsessed with death, often visiting the Paris morgue, then open to the public, to ghoulishly view the corpses. She asked for her coffin at this time, although she was to live sixty-four more years.

At this time, Sarah's future as an actress was first suggested during a "family conference," consisting of Judith, Tante Rosine, and four men closest to them—two of whom were Charles de Morny, Duc of Morny and half-brother of Louis-Napoleon, and Alexandre Dumas *père*. When one of the other two men ridiculed Sarah's wish to become a nun, the frail girl violently attacked him, shouting and screaming as she tore out his hair. After watching the dramatic display, the amused Duc of Morny declared Sarah a born actress and suggested that she be sent to the Conservatoire for training. The group decided to attend a performance at the Comédie-Française that evening where Sarah became so affected by the performance of Racine's *Britannicus* that she sobbed uncontrollably during the play. All members of the party but Dumas were embarrassed by her emotion; he understood her intense identification with the characters and comforted her, later fatefully saying, "Good night, little star."

Stage success was not immediate for Sarah, who studied at the Conservatoire and then made an unsuccessful debut in *Iphigenie* at the Comédie-Française in 1862. Given a second chance, Sarah was later forced to resign from the Comédie after slapping dowager actress Madame Nathalie Georges across the face after the woman had pushed Sarah's younger sister Regine into a column, cutting her head. Sarah agreed to apologize only if Madame Nathalie would apologize to Regine, but the management of the Comedie sided against Sarah. Less than a decade later, the theater begged Sarah to return.

Stories of Sarah's temper circulated and no one risked hiring her until in 1864, Regis Lavalie, a powerful friend of Judith's, interceded for Sarah at the Gymnase Montigny which specialized in light comedies. Miscast in comedy, Sarah left after one humiliatingly bad performance and contemplated suicide but listened to the suggestion of Alexandre Dumas *père* that a change of scene would be wiser. Armed with a letter of introduction, she left for Spain to meet the Bruce family. While there, she met and became the mistress of Belgian Prince Henri de Ligne. Called back to France when Judith became ill, Sarah realized that she was pregnant by the prince. Despite her profession, Judith was scandalized by Sarah's condition and she ordered Sarah to move into her own apartment, using half of the dowry from Edouard Bernhard. On 22 December 1864, Sarah gave birth to her only child, Maurice.

Sarah referred to the love affair with Maurice's father as the "abiding wound" of her life. Years later she told her granddaughter Lysianne that Henri wanted to marry her, but his family was vehemently against marriage to a unknown, half-Jewish actress. Without his knowledge, the family sent his uncle to reason with Sarah, and he convinced her that Henri's future was at stake and that marriage to her would mean the loss of Henri's position and fortune. Although there were many love affairs in her future, Sarah had only the one son and she only married once, in 1882, to Greek playboy-actor, Jacques Aristides Damala, eleven years her junior, whom her son bitterly opposed. The marriage was unhappy because of Damala's destructive morphine habit and feelings of inadequacy. He died in 1889.

Throughout the years, Sarah's name was linked with Prince Napoleon (known as "Plon-Plon"); Edward VII; playwrights Jean

Richepin, Edmond Rostand, and Jules Lemaître, and most of her leading men. So powerful was the charm of this illegitimate daughter of a milliner-turned-courtesan, that even after the passion had subsided, Sarah could depend upon these men to remain her friends and supporters. While her lovers, they could be counted upon to do her bidding. The Prince of Wales, later Edward VII of England, was an enthusiastic theater-goer and connoisseur of pretty actresses and he often arrived unannounced in Sarah's dressing room. One night in 1882 when Sarah was appearing in Sardou's *Fedora*, the Prince of Wales made an impromptu appearance in the play. At the urging of the actress, he played the part of the corpse in the scene in which Sarah as heroine cries over the body of her murdered lover.

The prince's name appears on lists of her dinner guests and he frequently visited her home. Both parties were extremely discreet in their relationship which remained friendly from its beginning in the 1870s through the 1890s when Edward VII was crowned. At that time, Sarah received a special invitation to the Abbey to sit in the king's box with several of his other female friends, including his current mistress, Alice Keppel.

When she was sixty-six, Sarah made Lou Tellegen, thirty-one and of Greek-Dutch parentage, her leading man for the American tour. He became her last lover. She always referred to him as *le Jeune des jeunes*, and he is generally described as being intellectually lacking, although he was physically very attractive. Sarah played both mother and lover to Tellegen who was panned by critics on both sides of the Atlantic. After the 1913 "Farewell American Tour," Tellegen remained in the United States when Sarah returned to Europe. He later married Geraldine Farrar, who divorced him after five years, and enjoyed brief success as an American matinée idol and silent movie hero. By 1934, he was alone and penniless, and he stabbed himself to death with a pair of scissors.

The "Divine Sarah" remained a trouper to the end, continuing to perform until five days before her death. In 1905, while playing in *La Tosca* in Rio de Janeiro, she went through the familiar scene in which she leapt over a parapet to enact a suicide attempt. The floor behind the parapet was usually covered with mattresses to protect her fall, but the mattresses were missing one night and Sarah fell heavily on her right knee, the same knee which had been shattered by her fall from the window at age four. The leg swelled badly, but she insisted on waiting to see a doctor until she reached New York three weeks later. The injury never healed and by 1908 she had difficulty walking. By 1913, stage furniture had to be arranged so that Sarah could lean every two steps and she frequently rubbed the knee with ether to deaden the pain. Finally in 1915, after her leg had been placed in a cast for several weeks, gangrene set in and her right leg was amputated high on the thigh. She refused to be restrained with a wooden leg or crutches and chose instead, to be carried dramatically in a specially designed elegant chair.

Sarah Bernhardt collapsed in her home in Paris during the filming of a Hollywood-financed film named *La Voyante*. Though too weak to go to a studio, she fought to keep working. The "Divine Sarah" died five days later and thirty thousand mourners filed past her body, lying in its rosewood coffin.

Bernstein, Aline (1881–1956), Aline Bernstein was forty-four, married, and the mother of two grown children when she met the boyishly handsome, twenty-five-year-old American writer, Thomas Wolfe, on an ocean liner returning from Europe. She had an established career as a theatrical designer while he was still four years away from his first successful novel, *Look Homeward, Angel*. Petite and alluring, she had gray streaks in her carefully styled hair, which contrasted sharply with his curly and tousled mop. At six feet, five inches tall, the unsophisticated Wolfe towered over her. Yet, they fell instantly in love at their first meeting, and Aline became Wolfe's mistress less than a month later after they had returned to New York City.

She remained married to her husband Theo, who patiently endured Aline's six years with Wolfe. She met her lover frequently, first at his apartment then later in a loft on East 8th Street, which Aline rented for their rendezvous. Their passion was, at first, insatiable and the two sometimes met twice in a day to make love. Wolfe was enchanted by his "plum-skinned wench," whom he also often referred to as his "dear Jew." He teased her about their age difference, calling her his "timeless mother" and a "lecherous old woman," but he told her how deeply she had become a part of him when he said that he could not get her out of his soul.

Wolfe often called Aline at odd times, both at home and at work, to make certain that she was remaining faithful to him (and to Theo, of course), but he continued to engage in brief affairs and he sometimes showed evidence of anti-Semitism. He vacillated between wanting Aline to marry him and having brief, anonymous sex with any available woman. In return, Aline soothed him, satisfied him, and helped him to succeed in his career. By 1931 his editor Maxwell Perkins urged Wolfe to end the relationship because it seemed to be taking its toll on his writing. When Wolfe left her, Aline tried to take her life. The attempt failed, and Wolfe wrote to her, telling her that he would love her forever, and that his heart would always remain hers. When he died in 1938 of tubercular lesions on his brain, his final words were only of Aline.

Aline lived for eighteen years after Wolfe's death. In 1951 she suffered several small strokes which left her increasingly paralyzed and debilitated until she finally died at the age of seventy-five, with her still-adoring husband at her side.

Bloomingdale, Alfred (1916–1982) See **Morgan, Vicki.**

Bonaparte, Napoleon (1769–1821) See **Bellisle, Marguerite Pauline; Deneulle, Elenore; Walewska, Maria.**

Bonaparte, Pauline (1780–1825) Fiercely devoted to her brother, Napoleon, Pauline was the only one of his three sisters to fight for permission to join him in exile on the island of St. Helena. Such loyalty seems to be one of the few virtues she possessed, for she was an exceptionally promiscuous woman, even for that licentious age.

All who knew Pauline Bonaparte agreed that chastity was a virtue with which she was unfamiliar. After she nearly created a scandal when, at sixteen, her flirting with Napoleon's General Staff became common gossip, Napoleon decided to marry her off to a suitable husband. His choice was a wealthy young military aide whose every move mimicked Napoleon's, twenty-four-year-old General Victor Leclerc, who welcomed the marriage in 1797 to his idol's sister and the possibilities for advancement which it offered.

Napoleon posted his new brother-in-law to Haiti, assigning him the task of restoring French control to the island and forcibly

Pauline Bonaparte (BETTMANN ARCHIVE)

reinstating black slavery. While there, General Leclerc contracted yellow fever and died, leaving the bereaved Pauline to return with his body to France and to resume her life alone. The new widow consoled herself with numerous handsome and virile young men, creating a scandal to which Napoleon again sought to put an end. Once more, he tried to save his sister's reputation, despite her wishes, and found her the twenty-eight-year-old Prince Camillo Borghese, inheritor of a great fortune and the owner of impressive diamond and fine art collections. Despite the prince's lack of intellectual attraction, Pauline agreed to the marriage because the material advantages were too great to resist. The pair were married in 1803, and Pauline promptly began to play the mistress to a series of men. She enjoyed a life of unparalleled luxury with an allowance of seventy thousand francs yearly from the prince, the use of two carriages, and the Villa Borghese at her disposal. Within a year, the disgusted prince separated from her and Pauline moved to Neuilly, where Napoleon added 130,000 francs monthly to her already large fortune.

Pauline reveled in luxury and sensuality. She owned six hundred dresses and millions of dollars in jewels. A young black male servant was employed to carry her nude body to her bathroom each morning and to place her in the tub which was filled with a mixture of twenty liters of milk mixed with hot water. As she bathed, she often entertained male admirers who might gaze freely at her breasts. Throughout the day, Pauline would wear the sheerest of shifts as she had her maids comb her hair, apply her perfumes, and complete her makeup while she spoke with male guests.

Rumors abounded that Pauline had committed infidelities because her prince was possessed of an underdeveloped sex organ and was unable to satisfy her sexually. Going to the other extreme, she became mistress to the intellectual and society painter, Nicholas Philippe Augustus de Forbin, who was rumored to be sexually overendowed. Their lovemaking proved so intense that Pauline's doctors prescribed rest and abstinence for a time, in order to allow her severe vaginal distress to diminish. Unable to broach the delicate subject themselves, the doctors asked her mother and sisters to bring up the issue with Pauline, and the young woman agreed to a temporary rest.

Music seemed a good source of consolation, and within weeks,

Pauline engaged a young violinist named Blangini to conduct her proposed orchestra. Because Pauline never hired the other musicians for the orchestra, Blangini was.instead called upon to join Pauline in bed. Her term as mistress to the conductor was followed by several years spent as the mistress of Armand Jules de Canouville, a young aide to Napoleon's chief of staff, an affair which was discreetly conducted for some time. When Napoleon finally learned of it, Canouville was quickly sent with the French army to Russia where he died in battle.

Pauline was mistress to one more man of note, the 24-year-old Sicilian composer, Giovanni Pacini, whose opera *Slave of Bagdad* enthralled her. She was forty when the affair began.

By the time she turned forty-five, Pauline was ill and alone, dying of a cancer which ravaged her famous physical beauty. With her brother Jerome at her side, in 1825 Pauline died with a mirror in hand bemoaning the loss of her looks. At her wish, her coffin remained closed at her funeral. Instead, she asked that Antonio Canova's sculpture of her as Venus be displayed, to remind the world of her lost beauty. The frankly naked statue with its perfectly curved breasts, graceful shoulders, and fleshy hips was said to be an exact image of Pauline in her prime.

Bonnemains, Marguerite de (1854–1891) Beautiful, blonde, and convent-educated, Marguerite de Bonnemains first met French Minister of War General Georges Boulanger while married to army lieutenant Vicomte Pierre de Bonnemains. When introduced at a small dinner given by a former schoolmate of Marguerite, the two fell in love. Marguerite obtained a civil divorce, but the two could not marry because the Catholic church would not grant her an annulment. Instead she became Boulanger's mistress.

During their first year together, Marguerite supported Boulanger's attempt to join with Royalists to overthrow the government and to establish a dictatorship. After a brief exile in the provinces, to which Marguerite followed and remained his secret lover and comforter, he returned to Paris to form the National Party, and to plot a *coup d'état*. When this failed in 1889, he fled with Marguerite to Brussels with an entourage containing eighteen servants, aides, and trunks full of his mistress' clothing.

Marguerite de Bonnemains (BROWN BROTHERS)

While in Brussels Marguerite became ill with pleurisy, an illness that worsened with their move to London, where Marguerite worked hard to obtain money to support them while Boulanger plotted his return and calmed his nerves with opium. To save money, they moved to the isle of Jersey where its dampness exacerbated Marguerite's illness, making her cough incessantly. Money was scarce, but Marguerite could not eat what little they could afford because of her coughing, and her body soon became skeletal. Near the end, when consumption had nearly claimed her, Marguerite gratefully endured a trip to Paris to collect an inheritance which she had only weeks to enjoy. She died in Brussels in 1891 of consumption. Two months later, Boulanger shot himself to death while standing in front of her grave. He had asked that his tombstone contain the following inscription "Could I really live two-and-a-half-months without you?"

Boulanger, Georges (1837–1891) See **Bonnemains, Marguerite de.**

Boulay de la Meurthe (1951 –) The slim blonde was 26 and a reporter for *Paris Match* when she met Sir James (Jimmy) Goldsmith, one of the richest and most successful businessmen in the world. Although the 44-year-old multibillionaire would soon marry his third wife, Annabel, he began a relationship with Boulay de la Meurthe that would produce two children and last until his death in 1997. Beyond beauty, the young woman brought an aristocratic heritage to the relationship. She was a Bourbon and the niece of the Comte de Paris, who was directly descended from King Louis-Philippe and the Pretender to the French throne. At the time of their meeting in 1977, Boulay de la Meurthe was living with her sister on the Left Bank in Paris. From the beginning, she assumed an important role in Goldsmith's life, travelling with him and serving as a sounding board. For several years, Goldsmith maintained a residence for her in Paris while his wife and children lived in England. In 1981, he made the decision to move to the United States, telling his wife and the press that he was disillusioned with both France and Britain. An equally important reason was that Boulay de la Meurthe had already moved to New York City to work, and Goldsmith was eager to join her. The two occupied a luxurious suite at the Carlyle Hotel for nearly a year, until Boulay de la Meurthe became pregnant. Goldsmith then bought a large brick town house on Park Avenue in New York and gave his mistress free reign to spend whatever she desired in filling it with all manner of luxuries. Their daughter Charlotte was born in 1983. In 1987, Boulay de la Meurthe gave birth to her second (and Goldsmith's eighth) child, Jethro. For his new family, Goldsmith built a personal paradise in Cuixmala, Mexico, and he invited his two previous wives and present wife, as well as the children from those marriages to join them, but Annabel and her children stayed in England. By 1991, Boulay de la Meurthe was spending part of her time in Paris, as the publisher of the Paris-based magazine *Point de Vue – Images du Monde*, an upscale periodical that Goldsmith owned. She also continued to travel with Goldsmith on most of his lengthier trips and remained the most important woman in his life. She was with him through his final, fatal bout with pancreatic cancer and early death at age 64.

Bourbon-Conti, Louise Henrietta (1726–1759) Cousin to King Louis XV of France, Louise Henrietta Bourbon-Conti, who became Duchess of Chartres in 1743 upon her marriage to Louis Philippe, the Duke of Chartres, was twenty-five years old, afflicted by acne, and a well-known nymphomaniac when she met the great lover Giacomo Casanova. In his account of their relationship in his *History of My Life*, Casanova refers to her solely by her title.

The Duchess was the president of the female Masonic lodges of France, and she appealed to Casanova for advice. In addition to lodge-related advice, Casanova also advised the Duchess in regard to her skin condition. He ordered her to restrict her food intake, to take vigorous exercise, to get plenty of sleep, and to wash her face frequently. This contemporary commonsense regimen seemed almost magical to the eighteenth century, more so when the acne condition disappeared. Impressed with her advisor, the Duchess eagerly rewarded him with her favors, which Casanova enjoyed for a time until his next conquest.

The Duchess of Chartres died at the age of thirty-three of the debilitating effects of venereal disease.

Bow, Clara (1905–1965) Labeled the "It Girl" after her 1926 movie *Mantrap* made her a red-hot star, Clara Bow was the first sex symbol of the American screen and fan magazines wrote continually about her

Clara Bow (NATIONAL FILM ARCHIVES)

sexual magnetism. Her flaming red bobbed hair, scarlet bow-shaped lips, and free spiritedness were copied by millions of American women who also wanted to have "It." She also titillated her readers and started a new undercover fashion by announcing to one movie magazine that she never wore underwear, a fashion tip which was to be repeated by later Hollywood sexpots.

The early life of the "It Girl" was substantially more somber and depressing than the carefree life and attitude which she projected. Born in the Brooklyn slums, she was the daughter of a usually unemployed father and a mother who locked Clara in the closet while she practiced prostitution to earn the food and rent money. Clara escaped from the tenements in 1921, after winning a beauty contest sponsored by the fan magazine, *Motion Picture*, and then proceeded to become one of Hollywood's most notorious stars.

Dubbed sexually insatiable by a string of one-night lovers, Clara had brief affairs with many actors and directors, as well as with most of her leading men. She was rumored to have had love affairs with as varied a group as Eddie Cantor, Gilbert Roland, Victor Fleming, Gary Cooper, John Gilbert, Bela Lugosi, and Broadway singing star Harry Richman. She was indiscriminate in her tastes, and the story of her regular sex parties with the University of Southern California football team made the rounds and was given credence when the coach posted a warning in the locker room that her home was off-limits to the team.

The wild "It Girl" image flourished, and Clara was often seen late at night speeding down Sunset Boulevard in her open red convertible, accompanied by one or more of her dogs and perhaps her monkey, all dyed red to match her hair.

The most enduring of her relationships was that with cowboy Rex Bell, later elected governor of Nevada for two terms, to whom she was mistress for several years before becoming his wife. When scandal destroyed Clara's career in 1931, after her former secretary, who was fired for stealing jewels and money from Clara, sold her memoirs to a tabloid, Bell was there to pick up the pieces. The memoirs contained detailed accounts of Clara's numerous men and provided graphic descriptions of the "It Girl's" cavorting. Depression-era America was shocked and that shock carried from the courtroom to the box office. Her studio contract was not renewed and her career was ruined. Clara had a breakdown and spent time in a sanatorium. Although she later tried to make a comeback, the "It Girl" never again achieved one small portion of the popularity which she had previously enjoyed.

Clara Bow spent many of the last years of her life moving in and out of mental hospitals. She died of a heart attack in 1965, five years after telling the media that she had passed the "It Girl" crown on to a new sex symbol worthy of the title, Marilyn Monroe.

Brady, James ("Diamond Jim") Buchanan (1856–1917) See **Russell, Lillian.**

Braun, Eva (1912–1945) As a child, Eva Braun was a mischievous student who wanted only to have a good time and who refused to learn any more than she needed to achieve that goal. When she began dating at fifteen, her father refused to let her go out, so Eva would sneak out to meet her boyfriends, until her father retaliated in 1928 and sent her to a convent school. The Catholic Young Women's Institute coincidentally lay across the Inns River from the small Austrian town of Braunau, the birthplace of Adolf Hitler, who was already gaining political fame.

Bored with learning and eager to experience life, Eva rebelled against the convent rules and was asked to leave a year later. Once back at home, the sixteen-year-old plump and pretty fraulein decided to change her physical appearance and to enter the "real world." She dieted, learned to use makeup, and looked for a career. An acquaintance informed her that a young and beautiful girl could easily find men who would give expensive gifts and money to young women who could make them happy. While looking for one of these generous benefactors, Eva took a job in a photography shop run by a short, heavyset Bavarian named Heinrich Hoffman.

For five years, since 1924, Hoffman had been Hitler's official photographer and unofficial pimp for the rising political star. Hired as clerk and bookkeeper, Eva was soon asked to entertain a friend of Hoffman's, Adolf Hitler. Politically naive, Eva was unimpressed by Hitler's name, but she was interested in his generosity toward her. From 1929 through 1933, while Eva continued to live at home, she met clandestinely with Hitler, sometimes staying overnight with him and lying to her parents that she was helping Hoffman on a

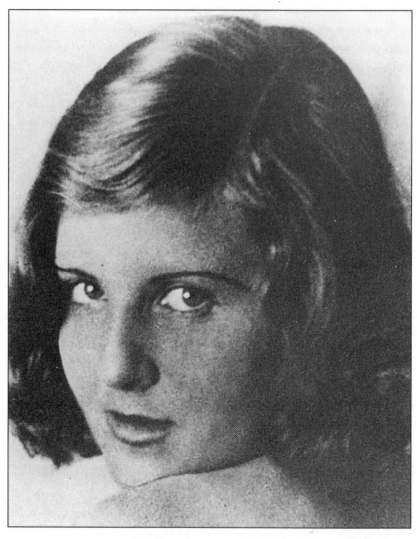

Eva Braun (NATIONAL ARCHIVES)

photography session. When Hitler became Chancellor of Germany in 1933, he arranged for Eva to have her own telephone line and secure telephone in her bedroom in her parents' house, so that the two could speak privately. When her parents finally realized that she was Hitler's mistress the expected tears and shouts occurred, but they gave in and she continued to live with them while seeing Hitler whenever his political activities permitted.

While living this backstreet existence, Eva learned to tread lightly on certain topics and she also had to end several Jewish friendships to avoid her lover's disapproval.

Hitler became bored at several points in the affair, but Eva was determined to keep her place in his life. Whenever they went too long without seeing each other, she bombarded him with letters. She attempted suicide three times, once with a gun and twice with pills, when she believed that she had lost his interest.

Finally, in 1935, Hitler moved her into a small apartment and demanded that one of her sisters live with her to maintain a respectable appearance. From that point until her death in 1945, Eva made herself fully sexually accessible to him. Within months, her lover moved her into a luxurious villa on the outskirts of Munich, where she continued to live in constant retreat, seeing only Hitler or her sister. Hitler bought her jewels, furs, cars, and other luxuries, but she knew that she existed only to meet his sexual demands and she lived in constant fear of being replaced. Although rumors of Hitler's alleged impotence flourished in 1930s Germany as a way of explaining his fanatical devotion to duty, accounts in Eva's diaries and reports of other women disproved them.

Meanwhile, as Hitler's political power increased and the newspapers printed numerous photographs of him, Eva was forced to stay out of sight or pretend to be his secretary. Any photographs which contained Eva were cropped to eliminate her image or banned.

Despite Eva's total sexual accessibility, Hitler had other affairs during their years together. However, the two were together when the end came in 1945. With Germany being overrun, Hitler decided that he would rather die and take Eva with him than suffer the fate of public degradation which had befallen Mussolini and his mistress, Clara Petacci.

On 29 April 1945, Adolf Hitler married his longtime mistress, Eva Braun, in a hurried, late-night ceremony. The next afternoon, the two committed suicide. Dressed elegantly in Hitler's favorite black dress with high heels and jewelry, her hair done perfectly, Eva took the phial of cyanide with which Hitler provided her. As Allied troops poured into Berlin, he also took the cyanide, then guaranteed his death by shooting himself with his pistol.

Britton, Nan (1896– ?) Young, impetuous Nan was fourteen years old and the daughter of a small-town doctor, and Warren Harding was forty-five and running for governor of Ohio on the Republican ticket in 1910 when she developed an obsessive crush on her hometown hero. She gushed over him, writing him fan letters and calling his home so frequently that Florence Harding, nicknamed "the Duchess" for her icy demeanor, warned Nan's parents that something must be done to protect her husband from such annoyance.

Coincidentally, Nan's English teacher was Daisy Harding, Warren's sister, and Nan wrote essays about him for class while garnering every detail of Harding's life. Everyone except Harding was worried about Nan's obsession, and Harding suggested that she visit him in his newspaper (*The Star*) office to help to bring the starry-eyed girl down to earth. Rather than to exorcise her illusions, the visit with Harding only plunged Nan further into love.

After Nan's father died and Harding was elected to the U.S. Senate, the relationship calmed. In 1916 Nan learned secretarial skills in New York City to support herself. She wrote to Harding in Washington, D.C., and asked if he remembered her. Harding enthusiastically responded and secretly met the now twenty-one-year-old Nan in New York City where they kissed in his hotel room. A few weeks later, they traveled discreetly together to Indianapolis, Chicago, and other Midwest cities, as Harding made speeches. Nan insisted on remaining a "technical virgin," so the pair only shared a bed, nudity, and passionate embraces.

Two months after they were reunited, they became full lovers, but their meetings were often hurried and frantic. Sometimes Warren went to New York City, while other times Nan met him in Washington. She reports in her memoirs that their lovemaking, such as it was, often took place on the floor of his Senate office, on the old couch in the corner, or on his Senatorial desk.

The possibility of using some form of contraception had never occurred to Harding, who thought that he was sterile; so when Nan became pregnant, his first move was to buy her some pills which he told her to take in the hope of inducing a miscarriage. Nan refused, and she went to Asbury Park, New Jersey, where her child Elizabeth Ann was born. With the baby, Nan then went to Chicago to stay with her married sister while Harding sent money for support.

When Harding went to Chicago for the 1920 Republican Nominating Convention, they resumed their relationship but the future president avoided the baby. Throughout the convention, Nan listened with rapt attention as her hero was nominated to run for president of the United States. Once it was official, Harding warned Nan that he would be followed and that it would be best for everyone if Nan's sister and brother-in-law would adopt their child. After Nan agreed, Harding sent her a short note with eight hundred dollars via a Secret Service agent, and Nan treated herself to a two-month vacation .

The lovers celebrated both Harding's fifty-fifth birthday and his election as President of the United States on 2 November 1920, by meeting and making love in a house in Marion, Ohio, which had been used by campaign clerical staff. With the help of a Secret Service man, they were able to outsmart the Duchess who waited patiently at home for Harding—a block or so away!

Harding had Nan smuggled into the White House several times, and one meeting nearly ended in disaster. In June 1921, a trusted Secret Service man brought Nan to the White House Cabinet Room, but there were too many windows so Harding took his love to a smaller room with only one window. They were still too conspicuous because the president's armed guard stood outside, so Harding led Nan into a roomy closet off the Presidential Office and there the pair made love. Once when in the same spot, they heard frantic knocking on the room door and the sounds of loud and insistent voices. The Duchess had appeared and demanded to be admitted, but Harding's trusted valet Major Arthur Brooks tried hard to stall her. As the Duchess rushed around to another entrance, the hurriedly dressed

Nan was hustled out the door and through a distant exit.

Harding died in office on 2 August 1923, of mysterious causes, but poison by the Duchess was suggested by many. After his death, the Duchess burned all implicating papers in a bonfire which roared for days. She insisted on burning them herself in the fireplace and using the poker to guarantee cinders. Through all the years of his infidelity, the Duchess had known about Nan and the child.

Nan was in Europe thanks to Harding's financial generosity when he died, but she headed to Marion as soon as she returned and tried to coerce both Harding's sister Daisy and his younger brother George to give her money for her child. She was roundly dismissed. In turn, in 1927, she wrote a tell-all memoir, *The President's Daughter*. Despite attempts by the Ohio political machine to suppress the book, it stirred up a storm because newsman H. L. Mencken devoted two newspaper columns to it and piqued the public's interest.

In later years, her name periodically appeared in the guest register at the Harding memorial.

Byron, Lord (1788–1824) See **Clairmont, Claire; Guiccioli, Countess Teresa; Lamb, Lady Caroline.**

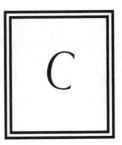

C

Caesar, Julius (100 B.C.–44 B.C.) See Cleopatra.

Callas, Maria (1923–1977) International opera diva Maria Callas was born Maria Anna Sofia Cecilia Kalogeropoulos in Manhattan's Flower Hospital on Fifth Avenue only three months after her parents arrived from Greece.

Her mother dreamed of a great career for her, so she whisked her back to Athens to receive the right training after fourteen-year-old Maria won several radio amateur singing contests. Soon after, they were caught up in World War II, during which Maria often sang to German occupation troops to obtain groceries.

In 1945 Maria and her mother were able to return to New York City where she met her husband, fifty-three-year-old Giovanni Battista Meneghini. Despite his wealth, the match was opposed by both families, but the couple married in 1949 and lef for Europe, where Maria trained her voice and changed her image. By the time she returned to the U.S., the trimmer, more fashionably dressed Maria

Maria Callas (BETTMANN ARCHIVE)

had already become a major star on the international opera circuit. From Milan to Buenos Aires, her performances were immediately sold out and her appearances were greeted by the raving bravos of the fans.

In 1957 she met Aristotle Onassis at a party given in Venice by society hostess Elsa Maxwell. Taken with the vibrantly alive thirty-four-year-old opera singer, fifty-seven-year-old Onassis diplomatically courted Maria, offering his motorboat and two sailors to her and her husband for their time in Venice. One year later when Maria was to make her debut in Paris, Onassis bombarded her hotel with huge bouquets of red roses, then pursued her and threw lavish parties in her honor. After a cruise on his yacht *Christina*, Onassis showed up under Maria's hotel window and serenaded her by repeatedly singing out her name. He also informed her husband that he intended to marry Maria, and he presented her with a heavy gold bracelet engraved TMWL (To Maria With Love).

Onassis became an obsession for Maria who had finally discovered true sexual fulfillment with a man who made her appreciate her sensuality. She loved to listen to him talk about his billion-dollar shipping business, and Onassis paid her the compliment of remarking that she was the only woman with whom he could talk business. Still, she also dreamed of having a real home and children, and their acquaintances fully expected that the two lovers would marry.

They had a stormy, brawling relationship which often erupted in public. When she reached forty, Maria wanted a home, but Onassis gave her parties, nightclubs, and galas. Onassis claimed that his children, Alexander and Christina, had been psychologically bruised by his divorce from their mother, Tina, and told her that marrying Maria would only cause more emotional upheaval. In fact, they publicly said that they hated her and referred to her scornfully as "the singer."

By 1963, Maria's whirlwind romance with Onassis had almost destroyed her opera career and she sang no onstage opera at all that year. She only wanted to be just Onassis' wife but, each time that she proposed to quit the stage, he pushed her to keep singing to feed his own ego as lover of the world's greatest opera diva. She returned to opera in 1964, her last stage performance ever, despondent because Onassis and her dream of family life seemed to be slipping away.

Maria was devastated when sixty-eight-year-old Onassis married forty-year-old Jacqueline Bouvier Kennedy in 1968, but a year later he was again being seen in Maria's company. Maria was also there to comfort Onassis when his son Alexander died in a plane crash in 1973.

Maria remained a vital part of Onassis' world until his death in 1975. In an interview with Barbara Walters, she called him the great love of her life. He may have felt the same because, on his final journey to the hospital, he wanted only one item along—the red cashmere blanket which Maria had purchased for him at Hermès earlier in the year. Although Maria could not join the family at Onassis' bedside, she received continuous progress reports from a friend .

Two years later, the great diva died, at the age of 53, unhappy and alone.

Carol II, King of Romania (1893–1953) See **Lupescu, Elena.**

Carpenter, Meta (1908–1994) Born in Memphis, Tennessee, and trained as a classical pianist, Carpenter met American literary giant William Faulkner after she went to California to work as a secretary and script girl for Hollywood director Howard Hawks. Faulkner had been turning out screenplays and was working as co-writer of the 1936 film *The Road to Glory*, and Carpenter was assigned to type the author's nearly indecipherable handwriting. Despite her best intentions to avoid the courtly charms of this married Southern gentleman – which she chronicled in her bestselling account of the affair, *A Loving Gentleman* – working together led her to lower her defences. Several weeks after they met, she agreed to have dinner with Faulkner, who was eleven years her senior, and the two embarked on a love affair that would continue, if sporadically, over a decade.

When the affair began, Carpenter lived at the Studio Club, an establishment that housed 74 young women under dormitory conditions. Faulkner's wife Estelle and daughter Jill had remained in Oxford, Mississippi, and he lived in a Hollywood hotel, so the couple's first sexual encounters took place in a hotel room. Carpenter describes the famous writer as stammering in surprise when she finally agreed to go out with him. After telling her that he and his wife had not shared a bed for years, Faulkner exhibited a "consuming sexual urgency" for Carpenter, to whom he told bawdy stories and whom he enticed with words that made her blush once they became lovers. Carpenter often spent weekends with Faulkner at the Miramar Hotel, where they would register under the names of Mr. and Mrs. Bowen; the names that they had also given to their sexual organs. Carpenter relates that she felt like a new bride during her first weekend away with Faulkner and that she was surprised when she entered their bedroom to find that he had covered their bed with gardenia and jasmine petals. Their relationship became an open secret among friends.

Less than a year after the affair began, he returned to Oxford, and thus began the series of arrivals and departures that would be the pattern of their affair. As Faulkner wrote letters that told of his unhappy life tied to a wife who was alcoholic, Carpenter gained hope that he would divorce Estelle to marry her. Carpenter and Faulkner reunited a second time in Hollywood, and their relationship deepened, but he soon had to return to Oxford and his family. When he returned to Hollywood with his wife and daughter, Carpenter realized that stolen moments with him would be the best that she could hope for. She allowed friends to introduce her to Wolfgang Rebner, a German-born concert pianist of Jewish faith who soon planned to return to an increasingly dangerous Germany. He fell in love with Carpenter, and she was attracted to him but would not allow herself to become involved until she finally realized that Faulkner would never be free to marry her, although he begged her to wait for him.

On the day that Carpenter and Rebner married, Faulkner went on a non-stop drinking binge and was rushed to the hospital suffering from an acute alcohol state. He then spent six weeks under medical care. Carpenter and her husband went to Germany, where she experienced first-hand the terror of the Nazi oppression. Fearful for their lives, the young couple returned to the United States, living in New York City for a time, and Carpenter resumed her affair with Faulkner.

In 1940, she moved back to Hollywood and became a script supervisor while her husband tried to obtain work. She learned that Faulkner had largely destroyed his reputation through heavy drinking on the job and surly behavior, and major studios had blackballed him. After she divorced Rebner, Carpenter made efforts to help Faulkner to re-establish his credibility as a screenwriter. From 1941 through early

1945, the two shared a rocky relationship during which Carpenter became a highly respected script supervisor and Faulkner drank ever more heavily. By late 1945, Faulkner had decided that the only way that he could produce any further writing of merit was to return to Oxford, so the two separated once more.

They would never meet again, although they would continue to write throughout the years until Faulkner's death. Carpenter remarried Rebner in December 1945, but the marriage did not last. On 6 July 1962, she was filming on location in Jackson Hole, Wyoming, when a co-worker casually mentioned the news that author William Faulkner had died the night before.

Caruso, Enrico (1873–1921) See **Giachetti, Ada.**

Casanova, Giacomo (1725–1798) See **Balletti, Manon; Bourbon Conti, Louise Henrietta.**

Castro, Fidel (1927–) See **Lorenz, Marita.**

Cattanei, Vanozza dei (1433–1509) Very little is known about the life of Vanozza dei Cattanei, aside from her role as the mistress to Rodrigo Borgia, who is better known to history as Pope Alexander VI. A native of Spain, she first met Borgia when he was a lawyer in Valencia and the lover of her widowed mother. She accompanied him to Italy where he became first a notary in the Vatican and then cardinal. During those early years before Rodrigo was elected Pope in 1492, Vanozza bore him four children, including Cesare Borgia and the notorious Lucrezia Borgia.

Although paternity by Popes and by those aiming for this office was hardly exceptional during the Italian Renaissance, Rodrigo desired to appear to lead an exemplary existence. Therefore, even as Vanozza remained his mistress, he married her off three times in succession to men who were husbands in name only, in order to protect Borgia as he rose through the Church ranks. Despite his high ecclesiastical office, however, Pope Alexander VI seems to have lacked the milk of human kindness. When Vanozza became too old for his tastes, he provided her with a pension and acquired a 15-year-old mistress, Giulia Farnese, to provide him with both new excitement and with three more children. He was already the Pope, so diplomacy was no longer required and Giulia became known throughout Italy as "The Pope's Whore."

As with many other women in similar situations in this period, little is known of Vanozza's life after her famous lover cast her aside with a pension, except for her treatment after death. When she died a few years after Borgia, at the age of seventy-six, she was buried with great ceremony in the church of Santa Maria del Popolo with the entire papal court present. She was treated as the pope's widow.

Chaplin, Charlie (1889–1979) See **Barry, Joan.**

Charles, Prince of Wales (1948–) See **Parker Bowles, Camilla.**

Charles II, King of England (1630–1685) See **Davis, Moll; Gwynn, Nell; Keroualle, Louise de; Villiers, Barbara; Walter, Lucy.**

Charles VII, King of France (1403–1461) See **Sorel, Agnes.**

Chatelet, Emilie Du (1706–1749) Well-read, considerate, and attentive, Emilie Du Chatelet was an expert horsewoman, a high stakes gambler, a translator of classics, an expert in Newtonian physics, a well-known hostess, and the adored of Voltaire. Together, Emilie and Voltaire used Voltaire's money to renovate her husband's chateau, and they shared intellectual as well as physical pleasure.

Emilie was also daring, even for her time. She wore dresses made of cloth-of-gold and cloth-of-silver. While most women were wearing low-cut dresses, Emilie went further to expose the greater part of her breasts and she rouged her nipples.

Before meeting and mating with Voltaire when she was twenty-six, Emilie had a parade of lovers, among whom was the Duc de Richlieu, whose self-discipline brought order into Emilie's chaotic life. Later, she met Voltaire through the Duc after the affair ended, but they maintained a correspondence to the end of her life.

Emilie was Voltaire's soulmate as well as his mistress, and her views were sought by the greatest scientists of the age. She conducted physics experiments in a specially built darkroom in her château, and she actively wrote on a range of philosophical and scientific topics. When the physical side of the affair cooled, Emilie was attracted by the tall, handsome soldier, Saint-Lambert, ten years her junior. His own eyes wandering, Voltaire was privately delighted. When Emilie announced that she was pregnant and noted that she could hardly blame it on her husband with whom she had not slept in years, Voltaire inappropriately joked that the child would have to be considered one of her miscellaneous works since no father had claimed it. Fate intervened, however, and Saint-Lambert came back from the Front in time to acknowledge the child.

On 1 September 1749, Emilie entered the throes of labor while sitting at her desk translating Newton. Seven days after giving birth to a daughter, she died.

Chilperic I, King of Neustria (539–584) See **Fredegond.**

Chopin, Frederic (1810–1849) See **Fuller, Margaret; Sand, George.**

Claflin, Tennessee (1846–1923) Lover of the very wealthy and influential Commodore Cornelius Vanderbilt and sister of Victoria Woodhull, the first woman to run for president of the United States, Tennessee Claflin was lighthearted and completely uninhibited. Her early life was spent in helping her mother to eke out a living through spiritualism, prostitution, magnetic healing, and claims of clairvoyance.

Eager to make their mark on the world, Tennessee and her older sister Victoria offered their services as miracle healers to Vanderbilt, whose tastes ran strongly to both sexually attractive young women and to psychic healers who would prolong good health and life. The sisters made their pitch successfully, and Victoria convinced the seventy-four-year-old commodore that she was a competent medium while Tennessee promised increased strength through physical contact as a magnetic healer.

Tennessee started her "healing" by placing her hands on the commodore's in order to pass the electrical energy from her body into his, and then she proceeded to join other body parts with his as she became his mistress. After about a year and a half, the commodore, who called Tennessee his "little sparrow," was willing to set the sisters up in a Wall Street stock brokerage firm which prospered due to the commodore's support and insider stock tips. Later, after Victoria had established herself as a stock speculator and feminist leader, he financed Victoria's unsuccessful bid for the presidency in 1872.

After they were done with the commodore, Tennessee and her sister involved themselves in a range of enterprises, from the suffragette movement to becoming publishers of the *Woodhull & Claflin Weekly*, which was first to publicize the Beecher-Tilton scandal which titillated Victorian America and in which Victoria had a major role. The sisters had attempted to convince fiery and popular preacher Henry Ward Beecher to publicly endorse Victoria's bid for the presidency by threatening to expose his affair with Elizabeth Richards Tilton. In a conciliatory attempt, Theodore Tilton became aligned with the campaign and appeased Tennessee and Victoria by publishing approving articles, writing Victoria's speeches, and becoming Victoria's lover. When Theodore stopped pacifying Victoria, the *Woodhull & Claflin Weekly* made the Beecher-Tilton affair public. Jailed for sending obscene material through the mail, the sisters were eventually acquitted, but not before creating a national uproar.

After the death of the commodore, Tennessee inherited both an oil painting and an unnamed sum of money to use with Victoria in advancing the study of spiritualism. He also left $95,000,000 to his eldest son William while his remaining son Cornelius and eight daughters shared $5,000,000. When the commodore's wronged children appealed to Victoria to testify that the commodore had mental lapses, his eldest son wisely paid the sisters a large sum of money to refuse, with the provision that the sisters leave for England until the matter was settled.

In 1885 Tennessee conducted a seance for a much older, wealthy English widower named Francis Cook. In it, the former Mrs. Cook communicated her desire for Mr. Cook to marry Tennessee. The two were married soon after, and Tennessee later became Lady Cook. When her husband died in 1901, Tennessee inherited the equivalent of $2,000,000, which she spent in trying to establish homes for reformed prostitutes, raising an army of women, building a school for fathers, and other projects during her numerous trips to her homeland. She died a rich woman in 1923, leaving Victoria half a million dollars.

Clairmont, Claire (1798–1879) Clara Mary Constantia Jane Clairmont changed the spelling of her first name several times as romantic fancy determined, yet her mother chose to simply call her Jane. Three years after her father died, Claire, her brother, and their mother moved next door to writer and publisher William Godwin, a widower and father of the infant Mary Godwin. The two widowed parties married and combined their families, then added a son, William.

The atmosphere of the new homelife was intellectually stimulating, and Claire watched and listened as poet Percy Shelley and others read their works and joined her stepfather in debates. Godwin was a leading free-thinker, but even he was shocked when the anarchist Shelley and Mary fell in love and ran away together. Not only didn't they marry, but they took along sixteen-year-old Claire, whose fluency in French would be helpful.

The trio spent six weeks walking through France and Switzerland, using what little money they had for food and cheap lodging as they traveled across the Alps. When they returned to London, Claire remained with Percy and Mary to avoid the convent to which her mother planned to send her. An introduction to the notorious Lord Byron changed her life forever, and she schemed to become his mistress. She was seventeen, physically attractive, and hopelessly in love. Byron was up to his neck in scandal as rumors abounded regarding his incestuous union with his half-sister and his deteriorating marriage.

Claire first wrote to Byron and asked to meet with him for advice regarding an acting career, for she knew that he was a member of the board of management of the Drury Lane Theatre. After he wrote her a letter of introduction to the theater director, she again wrote to Byron to tell him that she had changed her mind and now wanted to be a writer and she solicited his further assistance. This time, however, she suggested that they meet twelve miles outside of London, where they could be alone. Aware of her intentions, Byron told her that they could be as discreet and more comfortable if they used a house in town.

At first, Claire simply stole hours to spend with the still-married Byron, for he resisted any living arrangement which would increase his growing notoriety. When the scandals over his morals and his politics escalated to the point that he had to leave England, he refused Claire's pleas, that he take her with him. Finally, before he left in 1816, he agreed that she could visit him in Geneva if she were properly chaperoned. The ecstatic Claire convinced Mary and Shelley, who planned a trip to Italy, to stop over in Geneva with her.

In Geneva Claire continued to officially live with Shelley and Mary, as she tried to keep her role as Byron's mistress from reaching her family in London. By August, she was pregnant, and Byron ended the affair soon after. When Claire gave birth to a daughter in January, 1817, Mary wrote to Byron who replied that he wanted to name the child Allegra, and that he intended to have a hand in raising her. However, when the group went to Italy to take Allegra to her father, Byron refused to see Claire and sent a messenger for his daughter. He was already deeply involved with his new Italian mistress, Teresa Guiccioli.

Despite her misgivings, the despondent Claire reluctantly left Allegra to Byron's care, visiting her daughter as she was allowed until Byron committed the child to a convent when she was four-and-a-half years old. Claire begged Shelley to help her kidnap Allegra, but he refused. In 1822, when Allegra was five, Claire learned through Shelley that Allegra had died of typhus in the convent. Ten weeks later, Shelley drowned while sailing across the Bay of Spezia.

For ten years afterward, Claire earned her living as a governess in various wealthy families, first in Vienna then in Moscow, where in 1824 she read in a foreign newspaper of Byron's death in Greece. Although she had various brief affairs, no man ever again mesmerized her so completely as had Byron—nor did she ever come to hate any man so thoroughly as she finally came to hate Byron for having caused Allegra's death. After she returned to England in 1828, Claire spent the next twenty years as governess or tutor in Italian to a seemingly endless parade of rich children, hating every day of the work.

In 1844 Claire received a inheritance left to her by Shelley and she retired to Florence, Italy, where she could live less expensively. In her later years, her unmarried niece, Paula, joined her. Claire Clairmont died in 1879, and she was buried with Shelley's shawl, as she had requested.

Claudel, Camille (1864–1943) Brilliant, beautiful, ambitious, and seemingly independent, Camille Claudel was also a talented sculptor. Her brother, Paul Claudel, achieved fame as one of France's most celebrated poets and playwrights, but Camille found her own talents overshadowed by her lover, the sculptor Auguste Rodin. Even today, many experts question whether works credited to Rodin might have been created by Camille but signed by him as his own.

As a rebellious young woman, Camille left her quiet provincial background and went to Paris to become a sculptor. She was very mature at the age of nineteen and her art attracted the attention of Rodin, who took her on as his pupil. Although he already lived with his common-law wife Rose Beurat, the forty-year-old Rodin was strongly attracted to Camille and she soon became his model, muse, and mistress. For nearly a decade, she was also his collaborator and she worked on his sculptures as well as created many of her own.

By 1893 Camille had tired of her semi-official existence as Rodin's mistress. The age – and her increasingly critical mother and sister – demanded that she either be married or remorseful, so she sought marriage. Reports vary, but she is said to have had four children by the dominating Rodin, all placed for adoption, and several miscarriages. Rodin, however, refused to give up his freedom, a stance encouraged by Rose Beurat. Thus, Camille broke off the relationship, although they continued as occasional lovers until 1898, and she became determined to establish herself as an independent sculptor after ten years of Rodin's tutelage and domination.

Soon after the break with Rodin, Camille became mentally unbalanced, locking herself away for days at a time, disappearing without warning, and claiming that a conspiracy headed by Rodin existed to kill her and to destroy her art. By 1913 Paul Claudel and Camille's mother incarcerated her in an asylum where she remained for thirty years until her death as an old, miserable, and unknown woman in 1943.

Claudius I, Emperor (10 B.C.–A.D. 5) See **Agrippina.**

Cleopatra VII (69 B.C.–30 B.C.) Born into a family with a common name of Cleopatra, *the* Cleopatra was elevated to the throne of Egypt with her ten-year-old brother, Ptolemy XII Philopater, upon their father's death in A.D. 51. By law, the two were forced to marry, but three years later, the outspoken Queen of Egypt had so angered her brother's guardians and advisors that they tried to assassinate her and she fled to Syria.

While in exile, Cleopatra attempted to gather an army to fight to reclaim her throne, but she achieved little success until she met Julius Caesar. He attempted to negotiate on Cleopatra's behalf and invited her to visit him in Alexandria. Justifiably fearful of attacks by Egyptians who were sympathetic to her brother, Cleopatra secretly made her way to Alexandria and the legend remains that she asked a trusted servant to wrap her in a carpet, bind the roll tightly, and carry the package ashore as a purported present for Julius Caesar. Unwrapped at his feet, the beautiful Cleopatra excited the interest of Caesar and she soon became his mistress. Eager to please his lover, Caesar assembled his army and marched on Ptolemy XII Philapater's troops, turning them back and claiming victory for Cleopatra and for the Romans in 47 B.C. Philopater drowned in the retreat.

Ardent in his desire to please her, Caesar proclaimed Cleopatra to be Queen of Egypt, and she again ascended her throne. Due to custom, Cleopatra was forced to marry a second brother, eleven-year-old Ptolemy XIII, in order to rule jointly. Once she was certain that the government was stable, Cleopatra joined Caesar in Rome where she resumed her role as mistress and where she bore a son whom she named Caesarion, later Ptolemy XIV. After Caesar was assassinated in 44 B.C., Cleopatra returned to Egypt and had Ptolemy XIII murdered so that she could rule with her infant son Caesarion as co-regent. For the next three years, she kept abreast of happenings in Rome.

In 41 B.C. Cleopatra decided to win the friendship and loyalty of the new ruler of the eastern Mediterranean territories of the Roman Empire, Marc Antony. The two became lovers, and Marc Antony returned with Cleopatra to Egypt, carrying with him a desire to put

Cleopatra (BRITISH MUSEUM)

the power of his Roman troops and of the Empire itself to work for Cleopatra. They lived together for a time, with Marc Antony ruling at her side. Cleopatra bore two children as Marc Antony's mistress.

In 34 B.C. Marc Antony and Cleopatra married, and the last of their three children was born. The news of Marc Antony's actions infuriated the Roman Senate, and Julius Caesar's son, Octavian, later to be called Augustus, declared war on Egypt. The vicious battles which followed gave Rome the advantage, and Marc Antony's forces were crushed at Actium in 31 B.C. He committed suicide, leaving Cleopatra to contend with Octavian's revenge.

Planning to exhibit her as a spoil of war and drag her through the streets of Rome, Octavian had his prisoner heavily guarded. But she outwitted her captors. Legend declares that Cleopatra arranged to have a poisonous snake, perhaps an asp, smuggled into her room hidden in a basket of fruit. Ever regal and ever the queen, Cleopatra bathed, perfumed, and dressed herself, then provoked the snake to bite her in the breast as she reclined in a relaxed position. She was buried beside Marc Antony.

Cleveland, Grover (1837–1908) See **Halpin, Maria.**

Clifford, Rosamund (1157–1176) Numerous legends surround Rosamund both in life and death. Queen Eleanor knew fully of Henry II's promiscuity, and although she should have known that old queens must often simply tolerate young mistresses, Eleanor seems to have taken a particularly venomous view of Rosamund. So fearful was Henry for his sixteen-year-old Welsh nobleman's daughter that he had a maze built at his palace at Woodstock to protect her, but Eleanor is said to have sent a cohort to visit who allowed a silk thread to trail from a sewing basket; Eleanor found her way in later by following the thread. One legend tells that Queen Eleanor tried to murder Rosamund by having her bleed to death in a hot bath, while another story relates that she confronted Rosamund and offered her a choice of death – either poison or a dagger wound.

Popular opinion went in Rosamund's favor and the people referred affectionately to "Fair Rosamund," who had made their king so happy, but her life was brief. She died in 1176, at the age of nineteen. Devastated by his loss, King Henry gave a large sum of money to the nuns of a nunnery next to the River Thames in Oxfordshire to have Rosamund buried just in front of the altar, under the church choir. The sudden death of the youthful beauty stirred veneration in the nuns, who for years adorned the tomb with lamps, silks, and scented candles, until Bishop Hugh, rumored to be Henry II's illegitimate son by another mistress, visited them in 1191 and ordered the veneration ended. Rosamund's remains were exhumed and reburied in the nuns' chapter house. Even there, Rosamund could not rest for, during the intolerant Reformation which sought to eliminate all symbols of corruption, she was again dug up and her ashes were scattered in the wind.

Colet, Louise Revoil (1810–1876) Louise Colet was a literary figure in her own right, whose talents were admired and encouraged by leading poets and writers such as Victor Hugo, Leconte de Lisle, Pierre Jean de Beranger, Alfred de Musset, and Alfred Victor Vigny, as well as many lesser known literary, artistic, and political figures who frequented her salon. An earnest and prolific writer with many novels and volumes of poetry to her credit in later life, she kept detailed diaries and extensive letters which trace her relationship with French novelist Gustave Flaubert, telling us not only what they ate and when they made love but also giving us insight into the genesis of his great novel, *Madame Bovary* (1857).

Louise's first marriage was to her flute teacher, Hippolyte, which did not last long. Soon after they moved to Paris and she began to publish her poetry. Louise acquired the eminent mid-century philosopher Victor Cousin as her protector, mentor, and lover. He was a member of the French Academy and became Minister of Education in 1841. Cousin used his influence to convince friends in the Academy to vote for Louise's writing, and four of her poems won French Academy prizes which brought recognition for her work as well as financial reward. This use of influence angered a jealous pamphleteer named Alphonse Karr, who charged Cousin with fraud, claiming that the cabinet minister had raised the stipend for Louise whom he claimed was pregnant with Cousin's child. Hippolyte, although separated from Louise, felt impelled to defend his wife's honor and he challenged Karr to a duel. Louise moved quickly and caused a scandal when she confronted Karr with a knife and wounded him slightly. In her diaries, Louise maintained that Hippolyte was her child's father.

Louise continued her writing. At thirty-six she was posing for a bust by French sculptor James Pradier when Gustave Flaubert walked into the studio and the two met. He was twenty-five and living with his mother and niece in Rouen. Although he had had other experiences with women, he claimed that Louise was the first women whom he loved and possessed. Flaubert appeared unexpectedly at her apartment the day after they first met, and she agreed to dine with him. Afterward, they hired a carriage and watched the celebratory fireworks which commemorated the abdication of ultraroyalist Charles X in 1830.

Flaubert was tortured by the relationship. He feared a scandal if her husband were to learn of them because Louise was still married to Hippolyte. More troublesome were his feelings of conflict between his desire for Louise and his duty toward his mother. He had failed to tell his mother that he would remain in Paris overnight the first time that he stayed with Louise, and she had waited at the train station in Rouen all night to welcome him home. Each time that he took the train away from Paris and from Louise, his mother was waiting at the station.

The strains of meeting both demands upset Flaubert, who often suffered "nervous attacks," later diagnosed as epileptic seizures, after being with Louise. She demanded more time of him and her passionate tirades and letters made him feel guilty. After a year during which she charged him with treating her like a whore with whom he spent random afternoons and evenings, Flaubert proposed that they stay friends and write occasionally. He professed to love her, but he warned that love was not essential to his happiness and said that he could never make any woman happy.

The love-hate relationship continued in fits and starts even after her husband's death in 1851, and her private diary for that year shows that she followed Flaubert's movements carefully. She reports that Flaubert spoke of a new novel he was beginning, based on the tragedy of Madame Delamarre, a wife in the provinces whose excesses had ruined her husband. Letters from Flaubert reported his slow and painful progress in writing *Madame Bovary*.

In 1852, Louise won the French Academy competition with a long narrative poem, *L' Acropole d' Athenes*, which Flaubert had revised for her. Upset by Flaubert's coldness toward her, Louise became involved with French Romantic poet, Alfred de Musset, also forty-two, and she struck up an acquaintance with another member of the Academy who had also been twice the Minister of Education, sixty-two-year-old Professor Abel Villenaia. Piqued by her new relationships, Flaubert asked that they meet in Mantes, halfway between their two homes, where he shared his progress on *Bovary* while Louise read her new poems to him. Throughout 1853 they began to meet more boldly, sometimes spending a week or so together which the thirty-one-year-old Flaubert told his mother were spent with male friends. He worried constantly that Louise might become pregnant and frequently asked in letters "How are the English?" referring to the "redcoats," his euphemism for her menstrual periods.

As Louise agonized in letters over her love for Flaubert, he reported page counts as he progressed on his novel. As late as 1854, Louise complained that Flaubert had not kept his promise to introduce her to his mother, while he protested that he sought only to protect her from his mother's possible cold treatment. He increasingly asked in letters that she think more of mental rather than sexual gratification.

The relationship finally ended in 1854 when they met in Paris and Louise berated him viciously for his lateness, charging him with having been to a brothel instead of meeting her on time. As he reported in his *Correspondence*, she started to kick him and he thought of grabbing a log near the fireplace and beating her to death. Only the thought of court and criminal proceedings restrained him, and he chose, instead, to walk out and to never go back to her again.

Louise continued to write and published *Lui* in 1859, a fictional account of their love affair. *Madame Bovary* was published in 1857 so *Lui* created some interest, but this soon died down. She continued to write and periodically told mutual friends that she planned to publish Flaubert's letters to her, but she failed to carry out the threat, although she kept the letters with her until her death in 1876. The letters were finally published a few years later through the joint efforts of Flaubert's niece Caroline and Louise's daughter Henrietta who sought to make money from them.

Cooper, Gary (1901–1961) See Bow, Clara; Velez, Lupe.

Cortes, Hernan (1485–1547) See Tenepal, Malinali.

Craig, Gordon (1872–1966) See Duncan, Isadora.

Dahlinger, Evangeline Cote (1894–1974) Evangeline Cote Dahlinger was a longtime employee of the Ford Motor Company. Short, dark, self-confident, and attractive, she was of French-Canadian background and the first cousin of actor Tyrone Power. Forced to help to support her family at an early age, she had taught herself shorthand and obtained a job in the Ford Company at the age of sixteen. She rose to be head of the stenographic department only three years later and in 1913 attracted the attention of Henry Ford, who soon had her working late at the office in the role of his personal assistant. Evangeline was an exciting woman who was the women's harness-racing champion of Michigan and the first woman in the state to obtain a pilot's license. In addition, she usually carried a small pistol in her purse which she said that she would use on anyone who hurt Ford.

Numerous pictures survive of Ford and Evangeline together – with his wife, Clara, nowhere in sight – at baseball games, in celebrity groups, and at fancy occasions. Ford felt himself to be safe from criticism because he made everything very proper in 1917 by marrying Evangeline off to Ray Dahlinger, a Ford henchman and former chauffeur. The Dahlingers shared the same bed until the birth in 1923 of the baby boy, John, who occupied Henry Ford's attention. From that point, Ray Dahlinger slept alone in another part of the house.

Although Ford never acknowledged paternity, nor was he openly accused in his lifetime, he did pay particular attention to this child of employees. Not only did he give the Ford family christening gown to John for the baptism, he provided the wood crib in which he had slept as a baby, and he gave four-week-old John a Shetland pony. In addition, Evangeline's father and brother were provided with Ford dealerships, and Ray's mother received received a two hundred-acre farm beside a lake. Evangeline was given a one-hundred-fifty-acre estate, complete with a custom-built mansion, which was the second-grandest residence in Dearborn, as well as other holdings including a docking ramp for her personal seaplane.

After the baby's birth, Evangeline took an even greater role in Ford's life, and she was the person upon whom he relied to decorate all of the historic houses which he had transported to Greenfield Village. With Ford's death in 1947, Evangeline was "retired" from the company and Ray was let go after Mrs. Ford's death in 1950. In 1978, Ford's son by Evangeline, John Cote Dahlinger, wrote about the affair and of his mother's years as the mistress of Henry Ford.

Danilova, Alexandra (1906–) Russian ballet dancer Alexandra Danilova, known affectionately as "Choura," has been honored the world over for her talent, technique, and interpretive power. She trained at the Imperial School of Ballet in Saint Petersburg, then later became a soloist with the Soviet State Ballet. After leaving the Soviet Union in 1924, she became a member of Sergei Diaghilev's Ballet Russe and stayed until it dissolved in 1927 at Diaghilev's death. While a member of the Ballet Russe, Choura created leading roles in the ballets "Apollo," "La Pastorale," and "The Triumph of Neptune." She began to dance with the Ballet Russe de Monte Carlo in 1933, becoming the prima ballerina in 1938, and toured the United States extensively. She later appeared as a guest dancer with other ballet companies before taking her own company, Great Moments of

Ballet, on tour from 1954 through 1956 throughout Japan, the Philippines, and South Africa.

Choura won the 1958 Capezio Award for both her extensive repertoire and the unique nature of her characterizations which ranged from romantic roles through George Balanchine's highly stylized abstractions. Particularly noteworthy are her roles as the street dancer in "Le Beau Danube," the glove seller in "Gaité Parisienne," Odette in "Swan Lake," and Swanhilda in "Coppelia." Since retiring from dancing in 1958, Choura has given lectures, appeared in two movies, *Oh Captain!* (1958) and *The Turning Point* (1977), and taught at the New York City Ballet, as well as staged ballets for other companies. Further, as a member of the New York City Ballet faculty, Choura also staged with Balanchine, the company's artistic director, the complete "Coppelia" in 1975.

A member of the Maryinsky Theatre School in Saint Petersburg from the age of eight, Choura not only developed her talent there but she also met the man who would have a profound influence on her life, George Balanchivadze, whom the great ballet impressario Sergei Diaghilev later renamed George Balanchine. The children of the school became very close, seeking substitutes for the family life which they left behind in their dedication to dance. When the time came to leave the school, friendships remained strong.

Although Balanchine married Tamara Gevergeyev when he was eighteen and she sixteen, the friends continued to socialize. Choura also became a member of the group of young dancers, gathered by Balanchine after his graduation from the Petrograd Conservatory of Music, which presented a series of programs, called Evenings of the Young Ballet. On one of their evenings out, a gypsy fortune teller approached the group and told the newly-wed Balanchines that their marriage would not last long, because he would fall in love with a friend of his youth named Alexandra. Despite Choura's furious blushing at the time, the prediction did come true.

Choura left Russia with the Balanchines, dancer Nicholas Efimov, and former Maryinski opera company baritone, Vladimir Dimitriev, in 1924 as representives of the State Theatre under the name of the Soviet State Dancers. They had no bookings, but the man who organized their departure, Vladimir Dimitriev, hurriedly arranged several musical hall and resort engagements, private parties, and whatever else could be had in Germany. He finally obtained a booking for them at the Empire Theatre in London. Their act was canceled after two weeks, and they headed for Paris, despondent, when a telegram arrived stating that the great impressario Sergei Diaghilev wanted to look at them. The audition was a success and the four dancers became part of Diaghilev's Ballet Russe. After they had been dancing there for about a year, Balanchine confessed that he was hopelessly in love with Choura and that he was leaving his wife. Because the marriage papers had been left behind in Russia, George could not obtain a divorce, so Choura was forced to decide whether to leave her love or to move in with him and to relinquish her dream of being a bride walking down an aisle in a white dress.

During her years as the mistress of choreographer George Balanchine, Choura learned to refine her art, trained by Balanchine to dance with exactness. She also learned the value of establishing an independent career after Diaghilev's death in 1927. During the years from 1927 through 1931, while Choura lived with Balanchine, she did little dancing. Balanchine often left her in London for six months at a time to choreograph ballets, expecting that she would meet her expenses and those of their apartment while he spent lavishly.

In 1931, Choura finally went her own way, yet hoped that Balanchine would ask her to reconsider. Still upset a year after the breakup, she married Giuseppe Massera, an Italian engineer, but the marriage did not last long. Choura yearned to dance, and she earned a spot in the Ballet Russe de Monte Carlo in 1933. Balanchine, who had not been faithful to her while they lived together, married three times more during his lifetime, to young women under his tutelage. He created ballets for and had affairs with many more.

Despite their friendship in later years, the two never spoke about their love. Still, Choura continued to regret what might have been, and she speaks in her memoirs with longing affection of her days as mistress to George Balanchine.

Davies, Marion (1897–1961) Marion Cecilia Douras was born in Brooklyn, New York, on New Year's Day in 1897, and educated at the Convent of the Sacred Heart near Hastings, New York, until she turned sixteen. The stage and the Ziegfeld Follies beckoned and, three years after leaving the convent, chorus girl Marion had become the mistress of the man with whom she would spend the next thirty-six years of her life.

Thirty-four years her senior, the newspaper and real estate tycoon, William Randolph Hearst, bought Marion a film career by supervising most of her forty-five films and using his publishing empire to provide her with widespread publicity. He made certain that she played mostly virginal roles which would preserve her public reputation. He also installed her in his palatial West Coast mansion at San Simeon where she played the hostess to all of his guests while wife Millicent stayed on the East Coast. Only when presidents or royalty visited did Hearst fly his wife out to San Simeon to become temporary lady of the manor.

Throughout the thirty-six-year affair, Marion and Hearst slept in separate bedrooms and Hearst usually looked the other way while Marion had flings with leading men, among them Dick Powell, Leslie Howard, and Charlie Chaplin. In 1924, Hearst lost his tolerance when Marion became infatuated with Chaplin. During a party on his yacht Oneida Hearst followed Marion and the man whom he mistook for Chaplin down to a dimly lit cabin where he watched the two embrace. He took out a pistol and shot the man, who was actually movie producer Thomas Ince, in the head and killed him. The story was hushed up; the papers reported the death as a heart attack brought on by severe indigestion. Ince's body was cremated, and Ince's widow was provided with a trust fund.

Despite Hearst's patronage, none of Davies' movies were memorable, and few believed her talent alone won her the roles. Just prior to World War II, Marion left films to devote herself entirely to Hearst and became his constant companion. She acquired money, jewels, and real estate, as well as a knowledge of business which she put to good use after Hearst died in 1951 at the age of eighty-eight. Fifty-four years old, Marion was despondent and she rushed into marriage in Las Vegas with Captain Horace Brown, a former roustabout stuntman and merchant marine, only ten weeks after Hearst's death. She had millions of dollars in jewels and art treasures, expensive real estate, and a Beverly Hills mansion. Brown was the jilted suitor of her sister, Rose. Marion repeatedly regretted her move and filed for divorce after eight months. The pair quickly reconciled, but Marion sued for divorce several more times in their ten years of marriage.

At her death from cancer in 1961, the former chorine was worth twenty million dollars and left behind expensive real estate in New York City, Los Angeles, and Palm Springs. On her deathbed she told Horace that she had no regrets.

Davis, Mary (Moll) (fl. 1668–1669) Moll Davis met King Charles II of England at the Tunbridge Wells court in 1668 as one of several actresses, which included Nell Gwynn, offered for the King's perusal by the Duke of Buckingham. The court was there so that Queen Catherine could try the waters to cure her infertility. Moll quickly caught the king's eye, but she was only his mistress for a year before he generously pensioned her off and moved on to Nell Gwynn.

Moll was a member of Sir Willim Davenant's troupe at Lincoln's Inn and starred in *The Mad Shepherdess*, in which she sang a melancholy tune named "My Lodging is on the Cold Ground." So impressed was the King with her varied talents that he soon gave her a ring worth six hundred pounds and a house on Suffolk Street. She gave birth in 1669 to a daughter, christened Mary Tudor, who was married to the Earl Derwentwater at the age of fourteen. Upon Mary's marriage, despite having broken long before with her mother, Charles provided his daughter with wedding expenses and the money for the linens and furniture of her new home.

Diarist Samuel Pepys refers to Moll as being "the most impertinent slut in the world," but he praised her acting and thought her a better actress than Nell Gwynn. Her dancing was graceful, and her personality sweet. Charles seemed pleased with her, and his reason for sending her away is debated. Some historians say that he simply grew tired of her. At least one account places the blame on Nell Gwynn who is reputed to have laced Moll's sweetmeats with the purgative julap shortly before Moll was to dine with Charles. This ended their relationship.

de Barbin, Lucy (1936 –) Married off by her grandmother at the age of eleven to a brutal middle-aged husband, Lucy de Barbin was sixteen and the mother of two young children when she first met the King of Rock and Roll, Elvis Presley, who was then only an eighteen-year-old singer with the dream of wealth and fame.

As Lucy related in her story of the romance, *Are You Lonesome Tonight?*, Elvis repeatedly asked her to marry him from the beginning, but first her marriage, then her later fears of ruining his career by exposing the child which they had conceived prior to his entering the Army, kept her from agreeing to be his wife. Her only concession was to name their daughter Desiree, because that was the name of the one movie they saw together. It was after that movie that the two pledged their undying love and went through a self-styled wedding ceremony on a windy hilltop outside of Memphis, thus beginning a love affair which was to continue until his death in 1977. She never was able to tell Elvis that Desiree was his daughter, at first for fear of ruining his career and then because it was too late.

Lucy and Elvis drifted in and out of each other's lives over twenty-four years, years in which she divorced a brutal, abusive husband, then married another man with whom she had two more children but no happiness. Over the years, Elvis would call for moral support or unexpectedly send her peach-colored roses with the inscription she knew so well, "E.L. Lancelot." The E. L. stood for "Everlasting Love" and she referred to him as Lancelot for having been the knight in shining armor who gave her the courage to start a new life. He, in turn, called her Desiree.

In his early television appearances Elvis would bring his hand to his ear several times as a signal to Lucy. That signal had grown out of their habit of doing the same during their tender moments to hear their heartbeats through their hands.

After he had married Priscilla and she was pregnant with their daughter Lisa, Elvis called Lucy and confessed that he still loved her. He had tried to remake Priscilla into Lucy's image by having her dye her hair black and taking dancing and French lessons, for Lucy was a dancer and spoke French. Later, when his marriage was falling apart, he again called Lucy to urge her to think of a future with him.

Lucy hesitated because of the apparent inconstancy of Elvis' attention. Although he professed undying love, women moved in and out of his life and the newspapers continually reported new relationships. At the end, as Elvis drifted closer to his destruction from the over-prescription of drugs, he called Lucy from every stop on his tours, pouring out his heart and bringing her closer to revealing the secret of their child.

Finally, in August 1977, Lucy had gathered the courage to complete her divorce and she was going to tell Elvis about their daughter. He was to leave for a tour on August 16, and he had promised to call her before he left. She never received the call. Instead, their daughter Desiree called to tell her of Elvis' death.

Dedichen, Ingeborg (1900–1983) Ingeborg Dedichen was the youngest of seven children of Ingevald Martin Bryde, one of Norway's most prominent shipbuilders, and her mother was descended from Swedish aristocracy. When she and Onassis met in 1934, Ingeborg was about to shed her second husband, a bridge player and gambler, whose name she retained and whose vices had begun to diminish her fortune.

When the two met on the cruise ship *Augustus*, the tall, stylish blond Ingeborg told Onassis that he looked like a mobster. But Onassis showered her with his attention and the two soon became lovers. They traveled throughout Europe, fighting passionately in public and making up even more passionately in private. Onassis' manners appalled Ingeborg's friends and she was happiest when the two dined alone.

Privately, their relationship seemed close, and the two gave each other pet names. Ingeborg was called Mamita while Onassis became Mamico. When Onassis had to leave the country on business, he jealously cautioned her to guard her reputation and never to betray his trust. He insisted that she write to him daily and tell him whom she had met, with whom she dined, and how she spent her time. Calls in the middle of the night revealed his deep suspicions.

Onassis begged Ingeborg to marry him, but she was not yet legally divorced. At the same time that he was paying all of her bills, Ingeborg allowed it to be known that the two were lovers but she took offense if anyone referred to her as his mistress.

In the hectic pre-World War II years, Ingeborg and Onassis were often apart as he feverishly worked in Athens and she remained in her Paris apartment, refusing to join him in Athens. Still, she provided him with valuable business contacts in the Scandinavian shipping world.

In 1939, when WWII was imminent, Onassis pressured Ingeborg to leave Paris and to live with him in New York where many other wheeling and dealing Greek shippers had moved.

Once in America, the two lovers did the rounds of clubs, but he had flings with several Hollywood starlets while he watched Ingeborg closely. They shared an apartment at the Ritz Towers. Onassis also purchased a cottage at Center Island, which he named Mamita Cottage and to which their friends flocked each weekend.

In 1942, when both Mamita and her Mamico were forty-two, Onassis told Ingeborg that he loved her very much but that he wanted to see other women. He left for California to pursue a society girl who had become a starlet. To assuage his guilt, Onassis sent Ingeborg a check for $200,000 accompanied by a short, affectionate note. The starlet turned down his offer of marriage, and Onassis rushed back to his Mamita for comfort and to recoup the check which she had still not cashed.

By 1943 he no longer mentioned marriage, although Onassis continued to profess his love to Ingeborg. Worse, he started to beat her. Onassis claimed that many of his girlfriends had been excited by his rough treatment and that such behavior heightened his sexual pleasure.

A frightened Ingeborg moved out of the Ritz Towers and into an apartment on East 54th Street, but the affair – and the beatings – continued.

The slightest imagined affront set him off. Finally, one night Onassis battered Ingeborg so brutally that her body was swollen and bruised, her face was pulpy, and one hand was paralyzed from her attempts to protect herself. Onassis nursed her as her injuries healed, and later swore that he loved her and wanted a child with her. Ingeborg waited until she was alone, then attempted to take her own life with an overdose of Nembutal. Onassis found her in time and called for help. After recovering, Ingeborg ended the affair completely. She returned to Paris after Onassis paid her $35,000 and promised to provide her with a $500 monthly allowance for life.

Although she wrote Onassis letters over the years, he never

responded. In 1983, Ingeborg passed away alone in her Oslo apartment where her nephew found her the next morning.

Demetrius, King of Macedonia (337 B.C.–283 B.C.) See **Lamia.**

Deneulle, Eleonore (1787–1868) On December 13, 1806, Eleonore Deneulle gave birth to a son, proving finally that the child's father, the Emperor Napoleon Bonaparte, was fertile. Unremarkable as the rest of her life as mistress and woman may have been, this one act was to have a decisive effect on history. Had she not borne the boy Leon, whom Napoleon acknowledged as his son and for whom he provided substantial financial support, Napoleon would never have ousted the Empress Josephine and married Marie Louise. The result of his marriage to the Austrian princess was the breakup and redistribution of the empires.

Through countless affairs and in his marriage to the aging Josephine, Napoleon had worried that he might produce no legitimate heir to the empire he had built. With proof now of his ability to father a child, he moved to divorce his wife and to find a younger aristocratic wife.

For her part, the eighteen-year-old Eleonore had no clue to her importance to history because she certainly had little emotional importance to Napoleon. In the weeks during which she was his mistress, the young woman who was born Louise Catherine Eleonore Deneulle shared only Napoleon's bed. There was none of the intellectual or emotional sharing, the friendship, the passionate letterwriting or the tears and scenes which had marked his other affairs. Once Leon was born, Napoleon discarded Eleonore and refused to see her, although he provided for her financial needs and for Leon's care and education and he included the child in his will.

As he had with previous mistresses, Napoleon arranged a financially successful marriage for Eleonore, but she was never lucky in this or later marriages. Her son Leon also brought her great pain as he racked up gambling debts and repeatedly filed unfounded lawsuits in the courts. Despite the emotional difficulties, Eleonore lived to a comfortable old age, dying at the age of eighty, forty-seven years after Napoleon's death.

Deng, Wendi (1968–) Born in the northeastern Chinese province of Shandong, Wendi Deng continues to live a life shrouded in mystery. The mistress of Australian media mogul Rupert Murdoch, the young Deng first came to the United States in 1991 to study economics at California State University. The details surrounding her stay in the United States continue to be vague and contradictory. School friends report a wealthy American businessman husband, whom Deng claims to have met in China. The fact that Deng appeared very affluent during her college years, always in possession of the latest electronics equipment and the best and the fastest computer, seems to corroborate this story. However, none of her classmates or teachers can remember ever meeting her husband. Some classmates remember hearing Deng tell of having wealthy, influential parents, but the details are cloudy.

While at California State, Deng became known as one of the best and brightest minds to ever enter into the institution's economics programs. Former professors continue to rave about her knack for the subject, ranking her among the top one per cent of students the college has ever seen. She graduated from California State University in 1993 and entered into an MBA program at Yale University. To complete the degree, Deng was required to undergo a business internship, which she wisely decided to serve in Hong Kong as she felt that she would stand out more.

Ironically, on a flight to Hong Kong in search of an internship in 1996, either accidentally or by a deliberate ploy, Deng was seated next to News Corp executive Bruce Churchill, who was working with Star TV, China's main television network. The two began talking about the emerging global economy and China's current and future role in the scenario. By the end of the flight, Deng was offered an internship at Star TV's headquarters.

During her internship with the television station, Deng met Rupert Murdoch at a cocktail reception at the nearby Harbour Plaza Hotel. The media giant, who was reported to have long since relinquished anything more than a fleeting interest in the opposite sex, was captivated and mesmerized by the young Chinese national, who reportedly held his attention throughout the duration of the evening. Insiders report that the romance began soon after this meeting, although even those who had watched Deng's efficient rise from intern to 'business development manager, legal and "business affairs" and who were aware of her enthusiasm for cultivating links with senior management were surprised that she had set her sights so high. Murdoch and Deng began appearing together in public. To stem the discussions of impropriety, Deng would introduce herself as Murdoch's translator, but would decline to comment on any other questions from the media or friends. The couple travelled throughout China together, with Deng acting as his translator and counsel. On numerous occasions, Deng purportedly exerted influence and opinion over Murdoch in the development of New Corp's China's policy. News Corp Beijing staff report that various changes leading to the departure of Australian executives, and the employment of Chinese nationals at the company, were a direct result of Deng's influence over Murdoch. In 1998 Deng left her desk with Star TV to become a permanent fixture with Murdoch. Since Murdoch filed for divorce from Anna Murdoch, his wife of 31 years, in April of 1998, the couple have become more public with their relationship. The two married in June 2000 and she is now expecting his baby.

Dewey, John (1859–1952) See **Yezierska, Anzia.**

Diamond, Jack "Legs" (1895–1931) See **Roberts, Kiki.**

Dickens, Charles (1812–1870) See **Menken, Adah Isaacs; Ternan, Ellen.**

Digby, Jane Lady Ellenborough (1807–1881) Jane Elizabeth Digby's father was an admiral in the British navy who had fought under Nelson at Trafalgar and whose wealth had come from capturing Spanish ships laden with cargo. Her beauty attracted attention from the start, and her mother decided to trade on Jane's looks by arranging for an early debut from a Harley Street address when Jane was only sixteen. At her coming-out party in 1823, Jane met her future husband, the thirty-three-year-old flabby and stodgy Edward Law, Lord Ellenborough, who had already been a widower for four years.

While Jane dreamed of a romantic adventurer, her parents urged a union with the stuffy and unpleasant lord whose estates and income dazzled them. The innocent young Jane soon learned that her stuffy husband preferred the pastry cook to her inexperience. Despite numerous offers from young noblemen at the balls she attended frequently, Jane remained faithful to the marriage for the first two years. Once she began to stray, however, she did it with enthusiasm.

She soon became the mistress of Prince Felix von Schwarzenberg of Austria, a special attaché to the Austrian Ambassador to Great Britain. She was so deliriously happy with him that, a few weeks after she had begun to meet him at his rooms, she climbed on the roof of her home and shouted, "I am the mistress of Prince von Schwarzenberg!"

Three years later, she was pregnant with the prince's child and awaiting the outcome of her husband's petition to the English House of Lords for a divorce. The scandal and notoriety from the ensuing debate and publicity followed her for most of her life, for Lord Ellenborough had paraded a long line of witnesses to prove that he had been wronged. While the proceedings dragged on, Jane left for Paris to await the birth of her child and for a brief reunion with the prince. There the prince abandoned her, taking their daughter.

Stranded and alone, she became for a short while the mistress of French novelist Honoré de Balzac, who later based one of his most fascinating characters on her, Lady Arabella Dudley in *The Lily of the Valley* in 1835. Jane had already been used as a character in three earlier novels before the appearance of Balzac's novel. In 1826, Margaret Stanhope's three-volume novel about English society, *Almack's*, based its main character on Jane. In 1830, Lady Charlotte Bury wrote *The Exclusives*, which portrayed Jane's affair with Colonel George Anson. In 1835, just before Balzac's novel appeared, Lady Blessington's *The Two Friends* scathingly portrayed Jane as the spoiled, immoral seductress, Lady Walmer. Many agreed that this best-selling novel painted the truest portrait of Jane.

After their brief but intense relationship, Jane left in 1831 for Munich, where she became the mistress of King Ludwig I of Bavaria. To maintain a semblance of decorum, however, she married wealthy nobleman Baron Carl Venningen, which provided her with the new title of baroness. The marriage to the baron most likely occurred to prevent a scandal, for Jane gave birth to a son six weeks after the wedding and it was supposed that the Queen had issued the marriage order.

Three years after her marriage, Jane met Greek Count Theotoky, who had been sent to Munich to study German military techniques. Entranced by his romantic stories of Greece and Theotoky's pleas that she run off with him, obtain an easy divorce in Greece, then marry him, Jane became the count's mistress. They met clandestinely, but the baron passed them one evening while they were driving in a carriage as he returned unexpectedly from a diplomatic mission. A chase ensued, after which the two men dueled. Jane's husband won the duel, lodging a bullet just above the heart of the young count. Jane and the baron took the count – whose wound seemed mortal – back to their castle, where his presence and eventual recovery set tongues wagging throughout the countryside. Soon after, Jane asked to be free of her marriage, and the baron agreed but he kept their two children. The two lovers then left and Jane spent the next five years as Theotoky's mistress, living in France and Italy. Her divorce was then final and she had become a member of the Greek Orthodox Church in order to marry him.

The marriage lasted ten years, and ended when their youngest son Leonidas died from a fall, thus severing the final bond of their deteriorating union. As forty-four-year-old Jane awaited her divorce from Theotoky in Athens, she became the mistress of King Otto of Greece, son of King Ludwig I. After she became tired of Otto, Jane traveled around Italy, then returned to take a tour of northern Greece. There in the mountains, she fell deliriously in love with General Hadji-Petros, the seventy-year-old leader of the guerrilla fighters and governor of the province surrounding Lamia where he had fought to liberate Greece. As his mistress, she became bandit queen, sleeping with him under the stars, eating simple bread and cheese, and drinking from goatskins.

Jane became popular among the mountain people, but King Otto's wife extracted her revenge. She ordered the general suspended as governor for immoral behavior with Jane, then chastised him in person. Despite this, the affair endured, but Jane left Hadji when she learned that he was also sleeping with her maid. Heavyhearted, she set out for a tour of the ruins of Palmyra in Syria. While deep in the Syrian desert, she met the man who finally fulfilled all that she had been seeking.

Short, leathery, and bearded, Medjuel El Mezrab's appearance disguised an erudite and cultured man of aristocratic Bedouin lineage who spoke several languages. His brother Sheik Mohammed asked Medjuel's assistance in arranging an ambush and kidnap-ransom scheme to obtain the wealthy Englishwoman's money, but Medjuel refused. When his tribesmen went ahead with their plan as he guided Jane toward Palmyra, he fought fiercely to protect her. Afterward, he told her that he loved her and would divorce his wife to marry her. Jane refused, then returned to Athens.

They met again several months later when she returned to Baghdad, and Medjuel presented her with an Arabian mare and told her that he had divorced his wife and sent her back with her dowry to her family. He then asked Jane to marry him, and she agreed. They were married in 1855, after overcoming the objections and snobbery of both their families.

Jane lived happily and fully as Medjuel's wife for twenty-six years, during which they lived Western-style in a villa in Damascus for six months of the year and Bedouin-style in a tent in the desert for the other six months. She made only one trip to England during all of that time, and returned happily to her desert lover. She died in 1881 after a prolonged attack of dysentery and was buried in Damascus in the Protestant section of the Jewish cemetery.

Diogenes (412 B.C.–323 B.C.) See **Lais.**

Drusilla, Livia (58 B.C.–A.D. 29) Born in 58 B.C. to the highly respected, proud, noble Claudian family, Livia Drusilla married a nobleman of her family, Tiberius Claudius Nero, and bore two sons, Tiberius and Drusus. When civil war broke out in Rome, the Claudian family joined opposition forces which battled Julius Caesar and his son Octavian (later Augustus).

When relative peace had returned to Rome in 39 B.C., Livia became acquainted with Octavian and she set out to charm him. Although both were already married, they managed to carry on a passionate affair, aware of the scandal and political outrage that would erupt should they be discovered. Anxious to leave the shadows, Livia persuaded Octavian to leave his wife and she divorced her husband so that they could marry.

Helped by Livia's practical instincts, by 30 B.C. her husband had become ruler of the Roman Empire, strengthening his authority by assuming the title of Augustus. Livia not only enjoyed her role as ruling spouse, but she also sought to ensure that her son by her first marriage, Tiberius, would ascend the throne upon Augustus' death. When her stepdaughter Julia's husband died in 12 B.C., Livia pressured Tiberius to marry the young widow and to become stepfather to Augustus' two grandsons, Gaius and Lucius. Despite his objections, Livia ignored her son's desires and the marriage occurred, and Tiberius went into voluntary exile on the island of Rhodes soon afterward. When Tiberius tried to return a few years later, Augustus refused him because Gaius and Lucius were growing older and more knowledgeable in government policy, and he didn't want their stepfather to interfere.

Augustus refused to relent despite Livia's entreaties until Gaius and Lucius died. Although there was widespread belief that Livia had ordered their murders, she and her accomplices seem to have covered their tracks well. Soon after, Tiberius returned to Rome, and Livia manipulated Augustus into adopting her son as his heir.

When Augustus died in A.D. 14., Tiberius ascended the throne as figurehead ruler while his mother directed his movements. Livia jealously guarded her power, even to the point of eliminating another potential successor, her grandson Germanicus, whose father was Livia's younger son, Drusus Germanicus. There was no direct evidence to tie her to this murder either, although she was a prime suspect. Under Augustus and Livia, Rome knew perhaps its greatest flowering as the empire expanded, and a stable, honest government ruled the land.

Duarte, Eva (1919–1952) Better known as Evita, Marie Eva Duarte was born in the extremely poor village of Los Toldos, located on the pampas approximately one-hundred-fifty miles outside of Buenos Aires. Her parents were unmarried and young Eva had little chance of education, but she had a persistent desire to escape her poverty.

She spent her teens and early twenties sleeping with the right men to move slowly up the social ladder. Stories conflict as to whether or not she ever worked directly as a prostitute, but she was referred to as a "little whore" by many who knew her. Certainly, her earlier male companions were second-rate entertainers or businessmen who first took her out of Los Toldos, then provided her with a living in the larger city. Later, she lived with a series of men who helped her to become Argentina's leading radio actress.

Soon, Eva set her sights higher, on the man who would someday rule Argentina, Juan Peron. A widower and colonel in the army, Juan Peron was forty-eight when he met the twenty-four-year-old Eva who first conquered his body and then his mind. She became his mistress and moved in with him. As his inspiration and the intelligent sounding board who encouraged his ambitions, Eva supported Peron's goal to head Argentina. Her humble background won her the hearts and support of the people, and she gladly shared her popular support with Peron.

Eva and Peron were married in 1945 and a short time later Juan Peron became president of Argentina. She served as minister of health and labor from 1946 through 1952, and wielded great power over government policy. Evita used her newfound power to suppress all stories and pictures of her earlier life, rewriting her history as required. She championed the cause of Argentina's poor, winning their devotion as they watched one of their own who had achieved power, and her influence provided support for women's suffrage, the organization of workers, and social programs to help her people.

Eva was a dyed-blonde goddess in furs and diamonds to the "shirtless ones" who adored her. She died of uterine cancer at the age of thirty-three, and her nation mourned her deeply. Three years later, a coup removed Juan Peron from power. He tried to return to power in 1973, but the magic of Evita was missing and Peron was ousted once again.

Dumas, Alexandre fils (1824–1895) See **Duplessis, Marie.**

Dumas, Alexandre père (1802–1870) See **Bernhardt, Sarah; Menken, Adah Isaacs.**

Duncan, Isadora (1877–1927) Born Dora Angela Duncan in San Francisco in 1877, she was destined to create an expressive style of dance which provided the foundation for twentieth century modern dance. After making her professional debut in Chicago in 1899, she toured Europe, danced in U.S. dance recitals, established schools of dance in Berlin, Paris, and Moscow, and introduced the world to a radically different approach to dance. Inspired by waves, sounds, emotions, and nature, Isadora's techniques emphasized free-flowing movements which were supported by her diaphanous tunics and freely-swinging hair. Highly improvisatory, the techniques pioneered by Isadora influenced numerous choreographers, including Americans Martha Graham, Ruth St. Denis, and Ted Shawn, as well as Russian-born George Balanchine.

Isadora waited until the age of twenty-five before embarking upon her first affair. She was enamored of a young Hungarian actor, Oscar Beregi, who was playing Romeo in a Budapest stage production and in her private life. Her first experience with him stretched to all-day lovemaking, and the two were blissfully happy for several weeks until professional engagements forced them apart. The following year Isadora became the mistress of theatrical designer (Edward) Gordon Craig, son of English actress Ellen Terry, who had a special friendship with George Bernard Shaw. Isadora disappeared for two weeks into Craig's Berlin studio to indulge in her passion for him without telling anyone of her plans. Shows were canceled, newspaper articles appeared, and her family and manager were terrified that she had been harmed. Nine months later, Isadora gave birth to her first child, a daughter whom she named Deirdre.

Two years later, she met and became the mistress of the playboy son of sewing-machine tycoon Isaac Singer. For seven years, Isadora lived in luxury and her every material wish was granted by the adoring millionaire Paris Singer. The couple had a son, Patrick, in 1910; both children lived with them. Singer was extremely jealous and he stormed out of Isadora's life one evening in 1912 after walking into a seemingly deserted room and finding Isadora in a compromising situation with playwright Henri Bataille.

Only months later, her beloved Deirdre and Patrick were killed with their governess when the car in which they sat stalled, then

Isadora Duncan (BETTMANN ARCHIVE)

started of its own accord after the chauffeur had stepped out to investigate the difficulty. It rolled backward into the Seine River, drowning the helpless passengers.

Free-spirited, temperamental, and passionate, Isadora Duncan changed the nature of modern dance by infusing her personality into her work onstage and breaking through the rigid constraints of classical ballet and translating her feelings into an entirely new dance form. Onstage, Isadora danced barefoot, wearing brief and flowing nearly see-through tunics. She insisted that dance be natural and individual, and appeal to both the spiritual and physical senses. Using graceful, free-flowing movements rather than the stiff and mechanically rehearsed movements of the times, she brought an excitement to dance which titillated audiences while her personal life stimulated the same interest.

After several meaningless affairs, Isadora met pianist Walter Rummel when she returned to Paris in 1918. Although he was ten years her junior, the thirty-one year-old Rummel adored her, and she returned his love and called him her archangel. Unlike previous relationships, Isadora seemed to be completely happy and free of any power struggles with Rummel. They lived a very private life, only leaving their retreat to give concerts. Soon, however, Isadora learned that Rummel was carrying on an affair with one of her troupe of young dancers, the "Isadorables." She broke with Rummel and left for Moscow to found a school of dance.

Isadora married once, in 1922 at the age of forty-four, but her alcoholic husband, Russian poet Sergey Yesnin, made her life miserable. When they separated after a few months, she depended on the kindness of former friends for shelter and food. Despite the poverty of her final years, she continued to exude the enthusiasm for life which characterized her early career. She died in 1927 when her long, red scarf became caught in the rear wheels of the Bugatti in which she rode, crushing her larynx and breaking her neck. Only moments before, she had called out to friends as she left, "Adieu, mes amis, je vais à la gloire." ("Farewell, my friends, I am going to glory.")

Duplessis, Marie (1824–1847) Alphonsine Rose Plessis knew from nearly the start of her life that she would die young, and she often voiced this fear to people close to her. Delicately beautiful, thin, and pale, she had fine skin that was marked with the little blue veins which many people of the nineteenth century associated with consumption. Early in life, she renamed herself Marie in honor of the Virgin, and to give herself an air of financial worth she took the surname Duplessis, for she dreamed of one day attaining wealth and of buying the Plessis estate. Despite humble origins, Marie possessed a natural style which made her appear elegant, and she added mystery to the image by always carrying bouquets of camellias.

Born in the village of St. Germain de Clairfeuille, in Lower Normandy, she was the granddaughter on her father's side of a prostitute and a priest. Her father was a drunken brute who owned a draper's shop and her mother left the family to take work as a maid to an English family when Marie was young. Her father then shipped Marie to relatives who owned a farm. The relatives returned Marie to her father when she turned thirteen, and he quickly saw the financial possibilities of having an attractive, physically mature daughter. He gave his daughter to a seventy-year-old bachelor friend in exchange for payment. After a year, Marie was sent back to her father who promptly sent her out to make her own living. After working for a corset maker and an umbrella maker, Marie became a streetwalker. When she was sixteen, a fat widower named M. Plantier, who ran a small restaurant, gave her an apartment and made her his mistress.

From this point Marie began her social climb. Within a few months, she left Plantier for the Count Ferdinand de Monguyon. Soon after, she met Agenor de Guiche, who became the Duc de Guiche-Gramont and French Foreign Minister under Emperor Napoleon III, and became his mistress. A year later, at the age of seventeen, she gave birth to his son. In the manner of the upper classes, Guiche took the child to a wet nurse in the country, then later told Marie that the child had died of pneumonia. This seems unlikely for in 1869, twenty-two years after Marie's death, a young man aged about twenty-seven contacted Marie's older sister and asked permission to view a portrait of Marie. Emotions flooded his face as he gazed at the portrait, and the sister observed that his features were very much like the face of the portrait.

Beautiful, intelligent, and possessed of a natural sweetness, Marie attracted not only men of wealth but also men of intellectual prominence, such as novelist Dumas *fils* and composer Franz Liszt. Yet, she was not satisfied with those who adored her. She sought luxury, and this she found when she was twenty as the mistress of Count de Stackelberg, the Russian Ambassador to Vienna. Married, wealthy, and an octogenerian, he nonetheless indulged in occasional lovemaking but, more important, he discreetly paid all of Marie's bills. She also became the mistress of Alexandre Dumas *fils* for one turbulent year during which he ran out of money escorting her to dances, paying her gambling debts, and buying her presents. He insisted that she give up her wealthy Russian count and Marie retorted that she would – if Dumas would pay all of her bills. The affair ended bitterly. Yet, Dumas *fils* remained obsessed with Marie who inspired his creation of Margaret Gautier in his 1848 novel *La dame aux camellias* and the later play of the same name which was produced in 1852. Dumas's play inspired Giuseppe Verdi to compose *La Traviata*.

She also sought respectability, which she achieved in the year before her death when she became the wife of the Comte Edouard de Perregaux in 1846. Shortly after the marriage, the couple separated and Marie, left without support, became gravely ill. When she died in 1846 of consumption at the age of twenty-three, creditors stormed her apartment and pillaged what they could. Later, most of her belongings and even locks of her hair were sold at auction and even lowly items such as combs were purchased for amounts equal to their weight in gold.

Edward Augustus, Duke of Kent (1767–1820) See Montgenet, Thérèse-Bernadine.

Edward VII, King of England (1841–1910) See Bernhardt, Sarah; Greville, Frances Evelyn, Countess of Warwick; Jerome, Jennie; Keppel, Alice; Langtry, Lillie.

Edward VIII, King of England (1894–1972) See Furness, Lady Thelma; Simpson, Wallis Warfield.

Eisenhower, Dwight David ("Ike") (1890–1969) See Summersby, Kay.

Eliot, George (1819–1880) Mary Ann Evans was born the daughter of a land agent in Chilvers Coton, Warwickshire, England, and educated in the local school before being sent to a religious boarding school, a move intended to strengthen in her the

Evangelical Protestant religion of her father. Eliot was summoned home at age seventeen to care for her father after her mother's death, and this move closer to family ironically freed her of her strict religious upbringing. Largely self-taught from this point, she read voraciously and worked as a translator from German into English. In the early 1840s, she rebelled against this strict religious dogma after becoming acquainted with rationalist thinking and the new German theological scholarship which caused her to question her beliefs and to eventually break with her family. She translated D.F. Strauss' *Leben Jesu* (*Life of Jesus*, 1846). Her father died when Eliot was thirty, and she immediately relocated to London to begin a career as a free-lance writer.

She never expected to find romance. Physically unattractive and awkward, Eliot's large nose, dull complexion, and lank hair evoked little passion among casual observers, but those who spoke with her were soon enchanted by her animated and expressive blue eyes and her clever mind. A few years after arriving in London, and after two years as the assistant editor of the *Westminster Review*, she met writer George Henry Lewes, a married man with four children. All had been fathered by other men, yet he had already accepted the children as his own. Consequently he was unable to divorce his wife with the charge of infidelity. This obstacle did not deter them, however. Henry James wrote that Lewes was as physically unattractive as Eliot, but that he matched her in animation and quick intellect.

The couple went to Germany in 1854, then returned to Britain to openly live together. Although Eliot viewed herself as Lewes' wife throughout their twenty-four years together, she never expected nor received any of the privileges which marriage provided the nineteenth-century woman. The relationship, however, was extremely satisfying to both parties; the two apparently lived as equals. She took her lover's first name for part of her pseudonym and she shared all of her earnings. Their relationship provided adequate material for the novels about illicit love which were to become so successful.

Eliot's first published works were reviews, translations from German, and magazine articles. She did not publish her first fiction until she was thirty-seven, and she was urged to do so by Lewes, who encouraged and protected her from unfavorable reviews throughout their life together. She used a pseudonym when her first three stories, which later formed *Scenes from Clerical Life*, were published in *Blackwoods* in 1857. Influenced by her unconventional lifestyle and resulting precarious position in society, Eliot's novels not only reveal the social and moral problems of her era but they more importantly present the internal struggles of characters who seek to live life on their own terms. *Adam Bede* (1859), *The Mill on the Floss* (1860), *Silas Marner* (1861), *Felix Holt the Radical* (1866), and *Daniel Deronda* (1876) contain sensitively drawn characters who must contend with the rules and will of society.

Middlemarch (1871–1872) has been acclaimed her major achievement, and some critics view the novel as one of the greatest in the English language. The novel contains her most detailed description of provincial life and of the social, personal, and professional conflicts faced by individuals within that society. The desire for reform by the sensitive and idealistic heroine Dorothea Brooks conflicts with real life as she learns that she cannot fight her true feelings and desires. Happiness eludes her until she decides to put aside material concerns, here in the form of her husband's dictate in a will that she will lose his estate should she remarry to the man she loves, Will Ladislaw. She finds happiness when she is true to herself and gives up her property to marry Ladislaw. Other characters, such as Dr. Lydgate and Fred Vincy, must also struggle to exert their will against the restrictions of society.

Eliot's life with Lewes was liberating in other ways. Throughout her years with Lewes, veiled hints indicated that the couple enjoyed a highly sensual love life. Eliot wrote in her journal that she often received her best ideas after a satisfying night of lovemaking, while she lay quietly beside him in bed.

She lost her protector and buffer from the world when Lewes died in 1878, and she became a recluse, unable to write. Despondent, for comfort she turned to her banker John Cross, a man twenty years younger than she, whom she married two years after Lewes' death. Seven months after the marriage George Eliot died.

Elizabeth I (1533–1603) To many who have seen only the portrait of the first Queen Elizabeth of England in later age, her nickname as

Queen Elizabeth I (BETTMANN ARCHIVE)

the "Virgin Queen" appears understandable. Tightlipped, balding, and laced tightly in stays with the high ruffled collar standing stiff beneath her chin, she projects an irnage of impenetrable authority. The early life of Elizabeth I seems, however, to have been decidedly different.

Several scholars contend that her nickname is not meant to suggest that she remained forever sexually inexperienced, only that she never married. Politically, maintaining her virginal image also provided Elizabeth I with a powerful psychological advantage. Still, a look at her life shows that many men were intimate friends who frequently spent hours alone with her in secluded discussion.

The only child of Henry VIII and Anne Boleyn, she was three years old when her mother was beheaded and the marriage was declared annulled so that her father could marry Jane Seymour. Elizabeth was declared illegitimate because of the annulment. She was one of only three legitimate children of Henry VIII, with sister Mary, born of Henry's first marriage to Catherine of Aragon, and brother Edward, born of the marriage to Jane Seymour. Surrounded mainly by adults and starved for parental love, she acted more like a grave woman of forty than a child of six when presented by her father to yet another stepmother, Anne of Cleves. By the time that she was ten, Elizabeth had had four stepmothers. This certainly influenced her view of marriage, and may have hardened her against it.

The earliest man to capture her heart was Sir Thomas Seymour, one of two younger brothers of Jane Seymour, Elizabeth's second stepmother. Upon Henry's VIII's death when Elizabeth was thirteen, the thirty-year-old Seymour petitioned the Council to allow him to marry her but was firmly refused. So, he secretly married the King's widowed sixth wife Catherine Parr and lived with her and with Elizabeth who had joined her stepmother. Servants became concerned about the intimacy which Seymour showed the young girl, often bursting into her room, slapping her buttocks, grasping her, and kissing her playfully. Catherine admonished both her husband and Elizabeth, but the behavior continued even though Seymour proved to be a loving husband to his pregnant wife. The dashing, rakish Seymour dazzled the inexperienced and affection-starved future queen.

In 1548, eight days after giving birth to a daughter, Catherine died. Seymour again plotted to marry Elizabeth. His ambitions angered government officials, and he was thrown into the Tower and then beheaded. Elizabeth was extremely upset, but she also exhibited suspicious physical symptoms for most of that summer. Rumors abounded that she was pregnant, although an official proclamation denied it.

After the incident with Seymour, Elizabeth realized that she had to retain a spotless reputation if she were to win the trust and love of the English people. While they might honor a virile and promiscuous king, they would not abide such behavior in a queen even though it would be years before she would ascend the throne, as first her brother would rule as Edward VI, from 1547 through 1553, then her sister would hold the throne as Mary from 1553 through 1558.

As she matured, and later became queen in 1558, Elizabeth carried on a lifelong love affair with Lord Robert Dudley, first Earl of Leicester. The two openly teased each other, visited in each other's quarters, and engaged in passionate flattery. Although Elizabeth vehemently denied sexual intimacy with her "Sweet Robin," her subjects and palace attendants gossiped that the two were lovers and invented five children supposedly born of the union.

This lover, as well as other favorites Sir Walter Raleigh and Robert Devereaux the second Earl of Essex, reflected her first love, Thomas Seymour, for all were sexually vigorous, rakish, handsome men, yet none shook her resolve to remain the "Virgin Queen." All were politically astute and wise advisors. The reign of Elizabeth I was a time of strong national spirit and industrial, economic, and political prosperity. England became a major sea power, and foreign trade was encouraged. The monetary system was standardized and the Royal Exchange opened in London in 1566. Further, literature flourished, and writers such as William Shakespeare, Christopher Marlowe, and Sir Edmund Spenser created their great works.

In 1601, Robert Devereaux, the second earl of Essex, led a revolt against the throne, and Elizabeth was forced to order him executed. Her last years were unhappy and lonely as she saw her popularity wane because of heavy expenditures and the abuse of royal power due to weak or incompetent ministers. At her death at the age of sixty-nine, she had her wish and her epitaph proclaimed that, officially at least, she had lived and died a virgin.

Ellis, Havelock (1859–1939) See **Sanger, Margaret.**

Essex, Earl of (1566–1601) See **Elizabeth I.**

Fairfax, Sally Cary (1730–1811) The wife of George Washington's brother-in-law (his half-brother's wife's brother), Sally Cary Fairfax met the future father of our country when he was only a gawky youth of sixteen and she was eighteen and already married.

Tall, slender, and pampered, the brunette Sally with her high cheekbones and direct, penetrating eyes, was the daughter of wealthy, indulgent parents who gave her both fine clothes and the access to books which she desired. She spoke and wrote French, read novels and political journals which were imported from France and England, and exuded polished sophistication.

Sally saw promise in the young George and decided to take over his education. Under her patient tutelage, George read widely, declined French verbs, and practiced penmanship. She also inroduced him to English drama, and he often attended presentations of dramatic skits in her home at Belvoir.

The two declared their love for each other in letters when George was twenty-three years old. Letters between the two survive for

Sally Cary Fairfax

George always wrote a rough draft before completing a final copy to send, and he kept his rough drafts. In this same period, George Washington rented Mount Vernon from his half-brother Laurence's widow, a move which brought him next door to Sally. In the winter of 1757, he was ill with influenza, lingering on the brink of death, and Sally spent much of her time at Mount Vernon nursing him. Gossip traveled all the way to her husband who was in England, and many acquaintances wondered just how close the married Mistress Fairfax had become to the twenty-five-year-old gentleman.

Even when George married Martha Custis in 1759 when both were twenty-seven, the rumors continued. In many accounts their marriage is represented as being more one of a mutually satisfactory arrangement based on respectful affection than one born of passion. George states in at least one letter regarding his intended marriage that the time had come for Mount Vernon to have a mistress. For the wealthy widow, emotional rather than financial considerations prevailed. She had been married since the age of seventeen to one of the wealthiest plantation owners in Virginia, then widowed at twenty-five with two children. Later, George and Martha raised the younger two children of her son after his death in the American Revolution. Martha was an enthusiastic wife, often joining her husband in army camps and she was with him during the long, hard winter in Valley Forge. She was also a gracious hostess and she entertained lavishly while First Lady and later when they retired.

Despite the apparent happiness of the Washingtons, hints of a relationship continued. Neither Sally's marriage nor George's produced children and the two families were constantly dining and socializing with each other. The scandal simmered for many years, and a letter exists in which Sally's brother-in-law Bryan Fairfax rebuked her for her conduct.

Finally, in 1771, with war in the air, Sally's husband decided to close their home Belvoir and to return to England with Sally. The contents of the home were auctioned off in 1774 and George Washington outbid all others to obtain both Sally's bedroom furniture and the pillows from her bed. She carried her letters with her to England.

The two families corresponded, but Martha put pressure on both parties to dampen their interest in each other. Sally never returned to America, even after her husband died in 1787. George died in 1799 and Martha died two years later. After Sally's death in 1811, alone, infirm, and in financial trouble in England, her letters from George were found among her effects. They point to a hopeless yet passionate love between a married and honorable woman and a reckless but respectful man. A descendant of Sally wrote about the affair early in the twentieth century and said that theirs was a physical as well as an emotional relationship, "a crimson passion."

Farnese, Giulia (1474–?) Dark-haired, with penetrating black eyes and a round face, Giulia was the youngest daughter in a family of Italian provincial nobles whose family owned the castle of Capodimonte. At the age of fifteen, she was engaged to Orsino Orsini, the thirteen-year-old son of Lucrezia Borgia's governess. Because the fathers of both were dead, Lucrezia's father, Roderigo Borgia (Pope Alexander VI), invited the two to his palace to sign the nuptial contract.

After the religious ceremony took place a year later, the young couple moved into the Borgia palace on Monte Giordano with the ten-year-old Lucrezia and her governess Adriana de Mila, Orsino's mother. Pope Alexander took a fatherly interest and awarded the fourteen-year-old bridegroom a command in the papal army and a yearly allowance. Soon after Giulia became pregnant, her young husband became distant from her, moved to his family estate, and voiced the desire to make a pilgrimage to the Holy Land. Giulia remained at the Borgia castle where she gave birth to her child.

Guilia's beauty attracted the desire of the sixty-year-old Pope who frequently visited his daughter Lucrezia. He finally decided that the papal palace was too far from his sixteen-year-old flame, and he found one nearer the Vatican for his daughter and, of course, for the rest of the household. After the group moved in 1493 into the Palace of Santa Maria, which stood on the left side of the steps of Saint Peter's in the Vatican, Pope Alexander visited the palace several times daily. People spoke openly of Giulia as being "The Pope's Whore."

Despite his age, Pope Alexander was a still-virile and attractive man. Giulia bore him four children, in addition to those he had sired before her, and enjoyed an obscure but protected life. She remained on good terms with his daughter Lucrezia, who went on to her own infamy.

Faulkner, William (1897–1962) See Carpenter, Meta

Fersen, Count Axel (1755–1811) See Marie Antoinette.

Fields, W.C. (1879–1946) See Monti, Carlotta.

Fisher, Catherine (Kitty) (1738–1767) Pretty, intelligent, clever, and young, Kitty Fisher was rescued from the dullness of being a milliner's apprentice by an army ensign who gave her attractive gifts. After she became his mistress, however, the young man began to pinch pennies and Kitty moved on to wealthier patrons. Each man introduced her higher into society, until she had as admirers at different times Admiral Lord George Anson, General John Ligonier, and the brother of the future George III, Edward the Duke of York. While she accepted steady support from several of her suitors, Kitty was also an entrepreneur who charged nightly rates for her favors. At one point, her price was one hundred guineas, which she demanded of all her lovers. When the Duke of York handed her only a fifty-pound note after a night of lovemaking, she angrily put the note on her breakfast bread and butter and ate it. The duke was never again welcomed.

London courted her attention, and her actions at the theater or opera were eagerly whispered. The famous portraitist Joshua Reynolds was commissioned to paint her, then painted her a second time as Cleopatra. During her six years of public attention Kitty met most of the famous men of the period, but she became tired of this life and married John Norris, a Member of Parliament, despite his family's objections. She died of illness five months after the marriage, at the age of twenty-nine.

Fisk, James ("Big Jim") (1834–1872) See Mansfield, Helen Josephine.

Fitzgerald, F. Scott (1896– 1940) See Graham, Sheilah.

Fitzherbert, Maria Anne (1756–1837) Born Maria Anne Smythe in Hampshire, England, Mrs. Fitzherbert was a twenty-nine-year old widow with a comfortable income when she met the twenty-three-year-old Prince of Wales, later George IV of England. When she rebuffed his advances, he stabbed himself with a knife, feigning a suicide attempt to convince the devout Catholic widow to become his mistress. To escape him, she left the country and left the prince to his tantrums.

To assuage her conscience, he offered to marry her and employed an Anglican cleric who had recently been released from debtors' prison to complete the deed. The prince knew, however, that the marriage was a sham because the 1771 Royal Marriage Act had been passed to prevent any member of the royal family under twenty-five from marrying without the sovereign's consent – and the prince was only twenty-four. Thus, Mrs. Fitzherbert remained merely a mistress although the two remained happily together through ten children in as many years.

As Mrs. Fitzherbert aged and gained weight, George returned to his drunken, boorish behavior, often threatening her and chasing after her with a sword. He also engaged in numerous and indiscriminate affairs which depleted the household finances, forcing Mrs. Fitzherbert to pawn her jewels. Although George decided in 1795 that he had to marry a legal wife to repair his finances, he confessed on his way to the ceremony that he would never love anyone but the mother of his ten children.

Soon after his marriage to Princess Caroline, George returned to his Mrs. Fitzherbert, with whom he lived in apparent contentment for another decade, during which she grew even fatter and he engaged in other frenzied affairs. Finally, in 1811, George publicly dismissed her. Yet, he must have loved her as much as he could any woman for in the will he wrote in 1796, he described her as his "true and real wife," and it was a miniature of Mrs. Fitzherbert that he ordered to be placed in his coffin. Nothing is known of Mrs. Fitzherbert after her public dismissal.

Flaubert, Gustave (1821–1880) See **Colet, Louise.**

Ford, Henry (1863–1947) See **Dahlinger, Evangeline Cote.**

Foxe, Fanne (1936–) Dubbed the "Argentine Firecracker," the former Annabel Battistella was a thirty-seven-year-old striptease dancer in the Silver Slipper Club when she met the long-time chairman of the powerful Ways and Means Committee, U.S. Representative Wilbur Mills. It was lust at first sight, and Mills was ready to do anything, even buy the club if necessary, to make Fanne his.

The affair was marred from the start by Mills' indiscretion when watching Fanne perform. He often ran up liquor bills of hundreds of dollars. In 1974, he made the mistake of attracting police attention at 2 a.m. while speeding without his headlights on over the bridge of the Tidal Basin. Officers noted that Fanne Foxe had somehow fallen from the speeding car into the Tidal Basin, and Mills became implicated in an embarrassing media circus.

Fanne used the incident to boost her career, and she began to bill herself as "The Tidal Basin Bombshell" and clubs hired her at enormous fees, at up to $13,000 weekly, just to let their patrons see her strip. At one engagement, a tipsy Mills joined her onstage in a Boston strip club, further shocking his constituents and feeding the gossip mills. He finally announced in 1974 that he had an alcohol problem and entered a clinic for treatment. Despite all of the bad publicity, Mills was re-elected to his House seat that year.

By late 1974, Mills was sober and trying to reunite with Fanne, to whom he gave a Cadillac. The reconciliation didn't work, and the scandal didn't subside, for Fanne had published her own version of her time as Mills' mistress in a memoir, *The Congressman and the Stripper*, in which she alleged that she had become pregnant but had an abortion because she feared that the baby would be deformed because of Mills' alcoholism. Despite strenuous denial, the sixty-six-year-old Mills decided to leave politics in 1975 and vowed to use his energies to combat alcoholism.

Francis I, King of France (1494–1547) See **Laval, Françoise, Madame de Chateaubriant.**

Franklin, Benjamin (1706–1790) See **Helvetius, Anne-Catherine.**

Fredegond (?–597) Fredegond was a serving maid in the employ of King Chilperic I of Neustria, a kingdom of the Frank empire in the old Roman province of Gaul. She used her beauty to attract the king

Fanne Foxe (BETTEMANN ARCHIVE)

and her wiles to tempt him to risk everything to possess her. Only a few months after their affair began, the king became afraid that Fredegond would leave him unless he made their arrangement more permanent. To pave the way for marriage, Chilperic murdered his wife Galswintha, then placed Fredegond on the throne beside him.

After giving birth to a son, Fredegond ordered the murders of Chilperic's children from the first marriage. Despite the suspicions of the court, her sexual hold on the king so bewitched him that he refused to even consider that she was responsible for the savagery which paved the way for her son to become king. In 584, Chilperic was also murdered and, despite the strong probability that Fredegond had arranged the murder of a king who was no longer useful to her, she again escaped blame in the matter.

At Chilperic's death, Fredegond's infant son became Clothaire II, but his mother wielded power as regent while he was excluded from all government matters. Fredegond ruled the kingdom unchallenged for thirteen years, quarreling with neighboring Frank kingdoms and engaging her Neustrian countrymen in numerous military campaigns which they always won. She died in 597, leaving her son to take over the throne, and to carry on the courageous rule which an ambitious serving-girl-turned-queen had begun. The story attracted interest in eighteenth-century France, and the composer Hervé wrote and produced a widely popular *opéra-bouffe* named *Chilperic* which drew enthusiastic audiences.

Fuller, Margaret (1810–1850) Known predominately for her learning and feminist views, Margaret Fuller appears to be an unlikely candidate for mistress. Still, the woman whose aggressive intelligence often intimidated men ended her brief life under mysterious and romantic, if tragic, circumstances.

The daughter of a father who was both a congressman and a lawyer, Margaret had command of Latin grammar at the age of six and knew all of Virgil at the age of seven. She had mastered Shakespeare by the age of eight and could speak French, Italian, and Greek before she turned fifteen. She did not attend school until she was fifteen, and she then developed severe headaches, nightmares, and physical ailments. She also soon antagonized most of her classmates.

Her early adulthood was spent in employment for Bronson Alcott, teaching at his school housed in a Masonic Temple. When she was twenty-nine, she began to deliver her famous "conversations" at the bookshop of the Peabody sisters, then joined Ralph Waldo Emerson in publishing the transcendentalist literary quarterly *The Dial*. She also reviewed books for the *New York Tribune*, and antagonized numerous writers with her views.

Her early life had been empty of romantic involvement, but she suddenly became involved in affairs with several men when she turned thirty-five. During a tour of Europe in 1846, Margaret met and charmed Chopin and the Polish poet Adam Mickiewicz, who passionately professed his love and offered to divorce his wife to marry her. She encountered Italian revolutionary Guiseppe Mazzini who also proposed marriage to her.

Margaret met her grand passion in Rome when she was thirty-seven years old. The Marchese Giovanni Angelo Ossoli was a twenty-seven-year-old Catholic nobleman, and Margaret became his mistress soon after they met. Friends viewed their union with disparagement as mainly sensual, and, a year after meeting, their son was born. Although they led friends to believe that they were legally married, no ceremony ever occurred.

The couple sailed with their child for New York in 1850, aboard an Italian ship that contained tons of marble which spent a month at sea. As they approached the shore of New Jersey, the waters became stormy and the boat crashed off Fire Island, New York, on a sandbar. The weight of the marble shifted throughout the hull, causing it to break open and water poured in. As people on shore watched the horrifying scene, crew members and passengers tried to reach land. Margaret stayed with her family, unwilling to save only herself, and the sea swept all three under. Her son's body washed up onto the shore a few days later, but the bodies of Margaret and her lover were never found. The American and English intellectual communities publicly mourned their loss.

Furness, Lady Thelma (1905–1970) Born Thelma Morgan of a prominent American family, but known by friends as "Toodles," Thelma had all of the right connections when she went to England

Lady Thelma Furness (KING FEATURES SYNDICATE)

and began to mix with nobility. Her twin sister Gloria had married into the Vanderbilt family, and in 1926 Thelma had married British shipping magnate Viscount Furness. The marriage had deteriorated by the time that Thelma Furness met and charmed the Prince of Wales in 1929. Thelma joined the prince that summer on a safari to Nairobi, which she later wrote about as being the most romantic time of her life. The two made love under the stars and enjoyed their distance from the prying eyes of London.

While she remained the prince's mistress for five years, Thelma never had him exclusively to herself. Although he had decreased his attention to his former mistress Freda Dudley Ward, with whom he spent an erratic sixteen years, he had not wholly ended their relationship. Thus, while Thelma served as his unofficial hostess at his home Fort Belvedere, he also spent stolen romantic moments with Freda. The differences between the two women, however, were great. As the prince once noted, Frieda appealed more to his intellectual side while Thelma's appeal was physical.

In 1934, after five years as mistress to the prince, Thelma decided to leave England for a six-week visit with her twin sister Gloria. When she was about to leave, a relatively new member of her social circle in England remarked that the prince would be "so lonely" with Thelma gone, to which she replied, "you look after him while I'm away...See that he does not get into any mischief." These fateful words were spoken to Wallis Warfield Simpson, for whom Edward VIII later gave up this throne.

As Thelma returned to London via ocean liner, she enjoyed trinks and dinner with Prince Aly Khan. The prince learned of this dalliance and – now that he had fallen deeply under the spell of Wallis Simpson – used it as his excuse to end their relationship.

Thelma spent the next thirty-five years crossing the Atlantic, between her home and her adopted home, wondering until her death what would have happened if she had never made her fateful journey. She died in New York City in 1970.

G

Gambetta, Leon (1838–1882) See Leon, Leonie.

George II, King of England (1683–1760) See Howard, Henrietta.

George IV, King of England (1762–1830) See Fitzherbert, Maria Anne.

Giachetti, Ada (1863–1934) Married and ten years older than opera immortal Enrico Caruso, the sexually sophisticated Italian-born Ada Giachetti entranced the great singer and the two became lovers soon after meeting. Doomed by Italian law which prevented divorce, Ada remained married while she and Caruso lived together for nearly eleven years during which she bore him four children, of whom only two sons survived.

A successful opera singer in her own right, Ada was a striking beauty whose smoldering eyes, black curls, and magnolia skin gave her the appearance of a Delacroix gypsy. In her early thirties when they met, Ada gave up her own career to stay at home and to provide the temperamental tenor with a nest to which he could return from his extensive touring. The decision was not an easy one, and Ada was torn between her physical passion for Caruso and the regrets of having put aside her own ambitions. The lushly furnished Villa Bellosguardo and the jewels, furs, and servants provided by Caruso could not replace the thrill of the limelight. Jealousy complicated the situation. Although he flirted outrageously, Caruso swore to his Ada that he was ever faithful to her. Still, the separations while Caruso toured and Ada's continuous accusations of infidelity made life turbulent.

Ironically, the relationship ended when Caruso returned from a tour to find that Ada had run away to South America with his young and attractive chauffeur Romati. The note ending their affair came only days after he had been informed aboard ship that his father had died. Passion may have motivated the elopement, but Ada had also grown impatient to resume her own career. Ada's departure drove Caruso temporarily mad and he suffered a nervous breakdown. He tore up the sheets of their bed, destroyed her clothes, and sent telegrams to every city where he thought that she might be. He also contacted Ada's estranged husband, a prosperous Italian business-man, to tell him of the ruptured relationship and to acquire the other man's sympathy. Instead of sympathy, the cuckolded husband responded calmly, and he philosophically advised Caruso to learn to live with his loss.

Adding insult to injury, Ada later sued Caruso for stealing her jewelry, claiming that he had taken back the many expensive gifts which he had made to her over the eleven years. The suit was peacefully settled out of court, and Ada was granted a monthly allowance of $100 for life and support for their two sons. Despite their differences, Caruso loved Ada so that he could never mention her name without awakening great pain. Each month, his eyes filled with tears as he handed his secretary the monthly check "for the mother of my sons." So constant was Caruso's concern that he never missed a payment, and he often reminded his later wife to make sure that the money was sent out.

Ada sang intermittently in the years that followed, then died in poverty and obscurity in South America some years later.

Gilbert, John (1897–1936) See **Velez, Lupe.**

Gilot, Françoise (1921–) Françoise Gilot was born of a respectably bourgeois family in Neuilly. Her father was an industrialist and he had protested vehemently when she dropped out of college to paint. When she met Picasso in Paris in May 1943, she told him that she was a painter and he burst into laughter and told her that a girl who looked as she did could not possibly be a painter. She informed him that she currently had an exhibition at a gallery on Rue Boissy-d'Anglais to which she invited him, and he offered an invitation to his studio.

At first, his longtime valet Jaimie Sabartes, who had been with Picasso for forty years, viewed Françoise as merely another girl with "hot pants" and he treated her rudely as he did all the others. Intrigued and attracted by her, Picasso made inquiries and learned that she cultivated friendships with painters and had been living with one, a Hungarian named Endre Rozsda. He began to realize that she was not the innocent creature whom he preferred in his seductions. During his initial attempts, he berated her for submitting to him with the statement "I'm at your disposition" rather than fending him off. He angrily told her that he couldn't seduce anyone under those conditions if she wasn't going to resist! Try as he did to shock her, bring a blush to her face, or make her nervous by references to phallic images or sexual behavior, she cooly answered him in kind.

Françoise became his mistress a few months after they first made love. He had already been throwing out hints to others, especially to his current mistress Dora Maar, by placing Françoise's face into drawings and leaving them in full view. He also began to supervise her artistic growth. Françoise remained in her own apartment, while Picasso continued to live with his former mistress under strained circumstances. Early in their relationship, he took her with him to visit the impoverished widow of an old friend to whom he gave money and he pointedly told Françoise as if in warning that this woman had once been one of the most beautiful women in Montmartre.

In June 1946, Picasso waned to show Françoise the seriousness of his intent so he bought a house in Provence and made a gift of it to Dora Maar so she would leave their Paris residence, keeping a set of keys for himself.

He treated Françoise as a schoolgirl, and she dressed like one with her jumpers, pleated skirts, and flatheeled shoes. At the same time, he did more and more portraits of her using her as the model for all of his nude and dressed women in this period. She became his "Flower Woman."

He delighted in torturing her, as he did all of his mistresses, and he took her on vacation in 1946 to the home which he had bought for Dora. There, he talked continuously about his women until Françoise could take it no longer and decided to hitchhike to Marseilles. He surprised her by picking her up on the road and calmly telling her that she must be more understanding of him and that what she needed was a child. She eventually bore him two children, Claude in 1947 and Paloma in 1949.

They began to live together later in 1946 for, as Picasso reasoned, people who do not live together eventually drift apart. He began to use her as his model for all of his work of the late 1940s. He told friends that Françoise lacked training. By the early fifties, Picasso was looking for a new, younger model but Françoise was no fool. They quarreled frequently, and Picasso insisted that his freedom was sacred.

In 1953, knowing that Picasso had already begun meeting another woman, Jacqueline Roque, whom he would later marry, Françoise became argumentative. She disagreed with him regarding a portrait of Stalin, telling him that he was in the wrong to have portrayed the Communist leader as a playboy. No one disagreed with Picasso, and he charged that she was taking sides against him. Françoise blew up, calling him a has-been and condemning him for not caring about her or her painting. Within weeks, she joined the "Worker-Painters" group in Nice and took part in its first showing in the St. Denis Museum. A few months later, Françoise told Picasso that she was leaving him and he protested that a woman cannot leave the father of her children. Furthermore, what would she do without him? How could she desert the man who had made a woman of her by giving her Claude and Paloma?

Her response shocked him. Françoise intended to take the children. She overturned all of his previous confidence in dealing with women by being the first to stand up to him. She refused to accept her role as his slave and object and nothing more. Even harder to accept was her apparent indifference to his veiled hints of a new woman, his scattered drawings with a new face in the crowd, and his absences for which he had offered no explanations. He called her "a monster of indifference."

Following their break, Françoise returned with the children to the apartment on Rue Gay-Lussac. The following year, she married a young painter Luc Simon, but the marriage failed as both artists found gallery doors closed to their paintings.

Glass, Alice (1911–1976) A close friend and political supporter of United States President Lyndon Baines Johnson, Glass was born on 11 October 1911, in Lott, Texas. After graduating from high school in Marlin, Texas, she attended Texas Christian University and Columbia University in New York. Unhappy in New York City, she returned to Texas and enrolled for a second time at Texas Christian University then moved to Austin, where she worked as secretary to state senator William Robert Poage. Although she would marry five times, Glass was twenty when she met the man who later became her first husband, Charles Edward Marsh, co-owner of various newspapers throughout the Southwest, including two in Austin, the Austin *Statesman* and the *American*. The couple moved east, where they first lived in New York and Washington before settling finally in Virginia, where Glass would live most of her life.

The Marshes were friends and supporters of politician Lyndon Johnson, a fellow Texan, and Glass encouraged her husband to use his newspapers to support Johnson in his race for the United States House of Representatives in 1937. In 1938 she and Johnson assisted Austrian conductor Erich Leinsdorf, a refugee from the Nazis, to secure a permanent residence in the United States. Johnson, a notorious womanizer, and his wife Lady Byrd were frequent guests at Marsh's rural estate called Longlea, a house modeled on a Sussex country home that Glass had seen on a trip to England with Marsh. Johnson and Glass had a long-running affair known to everyone at Longlea except Marsh, who appears to have loved Johnson as he would a son, though biographers imply that Lady Byrd was aware as well.

Late in her life, Glass told relatives that she and Johnson had been romantically involved in the late 1930s and 1940s. Some Johnson biographies contend that the congressman considered leaving his wife and marrying Alice. Talk of a flirtation between the two was rampant among their friends at this time, though hard evidence in support of the rumors was lacking. The letters that they exchanged after Johnson left the presidency suggest that they had once been intimates but that their closeness had ebbed a good deal over the years. In the last few months of her life, Glass moved from Virginia to Marlin, Texas, where she died of cancer on 9 December 1976.

Godey, Manuel de (1767–1850) See **Maria Luisa, Queen.**

Godwin, William (1756–1836) See **Wollstonecraft, Mary.**

Goldsmith, Sir James (1933–1997) See **Boulay de la Meurthe, Laure.**

Goya, Francisco (1746–1828) See **Alba, Duchess of.**

Graham, Sheilah (1908–1981) Young, daring, and exciting, British-born Sheilah Graham was the mistress of American novelist F. Scott Fitzgerald during the last three years of his life. The middle-aged, Irish Catholic Fitzgerald was fascinated by Sheilah's uninhibited attitude toward sex, and the two shared what Sheilah described as a gentle, tender, happy sort of pleasure.

By the time they met, Fitzgerald was past his prime as a writer, drinking heavily, and working on screenplays in Hollywood where Sheilah was a columnist. At twenty-nine, she exuded the enthusiasm and life which Fitzgerald seemed to have lost, and he drew inspiration from their relationship. The exuberant Sheilah also served as a buffer against the world by helping him to deal with his guilt over his institutionalized wife Zelda and by becoming friends with his daughter Scottie and maintaining the ties between father and daughter.

Sheilah was emotionally destroyed when Fitzgerald died of a heart attack in 1940, which was rumored to have occurred while the two were making love. Although she eventually remarried and had a family, she always spoke with affection of her years with Fitzgerald, and she remained a friend to his daughter Scottie until the end of her life.

Greville, Frances Evelyn, Countess of Warwick (1862–1938)
Frances Greville was familiarly known as Daisy Brooke, after her marriage to Lord Brooke. Daisy and her husband already knew Albert Edward, Prince of Wales, the future King Edward VII, from their command yearly visits to Windsor Castle and through their political activities. However, in 1889, Daisy approached him alone to ask him for assistance in a very embarrassing matter. Still married, she had been carrying on an affair for several years with the married Lord Charles Beresford, who had fathered one of her children and who recently ended all relations with her. In her fury, she had dashed off a letter pleading for reconciliation and demanded that he meet her on the Riviera, but his pregnant wife had opened the letter and consulted a lawyer. Lady Brooke was warned that legal steps would be taken if she continued to bother Lord Beresford.

Distraught, Daisy appealed to the Prince of Wales for help and used her physical attractiveness to place him on her side. Twenty years older than Daisy and the father of five children, "Bertie" was no innocent. He took Daisy's side and used his influence to intimidate both Lady Beresford and her lawyer, to the extent that Lord and Lady Beresford were omitted from social functions for years.

Daisy was mistress to the Prince of Wales for nearly nine years, during which she and her tolerant husband were invited everywhere. Of all the prince's mistresses, Daisy appeared to pose the greatest threat to his wife Princess Alexandra because Bertie seemed to be truly in love. He and Daisy exchanged rings and he always referred to her as his "little Daisy wife." Daisy became an enthusiastic proponent of socialistic government and social reform, and her conversation became increasingly political as she tried to influence the throne. As her political ardor increased, Bertie's passion cooled until the two agreed that they had simply become good friends.

When Bertie ascended the English throne as Edward VII in 1901, Daisy tried to use her access to the king to obtain influence for her radical social projects. She learned that Edward VII the king had as little patience for left-wing evangelizing as ever.

The Countess of Warwick became an eccentric spiritualist Socialist who continued her feverish efforts toward social reform. When she died in 1938 she left only a small estate. In later years, she sold her paintings and art objects, and the former wealthy aristocrat resorted to advertising for a paying guest.

Guiccioli, Countess Teresa (1800–1873) One of five daughters of Count Gamba in Ravenna, Teresa Guiccioli was educated at Faenza in the Convent of Santa Chiara. When she was eighteen, her parents forced her to marry the wealthy, fifty-seven-year-old Count Alessandro Guiccioli, who had already buried two wives. She met Byron three days later, but no sparks flew between the two.

When they met in Venice a year later, Teresa was tired of marriage to an old man whom she addressed as "Signore" and who slept apart from her. Byron presented a romantic and adventurous figure to the unhappy young woman, and her voluptuous body and seductive eyes enchanted him. Soon after she became his mistress Byron wrote to Teresa that she would be his last passion.

Teresa returned to Ravenna and the count allowed Byron to move into his palace. Teresa's husband seemed to placidly accept her role as Byron's mistress, and graciously gave his blessings as they moved between Venice and Ravenna. Byron was unable to obtain a consular post which the count had requested and refused his request for one thousand pounds. Tearful scenes resulted, and the count asked the Pope to aid him. Surprisingly, the Pope granted Teresa a legal separation and ordered that Guiccioli pay his wife two hundred pounds yearly and that Teresa return to her father's house.

Teresa was inseparable from Byron for the next four years, and the two set up a comfortable household in Ravenna, where Byron worked contentedly. Teresa captured Byron's heart and held it far longer than any previous woman because she combined a highly passionate, sensual nature with the ability to nurture the volatile Byron and to soothe him. She was also well-read and provided an intelligent sounding board for his work.

She met Shelley and other literary friends, and she served as Byron's emotional support through the difficult days following his daughter Allegra's death and the drowning death of Shelley. Finally, in 1823, Byron sailed for Greece to help in the Greek fight for independence against Turkey. She returned to her father's house and cherished each letter from Byron. On 17 March 1824, she learned

Countess Guiccioli (CULVER PICTURES, INC.)

that Byron was dead. Inconsolable, she returned to her husband for five months, then left him forever.

As years passed, she took various lovers, but never achieved the same state of contentment which she had enjoyed as Byron's mistress. She occupied most of her remaining fifty-nine years in defending Byron's memory against detractors. When she finally remarried in 1847, she chose a French nobleman, the Marquis de Boissy, who always introduced her as the former mistress of Lord Byron. Their home contained a full-length portrait of Byron which Teresa would often study, becoming misty-eyed.

When she died in 1873, a mahogany box was at her side. The box contained a lock of Byron's hair, one of his handkerchiefs, and the copy of her favorite novel *Corinne* with the inscription *Amor mio* in Byron's handwriting.

Gustav VI, King of Sweden (1882–1973) See Baker, Josephine.

Gwynn, Nell (Eleanor) (1650–1687)

The daughter of Madam Gwynn, an enormously fat brothel keeper who drank and smoked to excess, and a yeoman about whom nothing is known, Nell Gwynn was launched into prostitution by older sister Rose who provided her with early connections. At the age of thirteen, Nell worked as a serving girl in a local alehouse where customers could enjoy liquor at their tables, or sex in one of the several side rooms where the serving girls supplemented their income. Customers there ranged from the trade to the nobility, including the king's companions. Thanks to her sister, who was mistress to a shareholder in a Covent Garden theater, Nell obtained a job as an orange girl in which she was permitted to sell fruits and sweets to theater patrons.

With talent and strong ambition, Nell soon moved up to acting on stage, a new opportunity for women, although the reputation of actresses was little higher than that of prostitutes of the time. Her first known stage appearance was in 1665 in *The Indian Emperor* by English dramatist John Dryden, who later wrote several plays with roles tailored to her acting talents. Although she was by nature well-suited to the vivacious female roles of Restoration comedy, talent was not enough to provide the theater roles and luxurious lifestyle she craved. By sleeping with the right men, she soon acquired a valuable wardrobe and visible stage roles which helped her to attract the attentions of wealthy men.

She was mistress to a succession of important men, but her major chance came when one of her actor-manager bedmates traded her for the promise of patronage to Lord Brockhurst, whose company greatly increased her social status and who taught her the social graces. When the short-lived affair ended, she was approached by the Duke of Buckingham, who was nothing more than a royal pimp. Buckingham selected several women at one time for Charles II to review, and Nell Gwynn was bypassed as another actress named Moll Davis was chosen instead. The rejection had nothing to do with Nell's attractions for the king; rather, it seems that she was overlooked because she asked the king for cash up front instead of waiting for royal favors to be bestowed later.

Despite her initial disappointment, Charles II invited Nell back. From this point onward, Nell Gwynn regarded herself as the "king's whore," although she was just his occasional partner for the first two years. In time, she had two sons by Charles II, Charles Beauclerk, Duke of Saint Albans, in 1670 and James Beauclerk in 1671. The Queen, Catherine of Aragon, received Charles' affection, but he reserved his passion for his mistresses of which there were many. Charles took Nell as his mistress after ending an eight-year relationship with Barbara Villiers, who gave birth to three sons and two daughters in that time. He learned through experience that Catherine, who suffered several miscarriages but never produced an heir to the throne, preferred to pretend that Charles' mistresses were no more than ladies at court. To this end, despite initial antagonism toward the earlier Villiers, she eventually became friendly with the king's loves and never visited his bedroom uninvited.

Charles II had numerous other mistresses, most of them Catholic, as he was. Because she was one of the few Protestant mistresses at court, Nell was courted, fawned on, and flattered in various songs, plays, and stories. Dramatist Aphra Behn dedicated her play *The Feigned Courtesan* to Nell in 1679

In 1681, Nell's carriage was mistaken for that of one of the king's Catholic mistresses, and the Protestant London mob surrounded the carriage angrily. Annoyed with the turmoil, Nell stuck her head out of the carriage window and told the mob, "Pray good people, be civil. I am the Protestant whore." The mob cheered her, blessed her, and allowed the carriage to pass.

Nell Gwynn died in 1687, not long after Charles II, and left behind one surviving son who had been made the Duke of St. Albans. She also left behind the memory of having been the best-loved of the king's mistresses.

H

Halpin, Maria (1838-?) Maria Halpin arrived in Buffalo, New York, sometime in 1871 and soon captured the amorous attention of Grover Cleveland, future president of the United States.

Slim, dark-haired, large-eyed, and full-bosomed, Maria was a widow who left her two young children living with relatives in New Rochelle, New York, to come to Buffalo to make her fortune. Her father was a Brooklyn, New York, policeman and she seemed to have some education. The first job she took was as a supervisor of the cloak department at Flint and Kent's Department Store. She lived in a boardinghouse near that of Cleveland.

The affair began in late 1872, when Maria was thirty-five and Grover was thirty-six. Their son was born on 14 September 1873. Maria begged Grover to marry her for economic as well as social reasons, for he was the most financially secure man she knew. He had other plans, and he gave the child the name of a friend, then allowed Maria to move in with him. She was the first female roommate which he had ever had.

As Grover continued to dodge marriage, Maria began to drink and her shocked roommate made her move out with Cleveland's son in 1876. She moved to nearby quarters, but alcohol fueled her continuous harrassment of Grover. She trailed him on his nightly round of the Buffalo saloons and demanded that he marry her. No extent of negotiation would change her mind.

Finally, in 1877, Grover conspired with a physician to have Maria kidnapped and committed to an insane asylum. Their child was placed in a Protestant orphan asylum where Grover paid five dollars per week for his room and board. Eventually, her brother-in-law brought her an agreement from Grover in which she agreed to give up her child and make no further demands on Cleveland in trade for the payment of five hundred dollars. Maria agreed and dropped out of sight.

The scandal, however, did not die. It lay dormant until Grover's 1884 campaign for the presidency, during which the opposing Republicans circulated widely the following rhyme

REPUBLICANS Ma! Ma!
                      Where's my Pa?
DEMOCRATS Going to the White House
                      Ha! Ha! Ha!

After the case had cooled in the 1870s, Maria dropped out of sight and was only heard from one more time. In 1895, after she had remarried and was living in New Rochelle, she sent President Cleveland two letters in which she demanded money to stop her from publishing the facts in her possession. He never replied, and the damaging letters never surfaced.

Hamilton, Alexander (1755–1804) See **Reynolds, Maria.**

Hamilton, Lady Emma (1765–1815) Emma Lyon was the daughter of a Chesire blacksmith and worked in a series of menial jobs before she bartered her physical attributes to better her position in life.

When a cousin's wife appealed to the seventeen-year-old Emma to help get her husband released from impressment on a British

Lady Hamilton (CULVER PICTURES, INC.)

warship, Emma succeeded by agreeing to be the captain's mistress. A year and the birth of a child later, Emma was again on her own and she became employed by Dr. James Graham in his Temple of Health. Billed as the doctor's "Goddess of Health," Emma performed erotic dances in the nude around the "Celestial Bed" which the doctor rented to impotent men who sought to revive their virility.

As word of Emma's beauty spread, she was hired as a model by artists Thomas Gainsborough, Joshua Reynolds, and George Romney, the latter of whom painted her in numerous guises. Her fortune appeared to be made when she attracted the Honorable Charles Francis Greville, a minor nobleman and Member of Parliament, whose mistress she became for four years. Under his tutelage, Emma learned to dress, act, walk, and converse with members of the upper class. Greville taught her how to act as hostess in his home, as well as how to appreciate art and music. They might have remained together had Greville not begun to have financial difficulties.

Eager to impress his rich uncle, Sir William Hamilton, who was the British Ambassador to Naples, Greville decided to introduce him to Emma. Greville hoped to inherit his uncle's wealth, but could do so only if the fifty-five-year-old childless widower did not marry again. His scheme was to make Emma Sir William's mistress, then to securely carry on an affair with her. Stupidly, he sent Emma and her mother to Naples to stay with Sir William, without informing Emma of his plan. When her pleas for Greville to come and rescue her from the older man's increasingly amatory advances were ignored, Emma finally realized Greville's plan. Angered, she decided to turn the tables on him and, a year after becoming Sir William's mistress, she married him and became Lady Hamilton. Greville's inheritance became hers.

Seven years after her marriage, while living in Naples, Emma met the British naval captain Horatio Nelson. Although sparks went off in their hearts, the two did nothing until five years later when a newly famous Nelson, fresh from his defeat of Napoleon, now a lord and an admiral, again returned to Naples while in pursuit of the French. The thirty-eight-year-old Emma was dazzling and her sixty-eight-year-old husband was the perfect host to welcome the hero who had lost an eye and an arm since their last meeting. The three spent a few weeks traveling overland to England, where Nelson returned to his wife and the now-pregnant Emma settled with her husband. Her habit of wearing low, flowing clothing disguised her pregnancy from her husband, and she managed to later give birth in secret and board the daughter out with a widow without Sir William discovering her indiscretion. The daughter was named Horatia.

After Sir William died in 1803, Emma lived with Nelson at their home called Merton Place, but duty again called and Nelson never returned from the battle with the French at Trafalgar in 1805.

Left with an annuity, her daughter, and her home, Emma lived a dissipated life of drinking, gambling, and wild parties.

Harding, Warren G. (1865–1923) See **Britton, Nan; Phillips, Carrie.**

Harris, Jean (1924–) Cultured, well-educated, and the highly respected headmistress of the Madeira School, a prestigious private girls' school in Virginia, Jean Harris spent fourteen years as the mistress of Dr. Herman Tarnower, a popular and wealthy cardiologist who had written the best-selling books on the "Scarsdale diet," before shooting him to death in 1980. She was then fifty-six and matronly, and she had endured continued humiliation as the long-suffering mistress of a man whose sexual promiscuity had made him have relationships with at least thirty other women in their years together.

Disgrace and scandal were not a part of Jean Harris' life, either as a young woman nor at the Madeira School, where the girls referred to her as "Integrity Harris." Little did her co-workers or her charges know of her private life, however, which revolved around Tarnower, to whom she raced from Virginia to visit in Westchester, New York, during her vacations and weekends. He once asked her to marry him, then canceled the wedding after she had elatedly begun to make plans. In addition, he constantly allowed signs of his other women to confront Jean. Underwear, dresses, and cosmetics left by his other bedmates were carelessly left in the bedrooms or bathrooms of Tarnower's home, and he made no effort to conceal them.

Jean became particularly distraught when Tarnower hired a much younger woman, Lynne Tryforos, to be his new assistant and sexual partner. Although Jean was verbally reassured as to her place, she became frightened that Tarnower would end their relationship and she frantically thought of ways to keep his interest, even the possibility of plastic surgery to make her more physically desirable.

Although she later claimed that she had gone to see Tarnower on March 10, 1980, with a gun that she had asked him to use to kill her to end her misery, the court viewed the situation differently. Despite much media sympathy for Jean as the victim in the situation, the court declared her guilty of second-degree murder and she was sentenced to fifteen years in prison.

Hart, Gary (1936 –) See **Rice, Donna.**

Hays, Wayne L. (1911–1989) See **Ray, Elizabeth.**

Hearst, William Randolph (1863–1951) See **Davies, Marion.**

Héloïse (1099–1164) The story of Héloïse and the philosopher Peter Abélard has come down through history as being a case of near-ideal love.

Héloïse was the daughter of a French physician who left her and his ailing wife in the care of his cleric brother to fight in the Crusades. Her mother died soon after, and ten-year-old Héloïse went to live with her uncle, Canon Fulbert, at the cathedral of Notre Dame until he arranged for her to be educated at the convent of Argenteuil. There she excelled in Latin and Hebrew studies. Fulbert intended that Héloïse become a nun, but his mistress Madelon strongly disapproved. Fulbert couldn't decide what his brother would have wanted for Héloïse. He thus recalled her to Paris from the convent so that she could experience the world before taking so serious a step.

Sixteen-year-old Héloïse met the brilliant thirty-six-year-old Peter Abélard, who was a famous lecturer and potential candidate for the papacy, when she attended one of his lectures at the Notre-Dame Cathedral. Soon after her uncle met Abélard and invited him to live with them and to tutor Héloïse in languages. Abélard fought his attraction for the innocent Héloïse, reminding himself constantly of the promise of a great church career which his future held, but the two could not fight the inevitable. They became lovers, secretly carrying on their affair whenever the canon was out of the house.

When Héloïse became pregnant, she left with Abélard and Madelon to return to Breton to bear the child. Abélard insisted that he would give up his future and marry her, but Héloïse refused and insisted that she would remain his mistress rather than destroy his possibility of rising in the church hierarchy.

Nonetheless, while Héloïse stayed with Abélard's sister in Brittany to await the birth of the son Astrolabe, Abélard confronted her uncle and promised to marry her if the marriage could be kept secret so as to keep his future with the church secure. The canon agreed, and Héloïse returned with Astrolabe to Paris where she refused violently to concur with their plans. She was afraid to harm his advancement and worried that marriage would destroy their love if Abélard later regretted giving up his ambitions. But her protests were overcome and the couple was secretly married.

After the marriage, the couple lived apart, but rumors circulated and news of the child became public knowledge. To protect his niece's reputation, Fulbert publicized the marriage, but to protect Abélard's career Héloïse swore to everyone that she was Abélard's mistress and not his wife. When the canon punished her for the humiliation, Abélard kidnapped her and took her back to the Argenteuil convent to hide.

Her uncle misunderstood the intention and thought that Abélard had locked Héloïse away in the convent to be free to be with other women, and he thought that Abélard was insisting that Héloïse become a nun in order to remain eligible for the priesthood. To avenge what he viewed to be lost family honor, Fulbert hired four ruffians. The four entered Abélard's bedroom, bound him, and castrated him with a razor. Two of the four were later captured, blinded, and castrated, and a third was imprisoned. Fulbert was chastised by a church court which confiscated all of his possessions.

Although Héloïse begged Abélard to pursue a church career, he refused and, instead, entered the order of the monks of St. Denis. Héloïse re-entered the convent, this time taking the veil but pledging that nothing would ever obliterate her love for Abélard.

Years later, Abélard's writings were criticized for being heretical and unorthodox, and he was forced at the age of sixty-three to travel to Rome to defend himself. On the way, he became ill and died. Now the abbess at a priory in Paraolete, Héloïse had his body buried in its gardens where she visited and looked after his grave. She died twenty-two years later and was buried next to him. In 1817, their remains were removed to the Père-Lachaise Cemetery in Paris and reburied in a single tomb. Their letters to each other have come down to us as the relics of great love.

Helvetius, Anne-Catherine de Ligniville (1719–1794) Madame Helvetius was already fifty-eight years old when she met the seventy-one-year-old Benjamin Franklin in 1777. He had been sent to France by the fledgling government of the United States of America as both Minister to France and as the American Consul whose job it was to acquire funding for his nation.

Madame Helvetius had the maners of a peasant and, despite her great wealth and family connections, she maintained a household so slovenly that most peasant wives would have been ashamed. Her family had been among the oldest in Lorraine, but they had also been among the poorest, so there had been no money to educate young Anne-Catherine. Although she acquired the manners, dress, and appearance of an aristocrat after having made a comfortable marriage at the age of thirty to a famous and very rich financier, Madame Helvetius spelled abominably badly all of her life.

While Madame Helvetius might have carried herself and dressed like a queen, her home and her manners remained those of a peasant. Her face had moles and wrinkles, and she reportedly rarely washed her face. The magnificent mansion at Auteuil was filled with animals which ran wild, as well as with an assortment of philosophers and monks who took advantage of the stimulating conversation and free food and drink. At one count, she had eighteen cats, ten dogs, and several birds to which she doled out unlimited affection, often stopping in mid-conversation to pick up her favorite dog Poupou to kiss him. When Poupou wet the floor, she would unceremoniously use the hem of her skirt to wipe away the damage. She seems to have had an aversion to only one thing in life – other women who might possibly become her rivals.

Although her habits were slovenly, her mind was clever, her body

Madame Helvetius (NATIONALE DES MONUMENTS HISTORIQUE)

was robust and energetic, and her wit was sharp. The aged Franklin fell deeply in love with her and spent as much time at the Salon de Auteuil as his diplomatic duties would allow. Finally, unable to restrain himself any further, in 1780 he asked Madame Helvetius to marry him. The request took her by surprise, and she slumped weakly against the mantlepiece, unable to answer for a moment. After Franklin left, she consulted with a former suitor who had been her trusted confidant for years. He told her that she would lose her salon if she married Franklin, and that answer made her decision. She adored Benjamin Franklin, but she had lived without him and could continue to live without him. She could not live without her friends and her salon .

Sadly, she and Franklin began to see less of each other, although he wrote her a sad farewell when he left France in 1784. They never met again, although journal entries which he made when back in Philadelphia show that in his mind he often returned to his love.

Hemings, Sally (1773–1835) For years historians have pushed aside rumors and letters alluding to "Dusky Sally and her tan brood," preferring to ignore Thomas Jefferson's more than thirty-year affair with mulatto slave Sally Hemings. Although the story was briefly and eagerly discussed during the 1802 presidential campaign, Jefferson's descendants successfully erased most mention in later years.

Sally was officially part of Jefferson's property and she and her children were counted yearly like the cattle and horses. The daughter of Betty Hemings, a slave belonging to the plantation of Jefferson's father-in-law John Wayles, Sally's father was probably the plantation's master – the father of Jefferson's wife Martha. Sally was born the year after Jefferson and Martha were married.

When John Wayles died, Sally and her mother were sent to Monticello as part of Martha's share of the estate, and Sally grew up in Jefferson's household. Martha died in 1782 when Sally was nine years old, but the young girl had frequent contact with the master and the mistress because she frequently ran errands to her sick room.

Two years later Congress appointed Jefferson a Minister of Plenipotentiary to negotiate a peace treaty with the British, and he went to Paris taking only his twelve-year-old daughter Martha and

Sally's brother James with him. He left his two youngest children at home. Later, he asked that his remaining child (nine-year-old) Polly be brought to him after he received word of baby Lucy's death. He also asked that a reliable older slave be sent with Polly, because he would remain in Paris for three more years as a replacement for Benjamin Franklin.

The designated slave became ill, and fourteen-year-old Sally was hurriedly picked to replace her. Once in Paris, Sally was very well treated by Jefferson. He ordered new clothes to be made for her by Parisian dressmakers and hired a French tutor for her brother James, allowing Sally to sit in on the lessons. When he left Paris to travel around Holland and Germany, he paid a French couple to keep Sally in their home and to watch over her, a move which many recent historians have interpreted as sexual jealousy. This can only be supposition, because all of the letters from 1788 as well as the index to them has disappeared from Jefferson's papers.

A few months before Jefferson was to return to America in 1789, Sally became pregnant with his child. Sally and James did not want to return to the U.S. and to slavery. In Paris, they were free, they spoke French, and James could support them both as a chef. Jefferson, however, cajoled them into returning with the promise that Sally's children would be free at twenty-one, so Sally relented. On 23 December 1789, Sally gave birth to a son whom she named Tom.

At Monticello, Sally assumed the duties of Mistress of Master's Chamber which required her to take care of his bed chamber and wardrobe, to look after the children, and to do light work and serving. Jefferson's black sons later wrote that the master never showed partiality nor affection toward them.

Sally bore Jefferson four more children. A son Beverly was born in 1798, daughter Harriet in 1801, Madison in 1805, and Eston in 1808. Harriet was born as Jefferson was sworn in as President of the United States.

The story of Jefferson's affair with Sally first began to circulate during the 1801 presidential campaign, as Northern reporters who did not subscribe to the Southern gentleman's code questioned if this virile, sophisticated, handsome widower really was acting shamefully.

After Jefferson was already president, Virginia reporter James Callender broke the story that Jefferson kept one of his slaves as a concubine. He named Sally and observed that her eldest son Tom bore a striking resemblance to the President. Jefferson neither confirmed nor denied the story.

Sally, fifty-three, was with Jefferson as Keeper of the Master's Chamber when he died in 1826 at the age of eighty-three. Years later Madison Hemings, Sally's fourth child, was interviewed as an old man by the Pike County (Ohio) *Republican* and told reporters that the Hemings family contained the only slaves freed when Jefferson died and the only slave family not sold at the auction block. Sally was also freed and spent the rest of her life with Madison and Eston in Virginia, until her death at the age of sixty-two.

Henry II, King of England (1333–1379) See **Clifford, Rosamund.**

Henry II, King of France (1519–1559) See **Poitiers, Diane de.**

Hitler, Adolf (1889–1945) See **Braun, Eva; Raubel, Geli.**

Hopkey, Sophia Christiana (1718–?) Sophy Hopkey was eighteen and the niece of the magistrate and keeper of public stores of Savannah, Georgia, in 1736 when she first met John Wesley, a thirty-three-year-old Oxford graduate and a professed celibate who had traveled to the New World as an Anglican missionary. She was simple, sweet-tempered, and impressionable – and she had promised some months previously to marry Thomas Mellichamp, who now sat in jail charged with counterfeiting. Mellichamp had warned her that someone would die if she broke her vow to marry him.

Her passionate mistake had upset her uncle, Thomas Causton, who turned Sophy over to Wesley, telling him "I give her up to you. Do what you will with her." He also told Wesley that he would offer a generous living to her future husband, hinting that marriage to Wesley might tame his niece. For her part, Sophy was unhappy living with her aunt and uncle and she was especially susceptible to marriage offers, despite her protests that she desired lifelong spinsterhood.

Wesley was not tempted. Instead, he took Sophy on his journey to the small Moravian settlement of Frederica, where she stayed with a friend while Wesley with his brother Charles, already in the town, ministered to its needs. He also set up a rigid schedule according to which Sophy attended early morning prayers at his residence, shared breakfast, took French lessons from him, listened to devotional readings, and discussed religion. He read to her from Law's *Serious Call*, Dean Young's *Sermons*, Hickes' *Reformed Devotions*, or *The Abridged French Grammar*. People wondered at their relationship which required so much time alone. She remained demurely enticing, while he struggled with his awakened sexual feelings. His journal of the time is filled with mention of her "large, warm expressive eyes," and he observes in several entries that his "heart was with Miss Sophy all the time."

In letters to his brother Charles, who left Frederica before him, he speaks of the temptations which surround him and asks "Pray that I know none of them in the flesh." Just before returning her to Savannah, after finding that she was tempting but not tamed, he noted that he needed "to break off so dangerous an acquaintance." They made the week-long journey back to Savannah, traveling by boat and over rough land. The notes in his journal for that period are provocative, for he speaks of their enjoying the beauty of a secluded grassy knoll and sharing looks under the stars. Nothing seems to have changed his views toward marriage, although Sophy pushed for commitment while Wesley continued with prayer sessions and religion lessons.

Less than a month later, in March 1737, she eloped with William Williamson, a newcomer to town who had arrived while Sophy was in Frederica. Soon after she began to miss church services and by July Wesley felt that she no longer qualified for admission to Communion. He wrote to the now-pregnant Sophy and observed "shortcomings in observing her Christian duties." A few days later, she miscarried. When she attempted to take Communion a month later, he turned her away. This was a public insult to Sophy which showed Wesley's vindictiveness. A warrant was issued the next day for Wesley to face the court on charges made by Sophy and William Williamson that he had defamed her character by denying her Communion. In addition, Williamson demanded one thousand pounds in damages.

The town fathers declared that Wesley had refused Sophy

Communion as revenge because she had married someone else and not waited for him. They took the opportunity to add other charges regarding the strictness of his ecclesiastical practices. He was acquitted of all but the defamation charges, and he waited six months for the case to come to trial. When he could no longer stand the delay, he left town clandestinely, taking an arduous ten-day journey through forests, swamplands, and plantations to reach the ship which would carry him back to England.

Once back in England, Wesley experienced a religious awakening which has been attributed to his experiences in Georgia. Sophy was the chief instrument in convincing him to start anew. He had gone to the New World as an arrogant, self-satisfied young missionary and returned as a man who would begin a great religious revival. There was no further mention of Sophy in his later writings, and the two never contacted each other again. However, as the mistress of his heart for his time in Georgia and as the great romance of his life, Sophy Hopkey played a vital role in shaping his convictions.

In Georgia Wesley struggled to keep his vow of celibacy as he was thrown into daily frequent contact with Sophy. The extent of the struggle and the frequent temptations were methodically recorded in his journal, but he used a pattern of shorthand, abbreviations, and ciphers which made the journal unreadable until the code was broken in 1909 by a British army chaplain, Reverend Nehemiah Curnock. The translation was published as *The Journal of John Wesley*.

Howard, Harriet (1823–1869) Born Elizabeth Ann Haryett, the future mistress of Napoleon's grandson, Louis-Napoleon, renamed herself to avoid family shame when she ran off with a well-known English jockey Jem Mason while still in her teens. When Mason tired of her, he continued to support her until he passed her on to a Major Martyn, who gladly took her on as a mistress, and he provided her with a grand house and servants. While the major's mistress, Harriet gave birth to a son whom she had baptized as her mother's child to avoid shame. The major, however, welcomed his child and lavished presents and even more money upon its mother.

Never the grateful mistress, the twenty-three-year-old Harriet abandoned her benefactor when she fell madly and hopelessly in love with thirty-nine-year-old Louis-Napoleon whose eyes locked with hers at a fashionable party. Taken with the pretender to the French empire, she took her four-year-old son, her fortune, and her entourage and set up housekeeping in an inconspicuous house in which Louis-Napoleon also lived. She placed her extensive financial assets at the disposal of this politically ambitious man.

Harriet viewed Louis-Napoleon as her ticket to royal society, and she hired tutors to prepare her for her intended position. So impressed was her new lover that he sent for his two illegitimate sons whose mother had been his laundress and he entrusted their care to Harriet. He also pushed her farther into the background, hiding their relationship as he spent her money in attempts to restore the Empire.

Returned to the throne, the Emperor Napoleon III dealt Harriet a heavy blow when, in 1853, he wooed and won another woman to be his empress. To offset threats of blackmail by Harriet, he asked her to undertake a secret mission to England. While Harriet was gone, the emperor's men ransacked her house and took every shred of evidence – love letters, political notes, paid bills – of their relationship.

Later, when the empress locked him out of the connubial bedroom, Louis-Napoleon would visit his former mistress. He also repaid her the money which she had freely offered him in his restoration. When the visits ceased, Harriet became obese, then married an Englishman whose only interest was her money. When she died, she left a large sum of money in her will to create a home for young girls who had been victims of seductions, a memorial to her own early life.

Howard, Henrietta, Countess of Suffolk (1688–?) Fleshy, married, and in her late twenties, this daughter of a Norfolk squire was a seemingly unlikely candidate to attract the royal libido, yet she served as mistress to England's King George II for over a decade. She married early to Charles Howard, the heavy-drinking, brutal, ill-tempered younger son of the Earl of Suffolk, but the young couple was forced to live in not-so-genteel poverty. Henrietta had to sell hanks of her luxuriant long hair to a wigmaker to acquire the money for passage to the Hanoverian Court in Germany, where they and others sought to curry favor in the last months of Queen Anne's life.

Once she met and charmed the king, however, their fortunes improved. Henrietta became influential at court and brought the title of Groom of the Bedchamber to her husband. He was not wholly pleased, and tried to make her return to his bed, even appealing to the queen, Caroline, for help. Caroline not only tolerated Henrietta but she also took her side when Charles Howard pursued his wife at court and threatened to carry her off. To discourage the often-drunk and frequently abusive husband, Caroline took Henrietta for rides in her carriage and chased him away when he approached them. Defeated, he agreed to accept a royal pension of twelve hundred pounds yearly in exchange for giving Henrietta her sexual freedom and allowing George II to install her in palace apartments with the official title of Lady of the Bedchamber. When Howard became the Earl of Suffolk in 1731, Henrietta shared his new rank which elevated her to Groom of the Stole to Caroline.

Plain but intelligent, Henrietta was respected by contemporary intellects, and Alexander Pope immortalized her friendliness and justice in his poem "To a Certain Lady at Court." As for the king, even a mistress didn't change his basically dull and plodding nature. On schedule each evening at nine o'clock, George II entered Henrietta's apartments where he would stay for several hours before returning to his own apartments and the queen.

For her services, Henrietta received a rension of two thousand pounds yearly, a villa outside of London, a few jewels, and the aggravation of combing the queen's hair in her official capacity. When she decided to leave George II in 1734, after a rather dull decade as mistress, the queen became upset and tried to persuade Henrietta to stay as her insurance against other, more demanding mistresses. George II, on the other hand, confronted Caroline and told her to "let the old, deaf, dull beast" go. Henrietta left and retired into obscurity.

Hsien Feng (1831–1861) See **Tz'u Hsi.**

Hugo, Victor (1802–1885) See **Ozy, Alice.**

Henrietta Howard (NATIONAL PORTRAIT GALLERY)

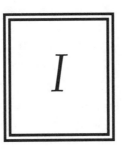

I

Isabella, Queen (1291–1358) Isabella was the daughter of French King Philip IV, and she became queen to England's King Edward II in 1308. Isabella was distraught to learn that she was burdened with an effeminate husband who openly favored his homosexual partners and who encouraged them in humiliating his wife. Disgusted with such treatment, she endured her marriage in name only for seventeen years. In 1324 she left for France with the Prince of Wales on the pretext of paying homage to King Charles IV. There, she met English noble Roger Mortimer who had escaped imprisonment in the Tower of London for his role as a member of the Marcher Lords, a group which had actively rebelled against Edward II's attempts to turn their lands over to his new favorite lover, Hugh Despenser.

The two fell instantly in love and lived as paramours in exile. When word reached them in 1326 that the English nobles were thoroughly disgusted with Edward and that rebellion was imminent, Isabella provided financial support for Mortimer and other exiled barons to raise an army with which to invade England. Isabella joined the invasion led by Mortimer in a surprise landing in London. Although Edward and his favorite Despenser escaped initially, they were later captured and Despenser was executed. Edward was imprisoned. Isabella and Mortimer convinced Parliament to force Edward to abdicate in January 1327, and the fifteen-year-old Prince of Wales was installed as King Edward III. In September 1327 Edward II was murdered at Berkeley Castle in Gloucestershire.

The young prince was just the front for the ambitions of his mother Isabella and her paramour Roger Mortimer, who held the true power in the government. In 1330, eighteen-year-old Edward III could no longer abide the situation. Leading a band of friends, he staged a palace coup in order to restore his political power. They fought their way into Mortimer's room, which lay next to Isabella's, and captured him. A hurried trial followed; Mortimer was publicly hanged. Isabella was confined to her home, where she stayed a prisoner until her death. She died at age fifty-three and was buried next to Roger Mortimer's remains at Grey Friars with Edward II's heart on her breast.

J

Jefferson, Thomas (1743– 826) See **Hemings, Sally.**

Jerome, Jennie, Lady Randolph Churchill (1854–1921) Jennie Jerome was born to wealthy American parents in Brooklyn, New York, and educated in Paris. In 1874, she married Lord Randolph Churchill, who offered only his titled name, a small salary as a Member of Parliament, one townhouse, and two horses without a carriage. Seven months later, their son Winston was born.

A year after marriage, Jennie and her sister Clara plunged into frenetic social activity. Biographers suggest that Jennie may have become aware that Randolph was suffering from syphilis, acquired in an early experience with a prostitute while at Oxford. She might also have become aware of his close male friendships and the rumors of homosexual activity which surrounded the trips he took. Whatever the reason for her social involvement, Jennie became good friends with Albert Edward, Prince of Wales, future King Edward VII of England, who paid attentions to her from early in her marriage.

Albert Edward made his interest obvious, and he gave Jennie presents of expensive jewelry which he gave to a woman only if they were intimate. Jennie was also a frequent guest at the Sandringham country home. When Randolph left for an extended trip to Egypt and India in 1884, Jennie saw more of the prince. They exchanged numerous affectionate letters, and his approval helped to ease her into British society. He was also solicitous during her mourning when Randolph died of the effects of syphilis in 1895. He didn't forget her after the relationship died down, for she sat in the King's Box during his coronation with other past and current mistresses.

Numerous other men paid court to Jennie, and she attracted all eyes whenever she entered a room. Her plethora of male companions created gossip and one column in *Town Topics* reported that her popularity with other women's husbands and fiancés had earned her the title of "Lady Jane Snatcher." Jealous gossip aside, Jennie was a beautiful woman and she loved male attention. When she was twenty-nine, she met the handsome, dashng Count Charles Rudolf Ferdinand Andreas Kinsky, four years younger, whose mother was a Lichtenstein Princess. He was a fiery young man, highly romantic and impulsive, and their relationship was to last for over a decade. Her husband Randolph at this point was ill in the third stage of syphilis, in which the mind begins to deteriorate, and she had begun to attend parties alone. By the end of 1884, their romance was a secret all over London. Kinsky was deemed the most eligible man in England. He had ridden his own mare in the Grand National and was the first amateur to ever win that race. Jennie had captured the hero of the hour, and her husband welcomed him as a friend. The lovers maintained a furtive romance, and Kinsky visited Jennie only when Randolph was away.

They parted when Kinsky returned to Berlin, but enjoyed a brief reunion when the Churchills visited Berlin in 1886. Over the years, Kinsky became a close friend to young Winston and became a substitute father, which was sorely needed, as Randolph sank increasingly into insanity. In 1894, Kinsky asked Jennie to go away with him, telling her that he could arrange to be transferred to any embassy in the world. Despite her husband's increased derangement, Jennie chose to stay with him and they took a one-year world tour.

During that year, they received a telegram from Kinsky which announced that he had become engaged to a woman twenty years younger than the forty-year-old Jennie. Jennie was crushed, and she later said that Kinsky had been the great love of her life who had been "like opium" for her.

Despite his marriage, into which he had been pressured by family, Kinsky continued to love Jennie. At her marriage in 1901 to George Cornwallis-West, a man only two weeks older than Winston, Jennie received a black-bordered card inscribed "Always in Mourning." In 1913 Jennie divorced George who left her for the actress Mrs. Pat Campbell. She and Kinsky reunited briefly, for his wife had died that year, but the magic was gone.

In 1918 at age sixty-three, Jennie married Montagu Porch, forty-one and three years younger than Winston. She retained her name Lady Randolph Churchill. At sixty-seven, Jennie was still learning all of the new dances and socializing with a young crowd. A fall that year, however, left her with a bad fracture of the left leg near the ankle. After considerable swelling which led to gangrene, the leg was amputated above the knee. Two weeks later, the main artery in the amputated leg hemorrhaged and Jennie died of loss of blood.

Winston Churchill spoke glowingly of his mother, and he attributed to her whatever greatness he might have attained.

Johnson, Lyndon Baines (1908–1973) See **Glass, Alice.**

Jordan, Dorothea (1761–1816) Dorothea Jordan was born in Ireland, to a Welsh actress mother and an Irish stagehand father who masqueraded as a former sea captain. She joined a Dublin theater company when she was twenty and was seduced by the company manager who deserted her when she became pregnant. Soon after she went to London to make a new start and became an instant star at the Drury Lane Theatre as the lead in *The Coutry Girl*, where she also became the mistress of the theater manager and bore him three children. During this time she was proclaimed the leading comic actress of her time.

Prince William first saw Dorothea in 1790, when she was thirty and he was twenty-six, and he pursued her for eleven months. Soon after becoming lovers the two set up a household in which, over the next twenty years, Dorothea gave birth to ten children. Life was difficult for the former star because the prince's civil allowance was inadequate to provide for the large family, and Dorothea returned to the stage between pregnancies because the future monarch could hardly be expected to take a job. Thus, Dorothea supported the household for much of her time as mistress to William. When she began to grow older and heavier with age, stage roles decreased and Dorothea's income also decreased. The ungracious Prince William decided to leave her in 1811 and agreed to a financial settlement, on which he later reneged.

Creditors constantly hounded Dorothea after the break with William, and she went to France to escape them. She died there impoverished in 1816, and her bed linen was sold to pay for her funeral.

Joyce, James (1882–1941) See **Barnacle, Nora.**

Jung, Carl (1875–1961) See **Wolff, Toni.**

Justinian I, Emperor (482–565) See **Theodora.**

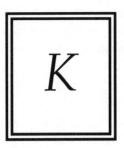

Katsura, Taro (1884 –1913) See **Okoi.**

Kaufman, George (1889- 1960) See **Astor, Mary.**

Keays, Sara (1948–) Keays has the distinction of ending the political career of Lord Cecil Parkinson, once the closest advisor to Conservative Prime Minister Margaret Thatcher, and of playing a major role in the biggest parliamentary scandal of Thatcher's time in office. A longtime private secretary to Parkinson, Keays first met the former Member of Parliament in 1971, when she was hired as a secretary in the House of Commons. She reported in her own account of the affair, *A Matter of Judgement*, that their affair began soon after. In 1974, Parkinson hired her as his private secretary, and the closeness of the working relationship led to a deepening of their involvement with each other. Keays claims that she tried several times to leave her job with Parkinson but that he refused to allow her to do so. Finally, in 1979, she left to work for Roy

Jenkins in Brussels. Whether intentional or not, the strategy appears to have made Parkinson realize what he might lose and he made time to meet with her and to tell her that he missed her when she returned briefly to London. Although he was still married, Keays claims that he asked her to marry him, but he also told her that they would have to be discreet and claimed that any move in the near future would seriously jeopardize his increasingly successful political career.

A few months later, even with no firm wedding date in sight, Keays returned to London and to a job in the House of Commons. While the affair intensified, Keays also became politically active and ran for a council seat in Southwark but lost. She then tried to gain the Conservative nomination for a seat in the General Election in Bermondsey, missing it by only a few votes. When the sitting member died and the candidate who had beaten Keays for the nomination was unable to run in the by-election, the matter of whether to choose runner-up Keays or to re-open nominations was left to the Conservative Central Office. Ironically, as chair of the Conservative Party, Parkinson would make the decision. He decided in late 1982 that a reselection would take place, thus destroying Keays' political chances.

Four months later, Keays announced to him that she was pregnant. In *A Matter of Judgement*, she claims that Parkinson ordered her to abort the baby and threatened to break all ties with her if she did not. In June 1983, Keays' father intervened and sent a letter to Prime Minister Thatcher, telling of the affair and of Parkinson's intentions, but he received no response. By August 1983, Keays and Parkinson were only communicating through solicitors, and political leaders were placing pressure on Parkinson. He stepped down as party chairman on 14 September 1983. After he issued a statement to the press on 5 October acknowledging his paternity and promising to provide for the child, public opinion turned in his favor. Keays was suddenly portrayed in the press and public comments as a scheming woman who had attempted to trap the politician. On New Year's Eve, 1983, Keays gave birth to a daughter, whom she named Flora. Although Parkinson settled £100,000 on Keays and Flora, he chose to remain absent from his daughter's life.

Keeler, Christine (1943-) Christine Keeler became the mistress to both the queen's Secretary of State for War, John Profumo, MP, and an alleged Russian spy, Captain Eugene Ivanov, the assistant Soviet naval attache in London.

Born into the English lower class, Christine hardly seemed the type to topple a government. Pretty, but not beautiful, she worked as a call girl in a cottage leased from Lord Astor by an osteopathic physician named Dr. Stephen Ward (who later committed suicide after his role became public). Christine and several other women used the cottage and the estate swimming pool for sex parties at different times during the summer of 1961.

England was shocked by the sexual antics of its Secretary of War, but the government was more seriously concerned that Christine might have been the conduit for vital military information from John Profumo to Captain Ivanov. No proof of this ever came out, yet Profumo was forced to resign and admit he had lied to Parliament. Ivanov was recalled to the U.S.S.R. Eventually Prime Minister Harold Macmillan resigned, and the shocked country rudely defeated his Tory party in the subsequent election.

During the Profumo trial, Christine's picture was in every paper and her Confessions were serialized weekly in the *News of the World*. She was approached and offered five thousand pounds by a variety show called "Turkish Delight" to appear as part of its cabaret format. The notoriety finally gave her the fame that she had long craved as it quickly destroyed the distinguished career of John Profumo.

When the ordeal was over Christine Keeler spent nine months in jail for committing perjury. She waited until 1983 to finally tell her story, in a book entitled *Nothing But . . .*

Kennedy, John F. (1917–1963) See **Meyer, Mary Pinchot; Monroe, Marilyn.**

Kennedy, Joseph (1888–1969) See **Swanson, Gloria.**

Kennedy, Robert F. (1925–1968) See **Monroe, Marilyn.**

Keppel, Alice (1869–1947) Alice Keppel was the last of Edward

Christine Keeler (BETTMANN ARCHIVE)

VII's many mistresses. Born in Scotland, she was one of the six children of Admiral Sir William Edmonstone, who had an aristocratic family background and extensive estates, but little money. Her marriage to George Keppel in 1891 was a love match, and they continued to love each other until her death in 1947 and his two months later. In 1894 Alice gave birth to the first of two daughters, Violet, who later became the lover of writer Vita Sackville-West and who herself published several books. In 1900 a second daughter Sonia was born.

Alice met the future king of England, Albert Edward, Prince of Wales, at the races in 1898 when he was fifty-seven and she was twenty-nine and married to Colonel Keppel. Referred to as "La Favorita" by the palace staff and "Mrs. George" by the King, Alice was amiably tolerated by the Princess Alexandra and remained Albert Edward's mistress for twelve years until his death. Her husband and their friends knew that she was the king's mistress and seemed to view her role as a social duty owed to the crown. Her husband never objected when she traveled with the king and seemed happy to share this indomitable and extraordinary woman with England's leader.

Warm-hearted and good-natured, Alice was humorous and discreet, and she acted as a buffer between the king and the rest of the world. She made few enemies and was not self-seeking, so there were no scenes nor recriminations ending in demands for expensive gifts. Unlike most other royal mistresses, she was never jealous or possessive, nor was her husband opposed to her relationship with the king. She also differed from earlier mistresses in that although she may have symbolized the Edwardian era, she did not influence the tastes of her time because her milieu was more populated by bankers than by writers or painters.

Her deep, throaty voice was siultaneously soothing and seductive to the king, and she loved him for himself and seemed to understand his numerous volatile moods. She was so successful in calming the king that Alexandra often called for her when he was in a state, and "Mrs. George" was always invited by the royal family to their weekend retreats to keep Edward VII in good humor. Alice watched over the king's temper as he played bridge and saw to it that he always won. The king was also a familiar figure in the Keppel home in Portman Square, London, and Violet and Sonia called him "Kingy" and raced buttered slices of toast down his trouser legs.

When the king was seriously ill in November 1910, Alice remained in her home to wait for news by telephone of his changing health. As he neared death, Queen Alexandra called for Alice to come to his sickroom and to join such friends of his youth as Sir Ernest Cassel and Mrs. Willy James. Edward VII died on 6 November, and Queen Alexandra notified Alice immediately and personally escorted her to the king's room. A few days later, the Keppels closed up the Portman Square home and retired to an estate in the country for a few months, to avoid the embarrassment of curiosity seekers and so that Alice could have her own private period of mourning. They then traveled to China. When they returned to London two years later, Alice's dark hair was completely white, yet she was only forty-three.

In the following years Alice managed her daughters' lives and lived contentedly with her husband. Using the advice given by Sir Ernest Cassel, she invested heavily in Canadian stocks and made a fortune which she used to buy an Italian villa, L' Ombrellino, in Florence, Italy, and to which the family moved. Alice Keppel died at the age of seventy-eight and was buried in the Protestant cemetary in Florence.

Keroualle, Louise de, Duchess of Portsmouth (1645–1734) When Princess Henriette Anne came to visit her brother Charles II in London, she brought along her maid of honor, Louise de Keroualle. Charles was smitten by Louise, but she resisted his early advances. As the princess prepared to leave, he suggested that she give him Louise. But the plump and beautiful Frenchwoman returned to France with the princess.

When Charles' sister died in 1610, Louise was offered the chance to leave court, but King Louis XIV of France convinced her to return to Charles. She was carefully instructed to use her influence in his bedroom to bring about an alliance between France and England. To do so, however, she would have to become the king's mistress.

Careful with her virtue, Louise took her time in yielding to the king and was extremely discreet in her behavior. It was not until a year after she arrived in England that the French manipulators had some hope of their success when Louise became nauseous during dinner and they hopefully suspected pregnancy. The nausea turned out to be just that and nothing more, so the French Foreign Minister decided that outside intervention was needed if an affair between Louise and the king were to occur. He personally escorted Louise to the race meeting at Newmarket which Charles attended alone because his current mistress Nell Gwyn was seven months pregnant.

Thanks to the minister's maneuvering, Louise became the king's lover, and she presented him with a child nine months later. The king bestowed the title of Duchess of Portsmouth on Louise, and their son became the Duke of Richmond when he turned age three.

Unlike her predecessor Lady Castlemaine, Louise was totally faithful to Charles II and not very tolerant of his promiscuity. Although she was designated Charles' "official mistress," she continued his eye. Try as he might to disguise his dalliances, Louise was blatantly reminded of them when he gave her "the clap." Her recovery was long and arduous, while Charles recovered quickly, but she manipulated him through tears rather than anger and found Charles generous in his guilt. The forgiving Duchess of Portsmouth provided a quiet sanctuary and she made no outrageous demands of him regarding fidelity or other compensation beyond requests for fine clothes and jewelry. At the same time, she influenced Charles to create treaties which favored the French and her efforts fulfilled the hopes of French politicians who had encouraged the relationship.

Despite obvious contentment, Charles II continued his adventures with other women until well into his fifties. For the last half of their seven years together, Charles treated Louise like a wife whom he would visit devotedly during the day but whom he would leave at night as he visited other women.

Still, Louise was his companion in later years when the thrill of the hunt was only a memory, and she was near him when he died. Charles II called upon his brother and successor, James, Duke of York, to be kind to his concubines and he especially named Portsmouth.

Krudener, Baroness Julie de (1764–1824) Born an aristocrat and married to a diplomat, Julie de Krudener lived an artistic life in Zurich and Paris before publishing her sentimental novel *Valerie* to great acclaim. After her husband's death in 1802 Julie adopted the religious beliefs of the Moravian pietists and she soon moved in high circles, telling of visions, apparitions, specters, and ghosts. She was small, graceful, and musical-voiced, and forty-seven years old when she first met the thirty-six-year-old Tsar Alexander. At their first encounter she verbally humiliated him into confessing all of his sins of pride and immorality. He installed her in the Elysée Palace in Paris after Paris fell to the allied Prussian and Russian forces. She wore white as she received her numerous royal guests and met privately with Alexander with whom she prayed, read the Bible, and discussed his shortcomings.

More than mystical, their relationship was also physical and the two were lovers. At the age of fifty, Julie was no longer a beauty, and she is described as skeletal with thin-boned eyes sockets and smooth, blue-veined eyelids. Still, she kept the thirty-nine-year-old tsar spellbound, who was not only the most prestigious monarch in Europe but also the most sought after by women.

Julie concocted with Alexander I the idea of The Holy Alliance, a plan aimed at making Alexander the saviour of the post-Napoleonic world. The intent was to unite all nations in a voluntary gesture of charity and peace. Compliance would be on a nation's honor. The world laughed, and the humiliated Alexander ended the affair.

Without her tsar, Julie and her disciples worked to help the poor, opening soup and bread kitchens, providing shelter, and preaching and converting people to God. She spent vast sums of money on the soup kitchens. Although she never met Alexander again, history reveals that only months after Julie died in 1824 in the Crimea, Alexander I made a journey to the Armenian Church where Julie was buried. He prayed a long while at her coffin in the bitter cold. Days later, he was severely ill with fever and died a month later of infection.

Lais (fourth century B.C.) Born in Sicily, Lais was first taken to Corinth as a slave and purchased by a sculptor to be his model. She worked in a brothel in her free time and learned the art of pleasing men. After three years, Lais went to Athens where she could model for the great sculptors. She was for a time the mistress of Myron, the creator of the "Discus Thrower," and she later took the philosophers Diogenes and Aristippus as lovers.

As she aged and her lovers discarded her, Lais turned to drink and sold herself to anyone who would offer even a few pieces of money. When she was seventy years old, she fell in love with a young man in his early twenties. She followed him around, eventually going after him to Thessaly and into the Temple of Venus where she offered her body to him. Onlookers were repulsed and they stoned her to death. A few years later, Athens erected a large tomb in her honor, despite her infamous end.

Lamb, Lady Caroline (1785–1827) Born Caroline Ponsonby, the daughter of the third Earl of Bessborough, she was sent to Italy with a

Lais (NEW YORK PUBLIC LIBRARY)

nurse at the age of three when her mother suffered a slight stroke. When she returned six years later, she lived in London with her wealthy aunt and uncle, the Duke and Duchess of Devonshire and their children – as well as the duke's mistress. As a child, Caroline was indulged with material goods and received no formal schooling. Doctors proclaimed her to be too nervous and high-strung to sustain the rigors of education, so she ran wild until she turned fifteen. At that point, Caroline began a program of self-education and soon discovered talents in music, art, and languages.

She also met William Lamb, a young Cambridge student who fell deeply in love with the petite, boyishly slender Caroline who aimed to shock everyone around her. He persisted for three years, and the two were finally married in 1805. Four years later, Caroline was bored with marriage, and she began to entertain writers in her salon. When in 1812 she read advance proofs of Byron's book *Childe Harold's Pilgrimage*, after hearing along with the rest of London of the passionate speech which Byron had made in the House of Lords in defense of working class saboteurs, she immediately demanded that she meet him. Several days later, the two were introduced at a ball, and later that night she wrote one of the most famous lines regarding Byron in her journal "Mad, bad, and dangerous to know."

Within weeks, Caroline had become Byron's mistress and the two were passionate lovers. Caroline welcomed Byron into the upper rooms of her home, and her husband remained tolerant of the affair. While Caroline flaunted her role as mistress at parties, and taunted her in-laws who begged her to stop, William Lamb refused to do anything to stop Caroline. At the same time, Caroline became all-consuming in her desire to be with Byron. She followed him around, begged him to meet with her when a day passed without a visit, and sometimes disguised herself as a page and slipped into his quarters.

Totally pliant, Caroline did whatever Byron asked of her, in attempts to please him totally. She gave up dancing and closed her salon at his command. She would not, however, stop her constant pursuit of him. Whenever she became insecure about his love, Caroline would fall into a tearful frenzy.

After five months, Byron could no longer stand her hysterics. He decided to make his break with her as dramatic as possible, so he openly began an affair with her one-time friend, Lady Oxford. When Caroline tearfully wrote him, he sent her a vicious farewell note, calling her pursuit of him an "unfeminine persecution" and telling her to exert her "absurd caprices upon others."

Caroline was mortified, and intent upon revenge. In a public ceremony for which she hired village girls to stand in white gowns, she burned a figure of Byron, then threw into the fire all the books he had given her, as well as locks of his hair and copies of his letters. She began to show up at odd hours at his rooms, walking in as soon as the door opened.

At a ball in 1813 Caroline moved close to Byron as he passed and pressed his hand against a sharp, pointed object which she had hidden in her hand, and told him that she meant to use it. When Byron ignored her, Caroline screamed out his name and slashed her arms with the knife. Several people stopped her, and she began to faint. When someone handed her a glass of water, Caroline immediately broke the glass on a table, then tried to slice her wrists with the jagged edges. Byron had already left the room and, when told of the incident the next day, he seemed indifferent and uninterested in the details.

When Byron married her cousin Annabella Milbanke two years later, Caroline rightly predicted that the marriage would fail. In the years that followed, she wrote a melodramatic novel entitled *Glenvaron* which was a thinly disguised account of the affair. Her husband was disgusted by her behavior and left her, and Caroline spent the next nine years involved in a series of degrading affairs. One of her last affairs was as mistress to the much younger novelist Edward Bulwer-Lytton, whom she forced to wear Byron's ring and to listen to her organ recitals.

Lamb temporarily returned to Caroline in 1824. During one of her daily rides, she stopped to allow a funeral procession to pass and, when she remarked upon it to her husband that evening, he told her that Byron's body was being carried in that coffin. She seemed to go mad, and she began to drink brandy heavily and to take drugs. In the months that followed, Caroline became abusive to everyone around her, often breaking dishes, wandering in the dead of night, and drinking and sobbing uncontrollably in front of a portrait of Byron.

Lady Caroline Lamb (BROWN BROTHERS)

In 1825, her husband again left her. When Caroline became ill two years later, Lamb moved her back to Melbourne House where she died in 1827 of dropsy.

Lamia (fourth century B.C.) One of the most famous of the early Greek courtesans, nothing is known about the life and true name of Lamia aside from the fact that she was the mistress of King Ptolemy of Egypt. After his death, and when she was already forty, she became the mistress of King Demetrius of Macedonia. Plutarch reports that her depravities earned her the name of Lamia, which means bloodsucker or vampire.

Whatever her sexual specialties, we do know that King Demetrius gladly acceded to her demand that he pay her 250 talents (approximately $300,000 in today's market) for her favors. To raise the money, he levied a soap tax on Athens. Despite the tax, Athenians became enamoured with her and built a temple in her honor, deifying her under the name of Venus Lamia.

Langtry, Lillie (1852–1929) Born Emily Charlotte Le Breton on the island of Jersey, Lillie Langtry, the "Jersey Lily," grew up tall and shapely, with a creamy complexion and thick reddish-gold hair. She was the original "pin-up queen" whose postcard images appeared in school dormitories, ships' cabins, and army barracks. She was among the first celebrities to do product endorsements, and her flawless complexion and fame as an actress made her a natural spokeswoman for Pears soap.

Lillie married a wealthy and jealous young widower, Edward Langtry, when she was twenty, to escape her oppressive home life, but she also found marriage stifling. Within a few years, the couple separated. Lillie arrived in London in 1877 and soon was asked by several society artists to pose. After John Everett Millais painted her as Effie Dean in a narrative painting based on Sir Walter Scott's sentimental *The Heart of Midlothian*, crowds formed to view it at the Royal Academy exhibition. The newly created celebrity attracted the attention of royalty, and the Crown Prince of Austria, English Prince Leopold, earls, dukes, and other assorted English bluebloods jockeyed for her attention. Albert Edward, the Prince of Wales, succeeded in winning her. He had been mesmerized by the Millais painting and arranged a meeting at the house of Artic explorer Sir Arthur Young.

As mistress, Lillie remained legally married to Edward Langtry but she spent most of her time with the Prince of Wales in a villa which he had built for her and where the two often entertained close friends. Lillie was the first of his acknowledged mistresses. While she remained faithful to the prince at this time, he continued to have affairs with other women, notably with Sarah Bernhardt who often pleaded exhaustion when unable to make a rehearsal, citing the prince as her reason.

After Edward Langtry went bankrupt, the prince began to roam more frequently and he strongly encouraged Lillie to become an actress, helping her more than a little to make the right contacts. She was highly successful in England, and then barnstormed across America to great acclaim.

Life after the Prince of Wales included numerous wealthy lovers, many of whom deluged Lillie with diamonds and roses as well as marriage proposals. She accepted the material gifts, but shied away from marriage even after Edward Langtry's death. Involved with Scottish industrial millionaire George Baird, Lillie frequently appeared with bruises and black eyes, which she claimed she tolerated because he paid her five thousand pounds each time he beat her. She became the mistress of Louis Mountbatten, Prince of Battenburg and nephew to Albert Edward, and had a daughter with him after which he promptly left her. Louis was the grandfather of Prince Philip, prince consort of Elizabeth II of England.

In 1899 "the Jersey Lily" married Hugo de Bathe who became a baron in 1907, thus making his wife Lady de Bathe. The unhappy marriage left Hugo to dally with chorus girls while Lillie acted occasionally, funded public projects, and travelled. She died alone and exceedingly wealthy in 1929 in Monaco, still a beauty by all accounts.

Laval, Françoise, Madame de Chateaubriant (?–1548) Fiery tempered and strong willed, Françoise Laval was recruited to be the mistress of King Francis I of France against her wishes. She married Jean Laval at the age of eleven and was a mother by the age of twelve. As she matured, Françoise became a breathtakingly beautiful woman whom many men desired. One of the royal pimps saw her and submitted her name to Francis I, who immediately asked to meet her.

When Francis I issued an invitation to the couple to visit at court, Françoise's husband Jean became suspicious. He refused, saying that his wife was much too shy to be presented to court. When a second, more insistent letter, arrived, Jean felt compelled to appear, but he left his wife at home. The disgruntled king demanded then and there that Laval write to his wife and invite her to come to court. Now Laval had arranged that Françoise would ignore all royal summons, even those written by him, unless the letter contained Laval's ring which he always wore. Foolishly, Laval bragged of the scheme to his valet. The valet, expecting a reward, told the story to the king who had the ring stolen and copied in order to outsmart Laval.

Thus, after Laval obeyed the king's orders and wrote to Françoise, the king secretly slipped the duplicate ring into the letter. Françoise arrived at court to find an ardent king and an angry husband who had been outsmarted. Within days, she was forced to become the king's mistress which she stayed until his death. Laval returned to Brittany to rue his misfortune. When the king died in 1247, Françoise returned to her husband, but he seemed to blame her for becoming the king's mistress and she was found dead shortly after her return to Brittany.

Lawrence, D.H. (1885–1930) See **Weekly, Frieda.**

Lenclos, Anne de (1620–1705) Referred to by Horace Walpole as a "veritable Notre-Dame des Amours," Anne de Lenclos became renowned as the foremost authority on the art of love in seventeenth-century France. She formalized this title by creating a School of Gallantry, in which she taught young noblemen the many facets of the art of lovemaking.

Intelligent, graceful, witty, and sensual in both appearance and nature, "Ninon" had numerous affairs, yet she was selective in bestowing her favors. Cardinal de Richelieu sought her body, but she wanted only to converse with the learned ecclesiast. Instead, she sent the cardinal her friend who quickly shared her charms and collected fifty thousand crowns as payment.

Ninon De L'enclos (CULVER PICTURES, INC.)

On the other hand, many other men of the finest of French lineage passed through Ninon's celebrated salon. She was mistress of both the Abbé Dessiat and the Maréchal d'Estrees when she became pregnant for the first time, and the two men eagerly sought to claim paternity. They tossed dice, and the Maréchal d'Estrees won the right to raise the boy. Famous statesmen shared her bed, among them La Rouchefoucauld, the Marquis de Sévigné, and the Duc d'Enghien. She lived for three years with the Marquis de Villarceux, who left her for a married woman, after which Ninon plunged into an affair with a man who fathered her second son.

Passion was her ruling emotion, and Ninon sent more than one lover packing when his lovemaking lacked fire. She wrote exultantly about the pleasures of love, claiming that life was more animated and passion more deeply felt when she was in love – and she fell in love with each man who shared her bed.

Ninon opened her School of Gallantry when she reached the age of forty. Mothers enrolled their sons to learn how to deal with a mistress or wife, what to expect of women, and the art of lovemaking. Individual verbal instruction was sometimes joined with personal demonstrations of the art of lovemaking in Ninon's own boudoir.

The only tragedy in an otherwise full life came when she was sixty-five years old. Her natural son, who didn't know that Ninon was his mother, consulted with her but he fell passionately in love with the aging mistress. When he refused to halt his gifts and notes of love, she asked to see him and revealed that she was really his mother. The distraught young man rushed into her garden and committed suicide with his sword.

From that time, Ninon reverted back to her original name of Anne and she bitterly lived out the rest of her life until her death at eighty-five.

Lenin, Vladimir Ilich (1870–1924) See **Armand, Inessa.**

Lennon, John (1940–1980) See **Pang, May.**

Leon, Leonie (1847–1906) Tall and striking, Leonie was a beautiful French woman who had left the provinces after her father's

Leonie Leon (CULVER PICTURES, INC.)

death to make a living in Paris. She left her first position as governess to the children of a government official after he seduced her.

Leonie first encountered one-eyed French statesman Leon Gambetta in 1869 when she went to hear him speak at the legislative body. He was a well-admired man who had helped to found the new republic after the fall of Napoleon III. During his speech, he noticed Leonie in the gallery, and sent her a note asking to meet him later. Her recent seduction had frightened her, and she bolted from the building in embarrassment. The pair met two years later at the home of a friend where Gambetta followed Leonie and proposed to her.

Her strong Catholic background demanded that only a Church-sanctioned marriage was acceptable, and she felt that Gambetta would not agree for he headed the anti-clerical party in France. Despite the danger to his career, however, Gambetta agreed to risk the repercussions of a church marriage. Ironically, it was Leonie who suggested that they exchange rings and pledge their devotion, leaving marriage to the future.

During their ten years together, Leonie encouraged her lover in his rise to president of the Chamber of Deputies in 1879. However, after three years Gambetta became tired of public life and resigned, intending to formally marry Leonie. He purchased Balzac's estate, and they set their wedding date. Only days before the marriage, Gambetta accidentally shot himself in the hand while cleaning a pistol and blood poisoning set in. He died on New Year's Eve in 1882. The distraught Leonie first entered a convent, then made her way to Paris to live, where her lover's supporters provided for her until her death in 1906.

Leopold II, King of Belgium (1835–1909) See **Otero, Caroline.**

Levassuer, Thérèse (1720–?) Thérèse was a semi-literate young woman who worked as a waitress and laundress in a boarding house – hardly the soulmate that one would expect for the famous French philosopher Jean-Jacques Rousseau. Yet, from the age of twenty-three and for thirty-five years, Thérèse played the concurrent roles of concubine, sick nurse, and cook/housekeeper to the great Rousseau who, nevertheless, never permitted her to eat at the same table as he and his friends.

Although the two were never legally married, Rousseau and his friends looked upon Therésè as his wife, which she became in his own eyes. After they had lived together twenty-five years, Rousseau solemnly acted the part of a priest and took Therésè as his wife in the company of a few friends.

Legal or not, Therésè acted the part of faithful and unquestioning wife. She stayed home while he dined and traveled with friends, and she fielded letters from his admirers and often had to mediate between women who pursued him. Therésè bore Rousseau five children whom he forced her to leave at the Foundling Hospital. He claimed that this action was done with selfless concern, because the world knew her only as his housekeeper, so he was saving her honor by abandoning their babies. He had declared at the outset of their long relationship that he would never marry her, and despite the solemnity of his self-styled ceremony, he never did.

After Rousseau's death in 1778, Therésè married the English valet on the estate of a marquis with whom they had been staying for the previous two years. Her life then faded into obscurity.

Lewes, George Henry (1817–1878) See **Eliot, George.**

Liszt, Franz (1811–1886) See **Duplessis, Marie; Montez, Lola.**

Lopez, Francisco (1826–1870) See **Lynch, Eliza Alicia.**

Lorenz, Marita (1939–?) Born in Germany in August 1939, Lorenz's turbulent life would lead her into the arms of a number of powerful men, including El Presidente Fidel Castro of Cuba. The youngest of four children born to Alice Lofland and Heinrich Lorenz, she appears to have been fated to enter the world of espionage. Two weeks after her birth, father Heinrich began commanding a German U-boat during World War II. Left alone with four children, Lorenz's mother became a part of the French Underground, and she was later recruited into British Intelligence. After both her mother and father became prisoners of war, young Marita was sent to a children's concentration camp in Bergen-Belsen. Shortly after the end of the war when the Lorenz family had reunited, seven-year-old Marita was raped by a deranged soldier. Friends and family report that this episode was key to the mistrust of men that would influence her later life. By the age of twenty, Marita was working with her father on cruise ships. On 28 February 1959, her father's ship, *The Berlin*, dropped anchor in Havana Harbor. The ship was greeted by a military entourage. Not wanting to disturb her father, and made curious by all the surrounding excitement, the young Marita asked the group leader the nature of his business. A young Fidel Castro smiled at the woman in astonishment that she did not know who he was. Marita, attracted to the dictator, offered to show him around the boat. The couple ended-up in her quarters, where Marita made love to him, her first lover.

Upon her return to the United States, Marita received phone calls from Castro, who eventually sent his private plane to New York to pick her up and take her to Cuba. For the next seven months, Marita lived with Castro at the Havana Hilton. She claims to have been more than the dictator's lover, and she would later tell friends that she had managed to become a political confidant of sorts. In April of 1959, Lorenz accompanied Castro to the United States for an unofficial meeting with President Eisenhower. During this trip, Lorenz discovered she was pregnant with Castro's child, an announcement to which Castro responded with joy. The couple returned to Cuba, where Lorenz was to make preparations for the birth of her child. Whether or not a child was actually born, however, remains unclear because of conflicting accounts given by Lorenz over the years. In one account, Lorenz claims that she gave birth to the child whom Castro kept and raised in Cuba and who eventually became a pediatrician. In another account, Lorenz writes that, with political controversy beginning to mount in Cuba, Castro, in apparent fear for his unborn baby's life, had Lorenz leave the island and return to the United States.

Upon her return to the States, Lorenz was hospitalized after falling ill and treated for the effects of an apparent botched abortion. Furious with Castro, and gaining the interest of the FBI and CIA,

Lorenz was recruited to infiltrate a number of pro-Castro organizations in the United States. She proved to be adept at espionage and was given the assignment of assassinating Castro. Armed with a botulism poison, Lorenz set out for Cuba to find her estranged lover and to kill him. However, upon arrival in Cuba, she realized that she could not kill Fidel and, instead, alerted him to the plot. The couple made love, and Marita returned to South Florida. After the failed assassination attempt, Lorenz remained in the shadowy world of espionage. In later years she would have ties to the Kennedy assassination and Watergate, and she would enjoy various romantic liaisons with small-time gangsters, political officials, and even dictators. While her stories are at times erratic, and often filled with missing details and contradictions, reports confirm that Lorenz and Castro did carry on a torrid affair during the late 1950s.

Louis XIV, King of France (1638–1715) See **Montespan, Athenais de.**

Louis XV, King of France (1710–1774) See **Becu, Marie Jeanne; Poisson, Jeanne.**

Ludwig I, King of Bavaria (1786–1868) See **Digby, Jane; Montez, Lola.**

Lupescu, Elenutza ("Magda") (1896–1977) When Elenutza Lupescu first met the future King Carol II of Greater Romania in 1921, she was the wife of Captain Tempeanu of his regiment in the northern town of Bistritza. Before embarking on a world tour, Carol purchased a costly brooch for her to indicate his interest despite the recent scandal involving Zizi Lambrino, a general's daughter with whom he had a child. Married and the daughter of a pharmacist, Magda Lupescu lacked the noble background needed for a potential queen. But the playboy king fell completely under her spell.

His parents, King Ferdinand I and Queen Marie, were horrified at the prospect that Carol might choose his low-born Jewish mistress over the throne. They hurriedly arranged for Carol to marry Princess Helen of Greece, a timid and unemotional girl who gave birth to their child

Michael less than a year later, then requested permission to return to her family. In this time, Magda quietly divorced her husband, who received a promotion, and she resumed use of her maiden name, Lupescu. Carol then made Magda his mistress and begged his wife for a divorce so that he could marry Magda. To forestall that possibility, Ferdinand spoke with Magda in 1925 and reminded her that the many anti-Semites of Romania would never accept her and warned that her presence in the country might lead to a mass slaughter of the Jews. Magda agreed, and went to Paris. But Carol followed his love, then wrote a letter to his parents in which he condemned the king's action and promised to never return to Romania.

The lovers enjoyed an active round of parties and social events in Paris, not returning home again for five years. After Ferdinand's death in 1927, the government proclaimed Carol's son Michael king and a regency of three was formally established to run the country. In 1928, Helen agreed to a divorce. By 1930, a coup had deposed the regency rule of Carol's son Michael. Carol promised his supporters that he would disassociate himself from Magda, and in 1930 he ascended the throne. However, as soon as he was securely in power, he brought Magda Lupescu back to Romania and installed her in the palace. The country soon grew to hate the king's mistress because of her extensive influence over the king, and because he seriously neglected his official duties to spend time with her. They superstitiously branded the red-haired Magda a "she-wolf."

Rather than keep her quietly in the background, Carol flaunted his love and permitted her freedoms with him in public. Magda frequently contradicted and criticized Carol in public. Rumors abounded that she beat him, and servants once reported that she had been seen waving a gun and chasing the naked king down a hallway of the castle. In 1937, at Magda's insistence, Carol had himself declared dictator, a move which he regretted in 1940 when he was threatened by the Nazis, Soviets, and Romanian Iron Guard fascists. All were threats to Carol's power and Magda's life. With the Romanian Iron Guard close behind them, Carol reappointed his son Michael king, then fled by train with Magda. The locomotive was forced to break through a border blockade, while Carol nervously guarded his mistress' life with his own body.

The couple settled in Portugal to enjoy domestic peace. During a serious illness in 1947, Magda requested that Carol marry her and legalize their union after twenty-four years, which he quickly did. Soon after the ceremony, Magda effected a miraculous recovery. After Carol's death in 1953 of a heart attack, Magda lived on alone for twenty-four years.

Lynch, Eliza Alicia (1837–1886) Born in County Cork, Ireland, in 1837 Eliza Alicia Lynch fled with her family for Paris during the great potato famine. There they married her off to a French army officer, Xavier Quatrefages, when she was only fifteen. Eliza spent the three years of her marriage in the dusty, hot desert of Algiers, then returned alone to Paris with the goal of snaring a rich man to support her.

Her golden blonde hair and statuesque body drew the attentions of numerous men. With the proceeds of her discreet services as a prostitute, she hired servants and set herself up in luxury. Unimpressed with the fickleness of French men, she decided to find a foreign "sugar daddy." She had calling cards made up which billed her as an "instructress in languages." Her servants left these cards at the foreign embassies in Paris.

Men began to call upon her and to view her home as a salon where only the elite were invited. One day, Eliza spotted an ugly, short man with brown teeth and a cigar clenched firmly in his mouth. She disdainfully asked another guest his name and was told that he was Francisco Lopez, extremely rich, twenty-nine, and the eldest son of the president of Paraguay. Her impression of him suddenly improved.

Lopez was dazzled by her attention, and they became lovers that evening. She listened as he spoke of his plans to become emperor of Paraguay, and he created an image of a virtual paradise in South America. When he asked Eliza to return with him, she agreed without hesitation.

Armed with a vast wardrobe of lavish Parisian gowns, crates of table service and china, opulent furniture, and even a piano, eighteen-year-old Eliza set out as mistress to the future dictator of Paraguay. Rather than the paradise which Lopez had promised, she found a hot and humid hell with a dilapidated and gloomy capital, Asuncion. She also found that her Parisian gowns were not the fashion in Paraguay where Lopez' sisters and mother dressed in frumpy black – not peacock blue silk. She further realized that the aristocratic families viewed her as only a whore and "Irish strumpet" and wanted no contact with her.

Eliza gave birth to her first son soon after the couple arrived. The joyous Lopez built her a pink-and-white palace, the first building of two stories in all of Paraguay. Seven years after she arrived, the old dictator-president died and Lopez took over the throne. The aristocrats no longer dared to ignore Eliza and Lopez demanded that they treat his mistress with all courtesies and honors due a wife. Eliza bore him six more children before she turned thirty-two.

As the other South American countries began to build up armies in 1865, Eliza urged Lopez to create a strong military presence which would allow Paraguay to withstand and conquer the others. Cabinet ministers urged peace talks, but the ambitious Eliza used pillow talk to push Lopez further to achieve the dream of making themselves Emperor and Empress of South America. Their aggressive stance soon pushed Paraguay into full-scale fighting, and Eliza used this event to wreak revenge on the aristocratic wives who had snubbed her only ten years before. She declared that all women, herself included, must give up their most treasured pieces of jewelry to help the war effort, and she personally collected the fine pieces from individual women.

Long before, she had memorized the owners of especially fine jewels. If these were not produced, she patriotically insisted to their owners that they donate them to the cause. But the jewels bought no guns – Eliza shipped them out to her agent in Paris, in addition to four caskets of gold coins from the Paraguayan treasury. When the loss was discovered, Eliza stood by unemotionally while her husband ordered the torture death and of his treasury officer whom he charged with the crime.

When Paraguay disastrously fell to Brazil in 1870, Lopez was killed and Eliza was caught trying to escape. Before sending her out of the country, the leader of the Brazilian forces ordered the would-be Empress to bury her dead husband and son – with her bare hands. Sometime later, she was placed on a ship bound for Europe.

Eliza went to London, where she lived for the rest of her life in comfort. Although most of her previously stolen wealth awaited her, she had to use legal means to retrieve additional money which had been sent with a doctor who conveniently forgot to hand it over to Eliza.

Although she had been Lopez's mistress for all of her years in Paraguay, when she died in 1886, her death certificate accorded her respectability in identifying her as the "widow of Francisco Lopez."

Mansfield, Helen Josephine (1840–1931) Josie Mansfield was born in Boston in 1840, the daughter of a newspaperman who moved his family to Stockton, California, in 1852. The convent-educated beauty made an early marriage to a small-time actor just to escape her restrictive home life, but they were divorced after two years when her husband accused Josie of infidelity. Josie drifted back to New York City and in 1876 she lived at the well-known bordello on Thirty-fourth Street run by Annie Wood. There she met "Big Jim" Fisk, a friend of political manipulator Boss Tweed and partner of American financier Jay Gould.

The blatant sensuality of the full-figured woman with the large, deep, bright eyes and purple black hair worn in massive coils captured Fisk's libido. He set her up in the manner of a grand courtesan and provided her with a luxurious apartment complete with butler, cook, chambermaid, and coachman, and an expense account for her whims. Behind Fisk's back, Josie was called "the Cleopatra of Twenty-third Street."

Although she was treated as a legal wife, Fisk observed the social rules of the day to maintain his business image, so he left Josie at home when he went to the "fashionable places" such as Delmonico's. At the same time, Fisk's wife lived quietly in Boston.

By 1869, Josie became bored with Fisk's frequent business concerns, and she secretly took as a lover a married young dandy, Edward Stiles Stokes, who was a part owner with Fisk and others in a Brooklyn oil refinery. Josie decided to leave Fisk for Stokes, but she first asked Fisk for a cash settlement. Her request led Fisk to refer to her as "Lumpsum".

Fisk tried to hang on to Josie, and refused to make a cash settlement or to share her with Stokes, as she suggested. Instead, he set out to ruin Stokes financially. The distraught young man sought to save himself by trying to extort two hundred thousand dollars from Fisk and embezzling twenty-seven thousand five hundred dollars from the company. He soon landed in jail.

Josie rescued Stokes' extortion letters from Fisk and, at the same time, she sued Fisk for fifty thousand dollars which she claimed he owed her from a business deal. Both suits landed in court, and the affair was blown wide open. Josie claimed that Fisk had damaged her good name, and she denied their living arrangement, claiming that she was simply a client of his brokerage house.

The legal battles ended on 6 January 1872, with Stokes branded a parasite and thirty-eight thousand dollars in debt with legal fees. Judge Pratt ruled a permanent injunction against the publication of Jim's letters to Josie, and a few hours later a grand jury indicted Stokes and Josie for attempted blackmail and put out warrants for their arrest. Stokes stalked Fisk that afternoon and shot him on the staircase of the Grand Central Hotel on Broadway. Fisk died on 6 January 1872, at the age of thirty-six. Stokes was captured immediately. He was tried and acquitted because the jury disagreed on the verdict. He received a second trial and was sentenced to be hanged, but the court of appeals set aside this conviction. In a third trial, Stokes was convicted of manslaughter and spent four years in Sing Sing prison. From 1876 when he was released until his death of natural causes in New York City in 1901, Stokes was a partner in a variety of businesses.

Josie left for Paris after Fisk's death, then traveled throughout

Europe for several years. In 1891, she married a rich, alcoholic New York City lawyer, Robert L. Reade, in London. They were divorced in 1897 after Josie had him declared insane, and she acquired control of his estate. She returned to Boston, then drifted with a brother to South Dakota in 1909. She returned to Europe and lived in Paris for many years until her death at the American Hospital there on 27 October 1931. Only three mourners were present at her grave, two serving women and an unidentified friend.

Maria Luisa, Queen (1751–1819) King Carlos IV of Spain enjoyed no mistresses, and once told his father that women of royal rank have difficulty committing adultery because of the lack of available men of equal rank. His wife, Queen Maria Luisa of Parma, was no beauty – but she went through many lovers, despite her beak of a nose, a pinched mouth, and dark, beady eyes.

After a string of brief affairs with assorted counts, dukes, minor ministers, and guardsmen, the indiscriminate queen became passionately involved with Manuel de Godoy, a provincial commoner and member of the Royal Bodyguard who was sixteen years her junior. This passion had tremendous ramifications for Spanish political history. Despite his humble origins, Maria Luisa maneuvered to make him financially secure and to make the king bestow upon Godoy the rank of general. Soon after, King Carlos elevated the twenty-four-year-old general to nobility as a duke and appointed him the Prime Minister of Spain.

Unfortunately for Spain, the queen's supreme passion was politically inept. His actions led to Spain's disastrous involvement in the French Revolution, the ceding to France of the Louisiana Territory in America, loss to the British navy at Trafalgar, and the invasion of Spain by the French under Napoleon. In 1808, Maria Luisa and Carlos IV were deposed, and the royal couple with Manuel went to Rome. Maria Luisa died ten years later, but her grand passion survived her by forty-eight years to become a shabby and lonely old man in Paris.

Marie Antoinette (1755–1793) Marie Antoinette was born in Vienna in 1755, a daughter of Holy Roman Emperor Francis I and Empress Maria Theresa. She was married to Louis, heir to the throne

Maria Luisa (NEW YORK PUBLIC LIBRARY)

of France, in 1770 in an attempt to strengthen an alliance between the French and her family, the Hapsburg dynasty of Austria. While married to Louis, who became King Louis XVI in 1774, she gave birth to three children, a daughter and two sons.

As queen, Marie became the scapegoat for all of France's ills. She was a foreigner which made her unpopular, a difficulty which she compounded by devoting herself to Austrian interests. She surrounded herself by reckless individuals with bad reputations, and she was extravagant. The French blamed their financial problems on the expenses accumulated in buying her gowns and diamonds and in redecorating the palaces.

Despite her extravagance and bad companions, historians have found that Marie was mistress to only one man in her lifetime and she respected her husband even if she did not love him. In 1778, Marie met tall, handsome, patrician Axel Fersen, a young Swedish nobleman whose family had a long tradition of court service. She was at the height of her beauty when they met, with her full blond hair, large blue eyes, and fresh complexion. Their meeting was significant, as Fersen noted in his journal, but it was not until five years later that Marie became his mistress. He had returned to France as a representative of the Swedish court after our years as aide-de-camp to General Rochambeau, the commander of French expeditionary forces which aided the American colonists. Service in the wilderness had toughened him and brought numerous military honors from both the French and the Swedes.

Marie invited Fersen frequently to Versailles, and he wrote at that time to his sister Sophy that all of his family's intentions to arrange a marriage should end, for he had found the woman he loved even if he could not have her. To ensure that he could be at Versailles without suspicion, he used family connections to become commander of the Royal Swedish regiment in the French army. He also became an aide to King Gustavus, with whom he traveled on official visits, and wherever he traveled he wrote to Marie.

In 1787, Marie ordered workers to begin alterations on her apartments at Versailles to give Fersen a place to live while on visits. The remodeling, which is recorded in the Service of the Royal Buildings, shows that she installed a Swedish stove for his comfort which was not only expensive but which required that part of a wall and a large area of floor be demolished.

The two often rode together and gossip spread regarding the frequency and length of their meetings. Louis XVI accepted Fersen's presence as due to his official status, but Marie remained discreet. In 1788 Louis received a packet of letters which charged Marie with infidelity and it named Fersen. He became physically sick, unable to ride out as he had planned. Although Marie suggested that they send Fersen away to end the gossip, Louis XVI refused. With increasing unrest in France, he had come to depend on Fersen as a statesman.

Despite other brief affairs, Fersen wrote in his journal that he thought of her constantly and he later showed the depth of that love when France erupted into revolution. Louis XVI was beheaded in 1793, despite all efforts by Fersen to spirit the royal family out of the country. Soon after, Fersen tried to help Marie escape, but she wouldn't leave without her children.

Marie was lodged in the Great Tower, as she awaited her fate. In late July, a monarchist, General Jarjayes, was able to see Marie and she gave him Louis' watch seal and wedding ring. She also gave him a memento for Fersen, a wax impression of her own seal which years before she had modified to contain Fersen's crest, a homing pigeon with the words *Tutto a le miguidu* ("Everything guides me to thee"). She asked the general to assure Fersen that the words of the seal remained true.

On 2 August 1793, Marie Antoinette was brought to trial. She went to the guillotine on 6 October 1793.

Mata Hari (1876–1917) Mata Hari was born Margaretha Gertruida Zelle in Holland in the peaceful Dutch hamlet of Leeuwarden. Her father went bankrupt when she was thirteen and her mother died when she was fifteen. The future world-renowned stunner went to live with a staid aunt and uncle who sent her to a kindergarten teacher's training college in Leyden.

As a young woman, the 5'9" Margaretha was overly tall for the time, and her small breasts, big shoulders, and wide hips gave her an ungainly appearance. She would stuff her camisole with stockings, and several times the loss of a stocking had embarrassing results.

Her looks combined with the absence of a dowry led her to marry the first man who asked. He happened to be Captain Rudolf MacLeod, a thirty-nine-year-old member of the Dutch colonial army whose career seemed to be stalled. Together, they had a son, Norman John, and a daughter, Juana Luisa. Stationed in the Dutch East Indies with MacLeod, Margaretha watched the Javanese temple dancers and learned the moves which would later make her famous.

She endured her husband's infidelity, drinking, and beatings, but the murder by poisoning of their son by a native soldier, who was distraught over MacLeod's seduction of his girlfriend, pushed her out of the marriage. She left her husband in 1903 and arrived in Paris at the age of twenty-seven.

Once in Paris, Margaretha renamed herself Mata Hari, "The Eye of Dawn," and created a new past in which she claimed to be the daughter of a fourteen-year-old Javanese temple dancer who had died giving birth to her. She also claimed to have been raised by temple priests who taught her sacred dances, and she titillated society with her story of having first danced nude before the altar of a Hindu temple at the age of thirteen. In order to secure her position in society, she hinted that her father had been a British lord.

Dressed in a metallic bra with bejewelled breast cups and a jeweled groin cover which trailed diaphanous veils, the dark-haired, dark-eyed Mata Hari undulated sensuously in feverish movements before her audiences, ripping off her coverings at significant moments. She made stripping exotic and artistic, as she justified her actions as integral to "temple dancing." She was sought after throughout Europe, although some audiences were scandalized. One director went so far as to insist that she wear a panty of red flannel.

The small breasts which had plagued the young Margaretha determined that the newly born Mata Hari always kept her breast coverings, no matter what else she might remove. When asked by intimates why the jeweled bra remained while the groin cover fell with ease, she hinted broadly that her breasts had been bitten and permanently disfigured by MacLeod when, in truth, she had so little to expose.

With the outbreak of World War I, her affairs with high German government officials marked her for surveillance by the French. She had had a long string of lovers, including Crown Prince Wilhelm of Germany, a rich but married German landowner, a wealthy French stockbroker, and a rich and married colonel in the Dutch Hussars. Her final passion began in 1916 with twenty-one-year-old Russian Captain Vadime de Masslof, whom she visited in Vittel, a French resort in the military zone where he was recuperating from a wound.

The French arrested her in February 1917 on the charge of acting as a German spy. In 1907, she had attended a school for espionage in Lorrach, and she had numerous liaisons with high-ranking Allied officers who possessed valuable military information. Yet, Mata Hari claimed that she was a double agent who had actually been working for the French while appearing in public with several high-ranking Germans. Biographers contend that no proof exists to dispute this claim. Several rich, aged lovers came to her support at the trial, but she was sentenced to death by a firing squad.

She faced her death with style. Dressed as if to go to dinner, she faced the firing squad at Vincennes without a blindfold. At the end no one came forward to claim the body of the celebrated toast of Europe, and it was donated to a medical school.

Menken, Adah Isaacs (1835–1868) Born in New Orleans, Adah Isaacs lived in poverty until she met the wealthy Austrian Baron Friedrich von Eberstadt. He promised to support her family if they let him take Adah with him to Cuba. Once in Cuba, the baron not only seduced her but abandoned Adah with no money so she turned to prostitution, raising her price until she had earned her way back to the United States.

Once back Adah took society and the stage by storm. Openly defiant of social mores, she smoked in public, took lovers, and cut her hair, purposely flaunting her unconventional lifestyle. Although she married four times, she did not give up her love affairs, and the public soon viewed her as a wild, immoral woman. Her performances were always sold out. She was called the "Naked Lady" because of the close-fitting, flesh-colored body tights which she wore on stage in the play *Mazeppa*, but her personal life earned her notoriety.

After conquering the eastern United States and California, Adah went to Europe, hoping to find a literary figure to back an edition of her poetry. She met and charmed Charles Dickens and Charles Reade, and had a brief affair with Swinburne. Her main goal, however, was to meet Alexandre Dumas *père*. For a few months in 1868, Adah spent weekends with the sixty-six-year-old Dumas in his estate or walking through Paris, holding hands and sharing kisses. The pair once scandalized his son when he found Dumas and Adah passionately embracing as he unexpectedly walked into a room, and Dumas *fils* stalked out indignantly. She was to be his father's last mistress.

Though he was thirty-three years her senior, she called him a "King of Romance," and the "child of Gentleness and Love." Adah always liked to have pictures taken of herself with literary celebrities. She and Dumas were photographed in several intimate and relaxed poses, which Dumas allowed for he expected the pictures to be for their albums only. He had not counted on the photographer making copies of the pictures and selling them to shops on the boulevard to be displayed in public.

Dumas was humiliated by the public ridicule which followed, and he sued the photographer for damages. Adah, on the other hand, benefitted from the increase in her popularity which filled her audience with curious onlookers. What she did regret was the loss of her lover, for Dumas *père* angrily ended their relationship.

Adah died later that year at thirty-three in Paris of what doctors diagnosed as internal abscesses which might have been brought on by syphilis.

Mercer, Lucy (1889–1948) The affair between Lucy Mercer and Franklin Delano Roosevelt began in 1916 and continued to his death in 1945. A tall and willowy blonde with large, tranquil eyes who looked very much like FDR's mother, Lucy was descended from signers of the Declaration of Independence and she was acquainted with everyone who mattered in Washington, D.C. Her mother was a divorced society beauty and her father was a moneyless gentleman who had founded the Chevy Chase Club. The money dissipated and Lucy had to work after completing a convent school education in Vienna.

Although she began as a social secretary for Eleanor Roosevelt in 1913, her beautiful and winning smile, soft voice, and talent for knowing how to please a man and to make his life agreeable soon won her FDR's attention. During the summer of 1916 when Eleanor left for the summer for Campobello, the affair between Lucy and Franklin began. The attraction was obvious to those around them, and the pair also met secretly as lovers. Nigel Law, an English bachelor, acted as an escort for Lucy to deflect gossip.

The next summer while on a cruise Eleanor became aware of the attraction and decided against going to Campobello that year; however, she gave in to Franklin's demand that she go. World War I was on, and Lucy enlisted as a yeoman in the U.S. Navy, and she was assigned to duty in the Department of the Navy in the office of the Assistant Seretary of the Navy, who just happened to be FDR.

Gossip reached Eleanor, who returned early to Washington on the pretext of helping the doughboys who were shipping out to Europe. Eleanor learned all of the details through the talk of the other volunteering society wives. She confronted Lucy, who left the Roosevelt household as an employee, but who remained in FDR's office until her discharge in September, 1917.

Eleanor appealed to her mother-in-law for help, and Sara used political connections to have FDR sent to Europe in 1918 to inspect navy facilities. Lucy sent letters to him which Eleanor found and read when he returned in September.

The angry wife demanded a divorce, to which FDR agreed, but Sara and his political advisors fought the idea. The result was an armed truce in which Eleanor agreed to act as FDR's wife in public if he would give up Lucy, but the marriage, after seven pregnancies and four children, became sexually abstinent.

In 1920, Lucy married Wintie Rutherfurd, a rich, well-connected, fifty-six-year-old widower with six children. She met him when he hired her as a social secretary and governess, and he proposed to twenty-nine-year-old Lucy after a year. Sixteen months after the marriage, daughter Barbara was born.

Over the years, Lucy and FDR kept in touch through friends, and Lucy watched FDR's first presidential inauguration in 1933 from a White House limousine. The Secret Service men accompanying her called her "ladylike to her toes." She also watched the third and fourth inaugurations from the same vantage point.

Lucy and FDR met secretly and frequently in Washington where they would arrive in separate cars at a secluded spot then drive off together, or friends arranged meetings. The presidential secretary knew that her calls should always be put directly through to the president, and FDR sometimes burst into excited French if visitors were in his office during a call.

After her husband died in 1944, Lucy began to appear at White House dinners when Eleanor was away, and the presidential train often detoured to Lucy's home on its way to the Warm Springs presidential retreat. Lucy was with FDR on his last trip in April 1945 when he died. Lucy, a photographer, and a portrait painter were chatting with FDR when he complained of a headache. All were hurried off the train before Eleanor arrived, but she learned that Lucy had been there. She also learned the sad truth that Lucy had been a frequent White House guest when daughter Anna had acted as hostess in her absence.

Despite feeling betrayed, when she found a watercolor of FDR a short while later, Eleanor sent it to Lucy. Lucy, in turn, wrote Eleanor a direct thank-you note, but there was no further contact.

Lucy died in 1948 in New York City of leukemia.

Mérimée, Prosper (1804–1876) See **Sand, George.**

Meyer, Mary Pinchot (1932–1964) Mary Pinchot Meyer was three years younger than John F. Kennedy and the two had known each other since college days. Mary was also a friend of Jackie Kennedy as well as the sister-in-law of *Washington Post* editor Benjamin Bradlee, a close Kennedy intimate. Rich and politically well-connected, she first met JFK at Vassar in 1949 or 1950.

In 1956 Mary moved into the small studio behind the Bradlees' Georgetown house after her divorce from Cord Meyer, Jr., founder of the United World Federalists, who later headed the covert action staff of the Central Intelligence Agency. It was then that Mary and the United States Senator from Massachusetts JFK, thirty-nine, began to meet at the small dinner parties which were frequently given by both the Bradlees and the Kennedys. Other close friends were sculptor Ann Truitt and her husband James, with whom Mary shared the details of her growing relationship with JFK. James Truitt revealed the affairs after both Mary and JFK were long dead.

JFK and Mary did not begin their sexual relationship until 1961, after he had already been president for a year. Within a few months, the sporadic meetings blossomed into regular visits to the White House by Mary whenever Jackie was away. Kennedy also managed clandestine visits to the studio behind the Bradlees' house, and the two managed somehow to take walks along a path of the Old Chesapeake and Ohio Canal, which paralleled the Potomac River. She was the last and most enduring of Kennedy's mistresses, and she acted as both lover and confidante.

Eleven months after Kennedy's assassination, on October 13, 1964, Mary Meyer was taking a midday walk on the path which she had shared many times with JFK when she was shot fatally in the head and in the chest. Police arrested twenty-five-year-old laborer Raymond Crump, Jr. for the crime. Although a witness testified to seeing Crump standing over Mary, no murder weapon was ever found and no motive could be discovered. Crump was acquitted and released.

Although she kept a detailed diary which is said to have contained numerous romantic references to JFK, we might never have known about the affair had not her best friend's husband made the affair public after her death. Mary had requested that her diary be destroyed upon her death.

Miller, Arthur (1915–) See **Monroe, Marilyn.**

Mills, Wilbur (1909–1992) See **Fox, Fanne.**

Mitterand, François (1917–1996) See **Pingeot, Anne.**

Monroe, Marilyn (1926–1962) Sex goddess and fantasy mistress to millions of men worldwide, Marilyn Monroe excited desire in every man she met. Her voluptuous body and little girl voice made her appear to be appealing and unthreatening.

Born Norma Jean Mortenson on 1 June 1926, at Los Angeles General Hospital, she was descended on her mother's side from James Monroe, fifth American president. Although her mother identified the child's father as her second husband, Edward Mortenson, Marilyn often told people that he died before she was conceived and that her

Marilyn Monroe (BETTMANN ARCHIVE)

real father was a man named C. Stanley Gifford who worked with her mother. In 1951 she located her father and called him, but his wife relayed his message that he didn't want to see her and suggested that she contact a lawyer if she had some complaint.

Her maternal grandmother and grandfather had suffered mental disabilities and both were eventually committed to asylums. Norma Jean's mother Gladys, who had worked in the Columbia Pictures film laboratory and as a film cutter for RKO Studios, was also in and out of institutions, leaving the future glamor queen at the mercy of a series of foster parents and, for twenty-one months, the Los Angeles Orphans' Home Society.

When Marilyn neared sixteen, her foster parents realized that the regular support money from Los Angeles County would end, so they pressured her to encourage the boy who lived in the house behind theirs to marry her. James Dougherty was a relatively naive nineteen, and both he and Marilyn yielded to the pressure. They were married three weeks after Marilyn's sixteenth birthday on 19 June 1942. Two years later Jim shipped out with the navy and Marilyn the young housewife moved in with her mother-in-law and also began to work in a defense industry plant, the Radio Plane Plant, first on the assembly line packing parachutes then later in the "dope" room where the cloth used for airplane fuselage was sprayed with liquid plastic. Army photographer David Conover visited the plant to do a photographic essay for *Yank* magazine on women in war work and took the photos which eventually launched her with the Blue Book Modeling Agency. By early 1946, she was divorced from Dougherty and modeling on the covers of such "girlie" magazines as *Swank*, *Peek*, *See*, and *Laff*, under the name of Jean Norman.

She occasionally used Baker, her mother's last name from a first marriage, in her modeling jobs and in screen tests. By late 1946 Ben Lyon, the head of casting for Twentieth Century Fox studios, had renamed her "Marilyn" in honor of his favorite musical star, Marilyn Miller, who had died at the age of thirty-seven in 1936, and "Monroe," her mother's maiden name. From that point, rumors abounded that Marilyn slept her way into starring movie roles. Her name was linked with comedian Ted Lewis, then influential in Hollywood, as well as chief of production at Columbia Pictures, Harry Cohn, in addition to numerous middle-management producers. In 1948, she had small roles in *Scudda Hoo! Scudda Hay!* and *The Dangerous Years*. She also became a steady date of sixty-nine-year-old Joseph Schenck, whose contacts moved her into Columbia Pictures for a time. William Morris agent Johnny Hyde was her real coup, and as her lover and mentor he helped her move into bigger and better parts in *The Asphalt Jungle* and *All About Eve* in 1950. She achieved star billing in 1953 with *Gentlemen Prefer Blondes* and *How to Marry a Millionaire*, which continued in such hits as *The Seven-Year Itch* (1955), *Bus Stop* (1956), *The Prince and the Showgirl* (1957), *Some Like It Hot* (1959), and *Let's Make Love* (1960).

In 1952 Marilyn met the man who would become her second husband, thirty-seven-year-old Yankee centerfielder, Joe DiMaggio, who had retired from baseball in 1951. The two were married on 14 January 1954, but Marilyn couldn't mold herself to the image of the happy housewife, content to bask in her husband's reflected glory. They divorced after nine months, but he remained in her life as a protector and ready shoulder to cry on until the end of her life. Each year on the anniversary of her death, red roses appear on her grave, compliments of DiMaggio.

Marilyn's third and final husband was playwright Arthur Miller, eleven years her senior whose works include *Death of a Salesman*, *The Crucible*, *A View from the Bridge*, and *All My Sons*. They met in 1950 while she worked on her first "co-starring" film, *Young as You Feel*, and the prize-winning playwright was negotiating a film script. She confided to her drama coach that she was in love and had found a man whom she could admire like a father. Miller and she corresponded for several years, and they also met six or seven times in the East. He was married and did not file for divorce until 1956, soon after which they married. In their six years as sometime lovers and caring friends, Marilyn confided in Miller and asked his advice as she prepared for roles, but she did interrupt their contact for her nine months of marriage to DiMaggio. The marriage faltered after a year, but in 1960 Miller wrote a screenplay for *The Misfits*, an unsuccessful film starring Marilyn and Clark Gable. The Millers had lived apart for nearly two years before they were divorced in January 1961. Friends have observed that Miller's play *After the Fall*, written in 1963, is his attempt to exorcise Marilyn's ghost and to explore the contradictions of their romance and marriage.

Marilyn Monroe remained an insecure and emotionally hungry woman who, despite love and support from several men in her life, needed to always feel loved. Many suggest that Marilyn's death was linked to her love affairs with the Kennedys. When she carried on a clandestine affair with John F. Kennedy and became too possessive and involved, the man who had been bred as American political royalty turned her over to his brother Robert, who could let her down gradually with no embarrassment or political damage. However, as several writers have suggested, Marilyn fell even harder for Robert's promises of marriage and of being the future First Lady, and she refused to accept his rejection when he first changed his private phone number then refused to take her calls at the Justice Department.

Threats of exposure, rumors of a red-covered diary containing incriminating notes, and tapes obtained from her wiretapped phone conversations are said to have placed pressure on Robert Kennedy to end the relationship and to destroy all evidence of association. The FBI, under J. Edgar Hoover, had tapped both JFK and RFK's phone lines, and underworld figures also threatened exposure. Furthermore, while carrying on her affair with RFK, Marilyn is reported to have undergone an abortion.

Citing RFK's suspicious appearances and disappearances around Los Angeles the night before Marilyn's death, coupled with the contradictory official statement that RFK had been in San Francisco or in the East, writers suggest that Marilyn was murdered to eliminate political embarrassment rather than that she committed suicide.

The jury remains out as to just what caused her death. Missing police and autopsy reports as well as the disappearance of some of her telephone records have strengthened the allegations that Marilyn was murdered, but the truth remains hidden.

Montespan, Athenais de (1640–1707) Born of French nobility, Athenais de Montespan was twenty-six, married, and the mother of two children when she met King Louis XIV of France. She was introduced to him at court and soon after moved into a special palace apartment. She was the king's mistress for twelve years.

Sophisticated, witty, voluptuous, and experienced, Athenais appealed to the Sun King who had grown tired of his arranged marriage with Maria Therésa, his Spanish cousin. Although Athenais was ambitious and a heavy gambler, her reckless sensuality appealed to Louis and he willingly provided her family with favors. She arranged for her father, the Duc de Mortemart, to become governor of Paris, and her sister was given the position of abbess in a rich convent.

To please the king, Athenais dyed her brunette hair blonde because Louis liked blonde hair, and she also invented a new hair style which featured curls on each side of the face to just below the ear, with small curls on the brow, and a braid of hair around the head entwined with pearls and ribbons. She also became close friends with the queen. During her twelve years as Louis' mistress, Athenais bore seven children, all cared for by a young widow named Madame Scarron, who would become the King's next mistress as Madame de Maintenon.

Everyone at court observed the uncanny power which Athenais had for arousing the king's passion. Rumors circulated that she was adding aphrodisiacs to his food and drink and that she used magic. In 1680 the daughter of a woman executed for using black magic spoke before the King's Commission and charged that Athenais had paid her mother to have spells said and love potions concocted to capture and retain the king's love. She also alleged that Athenais had asked her to deliver messages to the devil, and that she had tried to kill young rivals by impregnating their clothes with poisons which were absorbed by the skin. The accuser also stated that Athenais had participated in the Black Mass, lying naked on the altar and consuming the blood and flesh of a baby.

The horrified Commission condemned her actions, and the king dismissed her as his mistress and pensioned her off. In her later years, she packed her luxurious brocades and silks into her closets and wore only clothing made of coarse linen. She became concerned with the poor and distributed her fortune.

Montez, Lola (1818–1861) Maria Dolores Eliza Roseanna Gilbert was born the daughter of an army officer and a milliner in Limerick, Ireland. The family was transferred to India in 1818, where the child learned to ride and to handle a javelin, as well as to speak Hindi and several other dialects. After her father's death when she was six and her mother's almost immediate remarriage, Lola gained a more formal education from her stepfather Major John Craigie who tutored her in mathematics, Latin, and Greek, as well as Portuguese and Spanish. Vivacious, intelligent, and attractive, young Lola became too much of a competitor for her mother, so Mrs. Craigie packed her daughter off to her father-in-law's in Montrose, Scotland, where Lola's education continued. When Lola was twelve, her stepgrandfather suffered a heart attack and she went to live in London with the family of Major General Sir Jasper Nicolls, which contained two young daughters. Mrs. Nicolls delighted in showing off Lola's exotic beauty by dressing her in saris and encouraging her use of Hindi.

While living in Paris for a year when the Nicolls sought to broaden their daughters' and Lola's education, the young Betty Gilbert, as she was then called, realized that many of her schoolmates and even the nuns in the convent school thought of her as Spanish. So she began to call herself Lola, a shortening of her second name Dolores.

Soon after fifteen-year-old Lola was informed by her mother that a prestigious marriage had been arranged for her with a gouty, sixty-year-old lord, Sir Abraham Lumley. Although Lola protested, Mrs. Craigie arrived in England to buy Lola's trousseau and to collect her daughter. With Mrs. Craigie was a twenty-seven-year-old First Lieutenant Thomas James, who had attached himself to the older woman aboard the ship, hoping to advance his career. Young Lola and the dashing officer became infatuated and they eloped into what the later adult Lola remembered in her *Autobiography* as a painfully unhappy marriage which motivated her to advise all young girls contemplating such a step to "hang or drown themselves just one hour before they start."

Lola and her husband lived for a time in England, then went to India where she enjoyed the social life of an officer's wife. Within a few years the marriage ended with Captain James suing for divorce on grounds of misconduct and Lola returning to England. She made up her mind to become an actress and, using money given to her by Major Craigie, acquired an expensive wardrobe and took acting lessons. When she accepted the fact that she had no talent for acting, Lola traveled to Madrid to take dancing lessons and also spent time in the sidewalk cafes studying the movements of the women. She failed to realize that the women whom she mistook for ladies were actually prostitutes, for ladies still only left their homes in the company of a duenna.

When she returned to England several months later, she had renamed herself Lola Montez and spoke with a faint Spanish accent. She billed herself as the prima ballerina of the Teatro Real in Seville, and theater critics gushed over her exotic and perfect Spanish beauty. Her stage debut in 1843 was ruined when a male voice boomed out at the end of her dance after the applause died down that she was not Lola Montez, but only Betty James. Lola was booed off stage and couldn't obtain another engagement, so she scraped together the money for a one-way ticket to Brussels. There she began the first of the dancing engagements which would lead to Berlin then to the Warsaw Opera.

In early 1844 Lola went to Dresden for a dance engagement and she met and fell in love with Franz Liszt. The thirty-three-old composer and pianist was extremely popular and the city was soon buzzing with the news that Lola Montez had moved in with him. The two took no pains to hide their relationship and Liszt took her everywhere with him and wrote a sonata in her honor. Wherever they feasted, however, Lola forced herself into the spotlight by a series of bizarre acts such as dancing on the tables at a royal banquet. Unable to face the terrible-tempered Lola, Liszt left her in their apartment without warning and paid the landlord handsomely for the expense of the furniture which Lola was expected to destroy when she awoke and found Liszt missing.

From Dresden, Lola moved to the fast-paced, urbane world of Paris. Although the critics attacked her dancing as being without talent, Lola triumphed in love. Alexandre Dumas *père* courted her, escorting her to supper and the theater, but she arranged to have others present to avoid any hint of gossip of an affair. In her *Autobiography* Lola denies that they were ever lovers. She did, however, find a rich protector in the person of Alexandre Henri Dujarier, with whom she lived for several months until he was killed in a duel. After arranging a settlement with his wealthy mother, who gladly paid Lola 75,000 dollars after she gave up claim to the dead man's estate which had been willed to her, Lola left for Germany where, in 1846, she met King Ludwig I.

Most critics and audiences hissed her dancing, and for this reason she was denied permission to dance in the state theater of Germany. Angered by the rejection, she marched into Ludwig's office, slit her dress fully down the front, and showed him her matchless body. Two days later with the King present, Lola took center stage at the Court Theatre, dressed in a Spanish costume. Despite their monarch's presence, the audience booed Lola's performance, but she returned a second night with Ludwig's secret police standing guard to prevent a repeat demonstration by the audience. Even the king couldn't make the Court Theatre retain an act which would make it the laughing stock of.Europe, and Lola was well paid for the two performances and terminated.

The king called his new love "Lolita" and wrote poems to her which he circulated among his ministers while his wife, Queen Thérésè, lived in another part of the palace. By the time she was thirty, Lola had spent two years as Ludwig's mistress and was named Countess of Landsfield, Baroness Rosenthal. The ordinarily frugal monarch, who had filled his library with secondhand books and whose clothes were threadbare, gave Lola an Italian palace filled with rare paintings, a glass staircase, a perfumed fountain, and the necessary jewels and clothing to maintain her new image. Lola also began to dictate government policy, creating a *Lolaministerium* which caused great resentment among the populace who resented her influence on the king.

Wherever she went, Lola carried with her the whip with which she quickly disciplined anyone who defied her commands. Her heavyhanded treatment of university intellectuals created major student riots and helped provoke the Revolution of 1848. Lola was driven out of Germany and Ludwig abdicated the throne in favor of his son.

Lola drifted to England and into marriage with a man ten years her junior, the very wealthy George T. Heald, who had recently come into an annual income of ten thousand dollars, while Ludwig sent letters, love poems, and small pieces of jewelry. While on honeymoon in Scotland in 1849 Lola was summoned by a magistrate to answer charges of bigamy. Her young husband's sister had delved into Lola's past and learned that her divorce from Captain James had never been finalized. To escape legal action, the newlyweds left for Boulogne then moved on to Paris where Lola spent freely at dressmakers, jewelers, and perfumers. When they moved on to Barcelona the couple quarreled violently and Lola slashed him over the face, chest, and arms with the knife she always carried. A disheartened Heald left for England and died a year later in a boating accident.

The whole affair made a pariah of Lola, and male friends in both England and France avoided her. A trip to America during which she starred in *Lola Montez in Bavaria* at the Broadway Theatre revived her dance career. She was a celebrity and no one cared if she had talent. She then took her show on the road, charming only New Orleans before she cancelled the show and headed out for California, where she charmed gold miners with her "Spider Dance," in which she wore tights and black, calf-length silk skirts and wriggled and shuddered to dislodge and then stomped on the imaginary spiders as they fell to the floor. Unfavorable critics received a slash of her whip, but, in a later trip to Australia where the dancer had been booed off stage, one critic responded to Lola's whip with one of his own. She performed that evening with red welts across her face, arms, and upper chest.

In 1858 while in the United States, Lola underwent a religious conversion and she began a lecture tour which took her throughout the country. Gone was the flamboyant dancer, who was replaced by a drably dressed woman, with hair parted in the middle and pulled back, and who looked much older than forty. Her lectures were vague, dull sermons which, nonetheless, drew crowds who still remembered the old Lola. She also worked to rehabilitate prostitutes at Brooklyn's Magdalen Asylum, becoming a recluse aside from her volunteer work. In 1861 Lola suffered a paralyzing stroke and died ten days later. She was buried in Greenwood Cemetery in Brooklyn with only nine mourners present.

Montgenet, Comtesse Thérésè-Bernardine (1750–1830) Thérésè Bernardine St. Laurent, later the Comtesse Montgenet, was born in

Besançon, France, the daughter of a civil engineer Jean Mongent and his wife Claudine. She was the mistress of two French aristocrats before being called to Gibraltar in 1790 to serve as both a singer with Prince Edward's band and as his mistress, before he was made the Duke of Kent and Strathern in 1799. The prince's agent, Monsieur Fontiny, had been told to acquire a young woman for the prince, and he learned of Mlle. St. Laurent through an intermediary. Without meeting the prince, she eagerly agreed and for twenty-seven years she was the mistress of Edward Augustus, the Duke of Kent and Strathern, the fourth son of George III and youngest brother of British Kings George IV and William IV.

He was also the father of Queen Victoria of England. The Duke of Kent left Therésè to find a legitimate wife when ascension to the throne appeared a possibility upon the death in 1817 in childbirth of his niece, George IV's daughter Charlotte, Princess of Wales. Because William IV, another brother who would succeed George IV upon the throne, had no legitimate heirs and others of the seven sons of George III were either childless or unmarried, succession of the throne would pass from Royal Duke to Royal Duke – unless one of the brothers produced an heir. At fifty, the duke had never been married and, despite twenty-seven years with Therésè, he still didn't know that she was seven years older than him.

Therésè was extremely upset when she learned of the duke's plan, for she had suffered through very lean years with him. She had remained with Kent through military duty in Canada, to which he had been sent in exile for overly severe treatment of his troops at Gibraltar, and back to duty at Gibraltar where he was finally relieved of all future military deployment because of the same behavior. Afterward, Kent and Therésè lived in England for nearly fourteen years until they moved to Brussels, upon which Kent had insisted because of its low cost of living. Although he had a yearly allowance of twenty-four thousand pounds, he was constantly in debt.

When the Duke of Kent followed his older brother, the Duke of Clarence, and arranged a hasty marriage in 1817 to thirty-year-old Victoria Mary Louisa, Princess of Saxe-Coburg and sister-in-law to the late Charlotte, Therésè threatened havoc unless the duke promised to provide well for her, and he struggled to buy her off.

What Therésè didn't know was that Kent had been contemplating a royal marriage for at least two years previous to Charlotte's death because of his debts. A marriage approved by the Royal Marriages Act guaranteed not only an increased income from Parliament but money to clear his debts and funds to set up a household.

On the day that the duke left Brussels for England (on the pretence that he was needed by the royal family) Therésè left for Paris where friends influenced King Louis XVIII to make her the Comtesse de Montgenet. She took a lavish apartment and began to collect her pension from the duke. He sent letters of apology regarding what he called his painful duty which had disrupted their many years together, and he also provided money for her to maintain her lifestyle, although he had to take out a loan before marrying to do so.

When the duke died two years later, only eight months after the birth of the future Queen Victoria, his insurance money went to Therésè, who was listed with the estate as a creditor. The Duchess Victoria Mary Louisa had long been aware of Therésè's numerous years as her husband's mistress, and she honored that relationship by sending a note to Therésè upon the duke's death.

Therésè lived ten years longer than her lover, dying in 1830. Her lover's wife was informed of the death through her bankers, as well as through the gossip. In her death, the pension went to the duchess to help to raise her young daughter, Victoria.

Monti, Carlotta (1908–) Despite the public image of American comedian W.C. Fields as an alcoholic, grumbling old tightwad, his mistress of thirteen years revealed a more affectionate side to him in her story of their years together. The couple first met when twenty-four-year-old Carlotta became an extra on the set where the fifty-four-year-old comedian was filming. Impressed by her exotic good looks, the result of her mixed Italian, Mexican, and Spanish ancestry, Fields greeted her elaborately by taking off his hat, bowing, and kissing her hand.

Although Fields had been married since 1900 to his former vaudeville assistant Hattie Hughes, he told Carlotta that he had once been married but had not seen his wife in years. In truth, he continued to support his wife and son for over forty years. The young woman was charmed by both Fields and his fame, and soon became his mistress, moving into his Hollywood home and becoming his trusted messenger. He called her "Chinaman" because of the mandarin-collared dresses she wore, and she called him "Woody" because he looked to her like a "woodsy bear."

Carlotta learned to deal with Fields' often odd behavior. He was suspicious of everyone, and he often left large amounts of money around to see if he could trust her. His jealousy had annoyed previous girlfriends who resented being followed by private detectives, but Carlotta always spotted the detectives and played her own games by simply taking exceedingly long and circuitous routes that led nowhere and which increased his detective bills.

Despite his often unusual behavior and the heavy drinking toward the end which made his life difficult, Carlotta gloried in their lovemaking and said that Fields was a perfectionist in the bedroom. Carlotta apparently pleased her lover, because their thirteen years together was nearly twice as long as any other mistress had lasted. On his deathbed in 1946, Fields is reported to have uttered the following words "God damn the whole friggin' world and everyone in it but you, Carlotta."

Morgan, Vicki (1952–1983) Vicki Morgan was the mistress of multimillionaire Alfred Bloomingdale, grandson of the founder of Diner's Club and a close friend of then-President Ronald Reagan and other key government officials. Bloomingdale met the beautiful blonde in the late 1970s. He found that Vicki was fully willing to indulge his sexual irregularities. She freely participated in his sadomasochistic orgies, as long as he kept the money coming.

In 1982 when Bloomingdale was hospitalized with throat cancer, his wife Betsy learned that he had secretly been paying his mistress Vicki eighteen thousand dollars monthly and she put a stop to the payments. Vicki responded by filing a five million dollar palimony suit in which she claimed that she been Bloomingdale's traveling companion, business partner, and confidante. A short time later, her lawyer filed another suit for an additional five million for the abrupt termination of the monthly allowance.

Bloomingdale died before the palimony case could come to trial.

In her testimony, Vicki claimed to have videotapes of high U.S. government officials at wild sex parties. The judge decided that she had no real claim beyond that of "a young, well-paid mistress" who had been financed by "a wealthy, older paramour." Vicki was, instead, awarded a lump-sum settlement of two hundred thousand dollars.

Vicki was bludgeoned to death with a baseball bat by her homosexual living companion Marvin Pancoast after he became annoyed with her complaints about inadequate money. Her settlement from the Bloomingdale estate was passed on to her fifteen-year-old son Todd.

Mortimer, Roger (?–1330) See **Isabella, Queen.**

Murdoch, Rupert (1931–) See **Deng, Wendi.**

Musset, Alfred de (1810–1857) See **Colet, Louise; Sand, George.**

Mussolini, Benito (1883–1945) See **Sarfatti, Margherita.**

Napoleon III (1808–1873) See Bellanger, Marguerite; Howard, Harriet; Oldini, Virginia; Pearl, Cora.

Nelson, Admiral Horatio (1758–1805) See Hamilton, Lady Emma.

Nero Claudius Caesar Drusus (37–A.D. 68) See Poppaea, Sabina.

Nicholas II, Tsar of Russia (1868–1918) See Otero, Caroline.

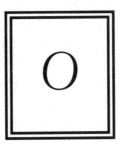

O

Octavian (63 B.C.–A.D. 14) See **Drusilla, Livia.**

Okoi (1870–1948) Okoi was born in 1870 to a mother who had broken with Japanese tradition and married for love, a transgression which resulted in deadly poverty and family ruin. Okoi's parents gave her up for adoption to a teahouse owner when she was four, and she later became the foster daughter to a geisha who determined to train the little girl in the art of geisha.

When Okoi turned thirteen, she joined the famous Omuja geisha house where she became very popular with the rich patrons, and Heizo Yajima took her as his mistress. Although he lavished money on her, she became involved with a rich actor of the period, Ichimura Uzaemon, whom she married. Once she left the life of geisha, Okoi found that she was only considered a drudge by her husband and her domineering mother-in-law. Okoi's husband then began a string of extramarital affairs which devastated her, and she divorced him. With borrowed money, she set up a small teahouse and began to attract wealthy and powerful patrons. One of these was the noble Prime Minister of Japan, Taro Katsura.

A major figure in Japanese-Russian peace negotiations in 1903, Katsura hosted a geisha party led by Okoi for his powerful political friends. When the Russo-Japanese War broke out in 1904, Prime Minister Katsura was deeply involved in war plans, politics, economic worries, and international affairs. Okoi became his peaceful center, and the two became devoted lovers. After Japan signed a peace treaty with Russia, Katsura and his cabinet fell into disfavor and were smeared as being the pawns of "white barbarians." Okoi was also labeled a traitor.

Angry mobs marched and rioted, and Okoi went into hiding. Katsura resigned his position and publicly announced that he was finished with Okoi, although the two carried on their affair in secret. By 1908, Katsura was again Premier of Japan, but he lost the title in 1911, then regained it in 1912, and kept it until his death in 1913 at the age of sixty-seven. During this period, he annexed Korea and helped Japan to create its world-class military. Katsura's death devastated the thirty-four-year-old Okoi, but she was strictly forbidden by the state to attend his grand funeral.

Throwing herself into the changes of the nation, Okoi ran the famous National Bar for five years on the Ginza main drag until the great earthquake of 1923 destroyed the city and the National Bar. After rebuilding the bar, she became tired of this way of life. She retired briefly, but was lured out of retirement to manage a teahouse in the Akasaka section of town. The teahouse was the scene of crooked political dealings and a scandal ensued which forced her into retirement. In 1938 she shaved off her hair and entered the Meguro Temple to become a Buddhist nun. In 1948 at the age of seventy, she died with few mourners to mark her death. Her few friends set up a modest statue of Kannon, the goddess of Mercy, on the temple grounds where it is identified as the Okoi Kannon for visitors who ask.

Oldini, Virginia, Countess di Castiglione (1837–1899) Virginia Oldini was born in Florence, Italy, of wealthy and powerful noble parents who neglected her. Her grandfather Lamporecchi was a famous scholar of the period, and he raised her in his palace, giving the extremely beautiful young woman the added benefits of intellectual training.

Paintings and written descriptions of the period show that Virginia, familiarly called "Nicchia," had lush brown hair, almond-shaped blue eyes, sensuous full lips, and a voluptuous and inviting body. Whenever the occasion permitted, she wore the sheerest, most deeply cut dresses, designed to carelessly allow others to catch glimpses of her ample breasts or, as in one instance at a costume party where Napoleon was present, her barely concealed pubic area.

Nicchia had her first affair at sixteen, when she clandestinely became the mistress of a young naval officer the Marquis Ambrogio Doria, while also playing the seductress with his two younger brothers. In her diary, Nicchia recorded her activities, using a code to remind her of how far she had gone with her various lovers so as not to become confused as she met with each. When her parents learned of her involvements, they hurriedly married her off to an Italian nobleman. Nicchia took an immediate dislike to the Comte Francesco Verasis di Castiglione, whom she viewed as a weakling and an imbecile; however the marriage did have benefits for her. Despite her personal view of the man, the count was important in the Italian government, for he was an aide to King Victor Emmanuel II. Two years later, after giving birth to a son and after spending her husband's fortune, Nicchia left him and her child.

Nicchia's cousin was Camillo Benso di Cavour, a major figure in Italy's unification movement. Cavour recruited Nicchia as a secret agent to seduce Louis Napoleon and convince him to support their cause. To convince King Victor Emmanuel II of her suitability for this job, Nicchia spent a night with him, after which he enthusiastically endorsed her talents.

In 1855 as the Countess di Castiglione, eighteen-year-old Nicchia took Paris by storm. After arranging an invitation to a gala at which Louis Napoleon was to be present, Nicchia made a dramatic entrance, wearing an elaborate and revealing ball gown which emphasized her endowments. She literally stopped all activity in the room as she entered the doorway, and waves of people stepped aside to allow her to pass. Men stood on tables in order to get a better look at her, and conductor Johann Strauss was so dumbstruck by her beauty that he halted the orchestra in the middle of a waltz. Louis Napoleon, as well, ended his conversation and walked immediately over to Nicchia to ask her to dance

Nicchia allowed Louis Napoleon some time to woo her. While he gave her a beautiful home in Paris and expensive jewels, Nicchia kept her distance, flirting just enough to keep him interested. She was determined to choose carefully the time to submit. That time came when Louis Napoleon invited her to visit the empress and him at their château outside of Paris. Nicchia feigned illness during the evening entertainment and went early to her room. A short time later, Louis Napoleon professed concern for his guest and went to her room to check on her. He found her waiting for him, wearing a finely made and delicate gray batiste gown trimmed with lace. She became his mistress that night.

Nicchia remained the official mistress of Louis Napoleon for the next four years, presenting him with a son during that period, who later grew up to be a successful Paris dentist. Eventually the emperor became annoyed with Nicchia's self-centered behavior and the publicity which she gave their relationship. He also complained that she frequently received visitors in her bedroom while wearing the monogrammed underthings which he had bought for her. They might have stayed together longer, but an assassination attempt against Louis Napoleon by an Italian was the final straw that convinced him to send his Italian mistress away. A bodyguard saved the emperor, and Nicchia was sent back to Italy.

Despite her ignoble return, Nicchia had completed her mission. Napoleon's arrny did go to war against the Austrians, and Italy became one nation under one king. King Victor Emmanuel II personally thanked her by making her his mistress. He gave her an apartment in the Pitti Palace in Florence and established for her a pension of twelve thousand francs per year. She lived happily as his mistress for two years, with never a wish to see either her husband Conte di Castiglione nor her son Giorgio. Two years after having been turned away, Nicchia returned to France at Louis Napoleon's invitation to become his occasional lover.

Dissatisfied with this arrangement, Nicchia became the mistress of Prince Henri de la Tour d'Auvergne, the French foreign minister, with whom she remained for four years. After leaving him, Nicchia spent the next fourteen years in a series of brief relationships, most notably as the mistress of the patriarch of the world's wealthiest family, the Baron James de Rothschild, who was seventy at the time. Nicchia profited well from this connection, but the baron was less demanding of her sexual favors than Nicchia wished so she also discreetly became mistress to his three sons.

As she grew older and daily found facing the mirror more difficult, Nicchia was haunted by her husband's warning that her beauty – and her admirers – would disappear as she grew older. Turning forty was traumatic, and Nicchia saw it as putting an end to her attractiveness. Despondent, she secluded herself in her rooms in the Place Vendôme, shuttering her windows and turning all mirrors to the wall. Her only human contact was with her servants who were instructed to turn away all friends and relatives who might visit. As she sank further into the surreal world which she had created, Nicchia became deeply involved in spiritualism, completely avoided daylight, and sat alone in her rooms remembering her past.

Soon she refused to permit even the servants into her rooms, allowing the garbage and dirt to pile up around her. Despite her still-great wealth, Nicchia lived as though she were impoverished. Finally, after hearing nothing from their mistress for several days, worried servants broke down the down to her room to find a horrifying sight. Nicchia had apparently died of a cerebral hemorrhage days earlier, and her body lay on the floor gnawed on by rats. She had lived out her husband's prophecy that admirers would desert her once her beauty had faded.

Onassis, Aristotle (1906–1975) See **Callas, Maria; Dedichen, Ingeborg.**

Otero, Caroline (1868–1965) Caroline Otero was born in the small town of Valga, Spain, where she was the daughter of the town prostitute. At eleven she was brutally raped by a man who had become excited by her innocent dancing.

At thirteen she left her home town behind and went to Barcelona and survived for a year as a prostitute before meeting a male dancer,

Paco Colli, who trained her for the stage by teaching her to dance, sing, and act, all while acting as her pimp. Paco asked her to marry him but she refused. Instead, Caroline put her stage training to good use and became a music hall entertainer. By 1890, she starred at the *Folies Bergères*. Her unique brand of dancing, which brought every part of her body into play, had captured public attention and Caroline's name was soon in the newspaper headlines.

With fame came access to rich and powerful men who would gladly pay ten thousand dollars to spend the night with the silky-haired, statuesque beauty whose firm breasts and long slender legs excited their libido. For those who wanted to make a greater claim on her time, Caroline willingly became their mistress in return for luxury accommodations and generous support. During her long life, she was the mistress of an impressive list of men.

The wealthy American William Vanderbilt, Cornelius' son, gave her two-hundred-fifty thousand dollars in jewels (in pre-1900 prices!) to keep her with him for a short while. He also offered her a yacht and other material temptations. The French Baron Lepic and she ascended in a hot-air balloon over Provence, France, and reportedly spent an hour making love while floating two hundred feet above the earth. In her old age, Caroline recalled this incident as her most exciting amorous adventure which made all further sexual activity with the baron pale in comparison.

She was the mistress of Prince Albert of Monaco for several years in the early 1890s, and he established her in a luxurious apartment and paid all of her bills. Caroline claimed that the prince was relatively impotent when they met but that she helped him to overcome that problem. For the next few years, he proudly escorted her and showered her with nearly one million dollars in jewels.

Soon after Prince Albert departed, Caroline became the mistress of Prince Nicholas of Montenegro, who moved in with her and paid all of her expenses. They were together for several years, during which the prince supplied the usual jewels, but he shared her with King Leopold II of Belgium, then sixty, who met with Caroline infrequently. Leopold gave Caroline a small villa in an exclusive resort in Flanders before she replaced him.

Caroline Otero blatantly exploited the wealthy and powerful men who sought her favors, and she never tried to hide her intentions behind the mask of feigned love. She spoke candidly of her distaste for two of her rich lovers whose mistress sbe, nonetheless, remained. During her five years as the mistress of the Shah of Persia, Muzaffar-ed-Din, Caroline found him to have poor personal hygiene as well as strange sexual tastes. He appeared punctually at two each afternoon and stayed with Caroline for three hours, then left. After each visit, he sent a servant to her with a gold box, lined in velvet, in which there was placed a valuable stone. Caroline would remove the gem then send the servant back with the box which would be filled again the next day.

The tzar of Russia, Nicholas II, also rated low on Caroline's hygiene scale for he rarely bathed and his face was badly marked. Not only did he smell bad, an assassination attempt some years earlier led him always to travel with numerous armed guards. Despite the heavy armed coverage, Nicholas remained a nervous lover who jumped at every sound.

There were others in Caroline's life, but the final member of royalty to make her his mistress was King Alfonso XIII of Spain. He was a nineteen-year-old virgin when Caroline and he first made love in 1905. In 1913, he made the forty-four-year-old woman his mistress, and gave her an apartment in Madrid.

In the years which followed, Caroline found that the men who wished to make her their mistress were less well-connected and less wealthy than those which she had attracted when she was younger. She retired in 1914 with a fortune in jewels and securities, but she eventually gambled all of this away.

"La Belle Otero" died alone in Nice, France, of a heart attack at the age of ninety-six.

Otto, King of Greece (1815– 1867) See **Digby, Lady Jane.**

Ozy, Alice (1820–1893) Julie-Justine Pilloy was the daughter of a jeweler whose parents found her to be so much of an encumbrance to their extramarital affairs that they placed her with a foster mother. Ten-year-old Julie-Justine was forced to join the foster mother's daughter in the attic, spending long days doing embroidery.

At the age of thirteen Julie-Justine's beauty convinced her foster

Madame Pillory (BIBLIOTHÈQUE NATIONALE)

mother to put her into a shop to draw customers. The innocent girl was soon seduced by the shop owner and she quickly found that offers of marriage were withdrawn when her seduction was known. At that early age Julie-Justine decided that her shame would prevent her from ever marrying, so she decided to make her experience profitable.

After a liaison with an actor who introduced her to the theater, Julie-Justine changed her name to the more melodious Alice Ozy. Although already in her early twenties, Alice projected a youthful innocence which attracted the nineteen-year-old Duc d'Aumale who had just returned from commanding a regiment in North Africa. At these times, Alice often dressed in men's clothes when the two roamed the streets arm in arm, and people frequently mistook her for the duc's brother. The young duc proclaimed his love publicly, to the extent of marching his regiment past her house and ordering the band to play "Kradoujah, ma maitress," a popular song brought from Algeria.

As the duc was not yet of age, he was not in control of his fortune. Therefore, when opportunity presented itself in the form of an expensively appointed carriage sent for her by the Comte de Perregaux, Alice left behind the young duc. The comte soon left Alice, though, for Marie Duplessis.

By 1847, Alice has sufficiently established herself financially to be able to decide freely who would join her in the sumptuously carved rosewood bed which was seductively draped in lace and covered with carved medallions of cupids. She entertained both the author Victor Hugo and his son Charles. However, she chose the son over the father, a rejection which the elder Hugo bitterly remarked upon in his recollections, although he remained a friend. Charles Hugo enjoyed Alice as his mistress for one summer, every day during which he wrote her a poem and copied it into a book bound in black morocco and secured with a lock.

There were other men – poets, sculptors, noblemen, and artists – as well as a German prince to keep her in style. As she aged, Alice found herself increasingly alone and she grew to be a dowdy, fussy, and stout old woman. Although most friends either died or forgot her, the Duc d'Aumale, whom she had left forty years before, remained an affectionate friend. She died at the age of seventy-two, leaving her fortune to provide for the children of needy actors.

Pang, May (1950–) May Pang had served for nearly three years as personal assistant to former Beatle John Lennon and his wife Yoko Ono, when the latter ordered her to become John Lennon's mistress.

Shock, disgust, and anger made twenty-year-old May try to diplomatically refuse the offer, but Yoko was insistent in her desire to handpick her husband's mistress in order to maintain control over his actions. May was told that her deliberate move into Lennon's life would save him from finding women who would be cruel to him – and allegedly she threatened that May's days working in the music business were numbered unless she agreed.

Within weeks, the affair had begun after Lennon made the first move, seemingly with his wife's approval. May Pang and John Lennon spent eighteen months together, moving from New York to Los Angeles, mixing with some of the top stars of rock and roll, and running from Yoko who called them several times a day with seemingly insignificant concerns. As time passed, the pair became exceedingly close as Lennon shared his deepest fears and secrets with May. He became interested in her Chinese heritage and soon began to use her Chinese name, Fung Yee which means phoenix bird. She became his sounding board as he returned to the recording studio to work on new songs, including those which eventually became *Walls and Bridges*.

In 1974 Yoko decided that she wanted Lennon back and she used all of her resources to achieve that aim. Within a few months, she was pregnant with their son Sean, and May was left alone. Still, whenever Lennon called, as he did periodically over the following six years, May answered and met him whenever and wherever he wanted to share a few hours of passion. When they were together, he spoke of having to sneak away from "Mother" or "Madam," his terms for Yoko.

May found herself blacklisted by the recording companies who admired her credentials and credits in record production but were too afraid of antagonizing John Lennon and Yoko Ono by hiring her. For several years she subsisted by taking a series of freelance jobs, until she finally gave up the record business and took a job as program director in radio.

Parker Bowles, Camilla (1947–) Born Camilla Shand, she was 25 years old when she met Prince Charles of England at a party in London in 1972 and informed him that they had a shared history. To the surprised Prince, she announced, "My great-grandmother was the mistress of your great-great-grandfather. I feel we have something in common." Alice Keppel was the longtime mistress of King Edward VII, and, like Parker Bowles, her husband tolerated and even encouraged the relationship. The lively post-debutante and the Prince were instantly attracted to each other, and the two shared six months before the royal naval officer had to return to sea duty in February 1973, leaving without making a commitment. Not one to wait, the lively blonde began to date army captain Andrew Parker Bowles, once a suitor of the Prince's sister Anne, and the two were married in July 1973. When Charles returned to London, he resumed his friendship with the newly married Parker Bowles and became friends with her husband, drawing both more fully into the royal circle.

In 1981, Prince Charles proposed marriage to Lady Diana Spencer in the garden of the country house owned by the Parker Bowleses. Throughout her marriage and the birth of two children, son Tom in 1975 and daughter Laura in 1979, the Prince and Camilla Parker Bowles maintained a close relationship, often speaking for an hour or more daily. Friends of the Prince have long considered Parker Bowles to be an ideal companion for him, because she shares his enjoyment in riding, fishing, and taking long walks in the country. While Princess Diana was alive, Parker Bowles and her husband led separate lives but maintained a marriage that many viewed as "extremely successful." Although wife and mistress often appeared at the same activities, such as Charles' polo matches, meetings between the Prince and his mistress remained discreet. The affair became public knowledge in 1992 when the London *Daily Mirror* published a few lines from an alleged telephone call between the two. The Australian-based magazine *New Idea* published a complete transcript of a conversation in which the male voice spoke of fondling Parker Bowles' body and stated, "I fill up your tank." The magazine, after consulting speech therapists, alleged that the voice was that of Prince Charles.

In 1995, Camilla divorced Andrew Parker Bowles and, after the Wales's divorce was finalized in August 1996, she began to make more frequent appearances as hostess alongside Charles at various social events. In June 1998, less than a year after the death of Princess Diana in a car crash in France, Charles arranged for Prince William to meet his mistress of 26 years, and the woman who had haunted the Wales marriage. Confirmation of the meeting by a spokesperson of the royal family led the press to believe that the Queen and other royals were beginning to grant some measure of approval to the relationship.

The couple made their first public appearance on 28 January 1999, when they allowed reporters to take their pictures as they left the London Ritz Hotel after attending a birthday party in honor of Camilla's sister. The couple achieved further acceptance when Queen Elizabeth was reported to have exchanged pleasantries at a weekend barbecue at Highgrove on 3 June 2000. Since then, they have been seen together in public numerous times.

Parkinson, Cecil (1932–) See **Keays, Sara.**

Pearl, Cora (1835–1886) Born in England in 1835, Eliza Emma Crouch was sent to a convent school in Boulogne when she was twelve, after her father left the family and emigrated to America. In the eight years of school, Emma learned only imperfect French but she did grow to love France. When her mother recalled her to England in 1854, nineteen-year-old Emma went to live in London with her grandmother where she she spent all of her nights reading travel books to her. She visited her mother on Sundays and she attended daily masses, escorted by a maid who waited outside the church for her.

One Sunday the maid was not waiting for her and Emma began to return alone to her grandmother's home. A man followed her and took her to a bar where the twenty-year-old girl accepted a drink. She lost consciousness and awoke in bed with him. This led to her lifelong distaste for men and sex.

Possessed of an excellent figure and shiny, thick, red hair, Emma decided that she couldn't return to her grandmother and she quickly found someone to support her, the proprietor of a notorious drinking den. The two later traveled to Paris where they took in all of the sights. While in Paris Emma changed her name to the more lyrical Cora Pearl and announced that she would stay in France.

The exuberant Cora was determined to achieve financial success and she began by entertaining less distinguished lovers as she worked her way to the top. In 1863 when another courtesan seemed intent upon interfering with Cora's conquest of an Armenian prince, the two women fought a whip dual from which both emerged with cut faces. While the two retired for several weeks to allow their faces to heal, the prince disappeared. Within only a few years, Cora had acquired a heavy gold chain upon which she wore tangible reminders of her wealthy and prominent loves, twelve lockets each emblazoned with the arms of the oldest and most prominent families of France.

By 1865 Cora had amassed a fortune due to the generosity of her male friends, and she also became the mistress of Prince Napoleon who gave her a key to the Palais-Royal. From 1865 through 1870, the last five years of the Second Empire, Cora was given two large and lavishly furnished homes and millions of francs worth of clothing and jewels. She carried on simultaneous affairs with Prince

Napoleon and with other equally generous nobles whom Cora played against each other.

Extravagant and wild, she spent countless francs on out-of-season flowers (which she would wantonly scatter underfoot) and hothouse fruits to please her guests. She introduced modern makeup to France, and her dyed yellow hair was the subject of popular gossip. She once had her dog dyed blue to match a dress.

Cora hosted well-attended masked balls and frequent banquets for which even the seemingly acceptable elements of society vied for invitations. Before one such dinner, Cora made a cash wager with her guests that she would serve them meat that they would not dare to cut, and they placed their bets against her wager. Nearly an hour after the bet was made, four footmen entered the dining hall bearing a huge silver platter with a cover. The platter was set down, and the cover was removed to reveal the naked Cora Pearl reclining with only strategically placed sprigs of parsley to cover her body.

She was finally banished from France after Alexandre Duval, a suitor ten years her junior, shot himself in despair. He had reached the end of his resources having given his money, jewels, and horses to Cora only to find himself dismissed by her. She had run through his entire fortune of ten million francs, then disdainfully sent him away. Although Duval recovered, the banishment remained.

Cora was ruined financially, although she tried to retain her spirit. She sold her *Memoires* in 1884, but made little money from it. She died of intestinal cancer in 1886, four months after her book appeared. In the end she had been homeless, alone, and forced to sell her body for any amount she could receive.

Peron, Juan (1895–1974) See **Duarte, Eva.**

Pericles (495 B.C. – 429 B.C.) See **Aspasia.**

Petacci, Clara (1912–1945) Born Claretta Petacci and raised as the cherished daughter of a successful Italian doctor, twenty-year-old Clara ran after Benito Mussolini's Alfa Romeo shouting "Duce! Duce!" (Mussolini's nickname, meaning "leader"). The leader of the Black Shirts was so impressed by her adulation and her physical attractiveness that he ordered his driver to stop while he stepped out to speak to her. They became lovers soon after.

The young woman met all of Mussolini's requirements for a mistress. She had green eyes, long legs, a husky voice, and the large, heavy breasts which he admired in women. Relatively unintelligent, she was, nonetheless, a generous and sensuous woman who became completely devoted to her man who, in turn, required that she be always ready to provide him with sex whenever his schedule permitted. Thus, she remained in her quarters, often reclining for hours upon the divan, playing romantic records or reading romantic novels, primping and waiting for the dictator's appearance which might occur at any moment or not at all on a given day. His visits to Clara were so frequent during the later years of their relationship that his ministers blamed his ill health and general debilitation on those visits which he seemed compelled to make.

The public knew Mussolini as a dutiful husband to his wife Rachele and a proud and attentive father to his five children, but he always claimed the Italian male's right to have mistresses. Clara had not been the aging dictator's first mistress, but she was his last. Still, by 1943 he had tired of her and tried to lock her out of the Palazzo Venezi, where he had installed her. She pushed her way past the guards and, with tears and pleading, convinced Mussolini to change his mind. As World War II went against him, Mussolini became increasingly abusive toward his devoted mistress, insulting her publicly and beating her when he chose. He also tried to push her further into the background to decrease the scandal of their relationship which added to his damaged credibility with the Italian people. They could tolerate numerous mistresses, but his focus on one woman and the favors which he had granted her family were unacceptable.

In 1945, as Mussolini's war effort crumbled, Clara's family begged her to accompany them on a flight to Spain. She refused. Her bullet-riddled body was hanged upside down next to that of her lover from the girders of the uncompleted roof of a filling station in Milan. People poked, shot at, and spat on her lifeless form.

Phillips, Carrie (1875–1960) Physically beautiful with a tall, slim figure, full breasts, and reddish-gold hair, Carrie Phillips married

James Phillips, the owner of the town department store, because she was tired of teaching school and of being poor.

Warren G. Harding was married to a bossy, tenacious woman six years his senior whom everyone referred to as "the Duchess," and the two families moved in the same social circles. The affair began when both spouses were hospitalized, and it continued through 1909 when the Phillipses and the Hardings toured Europe together. James and the Duchess seemed oblivious to what was going on. Carrie later became upset by the clandestine affair, and she offered Harding an ultimatum to either leave the Duchess or she would take her daughter and go to live in Germany. She made good on her threat and went to Germany for five years. The affair resumed when she returned to Marion, Ohio, in 1914 due to the threat of World War I.

Harding was elected U.S. Senator from Ohio in November 1914 and he told Carrie that he would vote to go to war over Germany. She had become a German sympathizer, and she threatened to expose him and their passionate love letters if he did. Undaunted, Harding voted for war and Carrie forgot her threat. The affair continued, but the Duchess learned of the affair and became threatening. She threw items at Carrie whenever she might walk near the Harding home, and while sitting on the dais with Harding during speeches she was frequently seen to stand up and shake her fist at someone (probably Carrie) in the audience.

When Harding became the official Republican presidential nominee in 1920, the National Committee sent advertising mogul Albert Lasker to speak with Carrie. He offered her twenty thousand dollars plus a monthly sum as long as Harding held office, so long as she kept silent and left the continental United States. She and her husband also accepted an all expenses-paid world trip with a long stopover in Japan.

Carrie returned to the U.S. when Harding died under mysterious circumstances in 1923. Her husband eventually lost most of his money during the Depression, and Carrie threw him out. He died of tuberculosis in 1939, a pauper.

Carrie lived until 1960 and she spent her later years in a home for the elderly where she had been committed because she was penniless and mentally vague.

Picasso, Pablo (1881–1973) See **Gilot, Françoise.**

Pingeot, Anne (1941 –) Longtime mistress of the late French Socialist president Francois Mitterand, Pingeot was born in a prominent family in Auvergne, France. She was an art historian who specialized in nineteenth century works, and she served for years as a curator at the Musée D'Orsay in Paris. Pingeot met Mitterand in 1973, while both were vacationing at Hossegor, a seaside resort in southwest France. Their daughter Mazarine, who is named after the library at the French Academy, was born the following year. Although Pingeot was Mitterand's mistress for over twenty years, she remained out of the spotlight, although not unknown to political insiders and discreet members of the French press. Danielle Mitterand, the French president's wife, and their two sons, Jean-Christophe and Gilbert, seem to have also known of the relationship but carefully orchestrated exits and entrances prevented meetings that might have embarrassed either of the president's families. Pingeot and Mazarine did occasionally stay for weekends at the presidential residence and at a government-owned château outside Paris, as guests of Mitterand – a revelation that raised objections in 1994 from political commentators, who complained that taxpayers should not be helping to maintain his second family. Although Pingeot gave her last name to the daughter she had with Mitterand, he finally did acknowledge Mazarine's paternity. In the final year of his life, while fatally ill with prostate cancer, Mitterand amended his will to give Mazarine the same share of his estate as his two sons received.

Poisson, Jeanne Antoinette, Marquise de Pompadour (1721–1764) Jeanne Poisson, whose last name means "fish" in French, was born in Paris to middle class parents. She married at twenty to a banker and became Madame d'Etoiles, but her ambitions were with the throne. Tall, slim, and elegant, she gathered leading middle class intellectuals, including Voltaire, to her home. Once she became the mistress of King Louis XV of France, her influence extended to all affairs of state.

Jeanne deliberately set out to meet Louis, and drove through the forest of Senart near the Etoiles estate in a brightly painted blue coach each time that she knew he was hunting there. After he finally noticed her, the twenty-five-year-old beauty was introduced formally to the thirty-five-year-old king. Although she was amusing, intelligent, sensible, and dressed in an elegant manner, the court was shocked that Louis would make a low-born woman his mistress. As official mistress, she would rule over all the titled women at court. Pamphlets of protest flooded Paris and the provinces. Louis solved the problem by elevating her to the ranks of the aristocracy by making her the Marquise de Pompadour, taken from the manor of Pompadour which the king purchased for her.

In addition to mistress, she also acted as executive secretary to Louis and became a power center. She determined who received appointments, made and unmade ministers, and advised Louis on affairs of state. She influenced the king to support a diplomatic arrangement in the Seven Years' War in which France fought on the side of its hereditary enemy Austria.

In 1752 she was made a duchess, a titled lady with new privileges to have a coat of arms, ducal coronet on her carriage, and to precede all non-titled individuals. In 1754, upon the death of her daughter Alexandra, she turned to the church and stopped sleeping with the king. She remained his best friend, however, and later worked as his procurer. He trusted her absolutely.

After twenty years of power, the Marquise de Pompadour died in 1764 of lung disease, after a year of suffering from shortness of breath, loss of appetite, and exhaustion.

Poitiers, Diane de (1499–1566) The future King Henry II of France met Diane de Poitiers when she was thirty-one and he only a boy of eleven. What started as an adolescent crush at that age escalated into full-scale obsession for Henry, who courted Diane as he grew older, finally winning her when she was thirty-nine and he was nineteen. Catherine d'Medici, the substantially younger Florentine noblewoman whom he married in 1533, was mystified that her husband could be passionate and devoted to a mistress who was so much older, and she schemed to discover Diane's methods of lovemaking which had mesmerized the king. Catherine ordered royal workmen to pierce small holes into the ceiling of Diane's room, and through these Catherine would spy, trying to discover Diane's tricks in the bedroom. After hours of watching her husband and his mistress making love, Catherine remained mystified and she never did discover the nature of Diane's attraction. A likely possibility is that Henry II desired both the passionate sensuality of his older mistress, and the stable nurturing which she had developed with age. Whatever the reason for his attraction, Diane de Poitiers remained the major love interest for Henry II until his death in 1559. At that point, his wife had her revenge and she demanded that Diane return the crown jewels which Henry had generously given his mistress. Diane was left to fend for herself during the seven years she lived after the death of her lover.

Poppaea Sabina (A.D. 35–A.D. 65) Poppaea Sabina was the daughter of Titus Ollius, who was killed in the earlier purge by Tiberius. She took her name from her grandfather on her mother's side of the family, Poppaeus Sabinus, who had been a government consul. She was beautiful, charming, intelligent, and ruthless. Once that she decided that she would marry the Emperor of Rome, nothing stood in her way.

In A.D. 58, Poppaea was married to a Roman knight, Rufrius Crisinus, with whom she had a son. She soon became the mistress of a young man named Otho, who was close to Nero, the future emperor. Poppaea discarded both her husband and her child to become Otho's wife. Nero soon noticed her and, while she encouraged his advances, she made it clear that because she was a married woman, he would have to treat her with greater respect than he treated his slave girls. Playing hard to get, Poppaea drove Nero mad with passion, and he assigned her husband Otho to the governorship of Lusitania. With Otho out of the way, Poppaea became Nero's acknowledged mistress, despite the disapproval of both Nero's wife Octavia and his mother Agrippina.

Poppaea tormented the twenty-one-year-old ruler, telling him that Octavia was a wife only in name and that his mother Agrippina made him dance like a puppet. She threatened to return to Otho unless Nero divorced Octavia and took greater control as emperor. Agrippina warned him that Poppaea was dangerous and urged him to remain in his arranged marriage with Octavia. Nero was too much in love with Poppaea to listen to reason. At his mistress's urging, Nero had his mother killed in A.D. 59.

In A.D. 62 after living with Nero for four years, Poppaea became pregnant. Anxious for an heir, Nero banished Octavia from the palace and aides spread lies that she had been unfaithful to him. Later that year, she was executed. Poppaea became his wife and in A.D. 63 she gave birth to a baby girl whom they named Augusta. The baby died four months later.

Poppaea became pregnant again in A.D. 65. Nero was losing his hold, and revolts in Britain and Judea were shaking the stability of Rome. Nero became the enemy of Roman aristocracy and its wealthy. In a fit of anger, after returning from the quinquennial games, he kicked the pregnant Poppaea to death. He later expressed great grief for his action and she was pronounced a goddess by the state.

Presley, Elvis Aron (1935–1977) See **de Barbin, Lucy.**

Ptolemy, King of Egypt (367 B.C.–283 B.C.) See **Lamia.**

R

Raubel, Geli (1908-1931) A vivacious and half-Viennese brunette, Angela Maria (Geli) Raubel was the daughter of Adolf Hitler's widowed half-sister Angela, and he took the pair into his home when he found that they were living in deep poverty.

Although Hitler's sister, Geli's mother, also lived in his household, Geli's room was situated next to his and it was to her that he showed the rare signs of physical affection. Despite Hitler's insistence that he kept Geli and her mother in his home only because he needed Angela's housekeeping services, party members grumbled about the relationship which hinted of being an affair. Therefore, Hitler professed that Geli had come to Munich to study music and needed to stay with him because she had no money for other lodgings. To continue the subterfuge, he hired a party member to provide singing lessons, but Geli viewed the lessons as a joke and neither practiced nor showed any talent. Hitler found another instructor who subtly made it clear that Geli had no talent despite Hitler's insistence that the lessons continue.

Rumors abounded in Munich in 1931 about Hitler's incestuous affair with his niece, and they were confirmed when sketches Hitler had made of Geli were found in which she appeared in numerous pornographic poses. Geli seems to have enjoyed the relationship. Hitler gave her freedom to come and go as she pleased, and she received substantial money to buy clothes and jewelry.

Geli also engaged in her own secret affairs with men as varied as violin players and ski instructors. When Hitler went away to political rallies, Geli would go out with other men, and she also carried on an intermittent affair with the officer who guarded Hitler's apartment as her bribe to him to say nothing of her forays.

People close to the household reported that Geli was willing to do anything to remain Hitler's favorite girlfriend, including performing acts she termed sickening. It was rumored he had her urinate on him, whip him, and strenuously kick him as he lay crouched on the floor.

In 1931 Eva Braun appeared to be gaining a hold on Hitler's affections. Geli quarreled with Hitler, demanding that he take her with him when he traveled, as her way of keeping Eva at a distance. He refused. Despondent over her waning hold on the increasingly popular leader, at the age of twenty-three she shot herself through the heart with Hitler's Walther .635. After her death, Hitler ordered that her room be kept just as it had been when she was alive, and the housekeeper was ordered to place fresh flowers there daily.

Ray, Elizabeth (1944–) Elizabeth Ray, a former stewardess and aspiring actress, was hired as a staff aide for the House Administration Committee by its chairman Representative Wayne L. Hays at a salary of fourteen thousand dollars a year. The problem was that she couldn't type, didn't take dictation, never learned shorthand, and rarely went to the office. She reported her duties ran to dinner twice a week with Hays, after which they would return to her Arlington, Virginia, apartment to make love. She also admitted to private parties on yachts and at summer homes where, at Hays' directive, she had seduced other government officials whose influence would help him.

Thirty-two-year-old Elizabeth first exposed her role as the Congressman's secret mistress in an exclusive interview to the

Elizabeth Ray (BETTMANN ARCHIVE)

Washington Post only weeks after Hays' marriage to the longtime director of his Ohio office, Pat Peak. She gave out interviews in which she painted a picture of small-town virtue gone wrong in the big, immoral city of Washington, D.C., and tried to draw sympathy by pointing out that she had no choice but to submit so that she could survive financially. When Hays at first denied that she was his mistress, she gave repeated interviews. He finally bid his career an emotional goodbye after colleagues moved to strip him of his role as chairman of four House committees. In desperation, Hays took an overdose of sleeping pills in June 1976, and fell into a coma but survived to resign in September 1976.

Elizabeth wrote a book, *Washington Fringe Benefit* and posed for *Playboy*. She put together a stage act which played briefly to crowds, who came out of curiosity about the Congressman's mistress, but her singing brought few repeat customers. Elizabeth Ray faded into obscurity a few years after the scandal died down.

Reynolds, Maria (1768–?) In 1791 Maria Reynolds asked the first U.S. Secretary of the Treasury, Alexander Hamilton, for help in returning to her family in New York City. Claiming cruel treatment and abandonment by her husband, the twenty-three-year-old woman visited Hamilton at his Philadelphia home with her request. Hamilton obtained money and brought it to her lodgings.

With his wife and children away in Albany, Hamilton was free to carry on an affair all of the summer and into the autumn. When his family returned and Maria hinted that her husband wanted a reconciliation, Hamilton eagerly encouraged her to agree to it. Their relationship, however, continued because Maria protested that she could never give Hamilton up and she countered his plans to break off with her by increasing her attentions to him during visits and bombarding him with letters.

Maria's husband showed up in Hamilton's office to demand retribution for loss of his wife's affections. He claimed that Maria loved only Hamilton and threatened to take his daughter and to disappear. Hamilton gave Reynolds thousands of dollars over a two-year period to keep him quiet. The blackmail would have continued had Reynolds and his partner Jacob Clingman not been involved in illegal speculation and attempts to defraud the government of money, which landed them in jail. When Hamilton refused to intercede, Reynolds told all, even implicating Hamilton in his crimes.

Maria was called to testify before a congressional committee, and she wept piteously as she denied that she had ever been Hamilton's mistress. Rather, she claimed that both her husband and Hamilton were deliberately blackening her reputation by inventing the affair to cover up their illegal speculation activities. Five years later, after the air had cleared, an acquaintance informed Hamilton that Maria, now married to Clingman, had asked him for a reference to clear her name. When he refused, she condemned him and said that her only fault in life had been to marry Clingman one half hour before her divorce from Reynolds was finalized.

Rice, Donna (1958–) In the thick of campaigning for the 1988 party nominations for the American presidency, the *Miami Herald* published a story that the contender for the Democratic nomination, Gary Hart, had entertained Donna Rice, a twenty-nine-year-old actress and model overnight at his Washington, D.C., townhouse. At first, criticism was heaped on the newspaper for having staked out the townhouse in the effort to prove previous suspicions, and much was made of the fact that for a part of the evening there was no surveillance.

Soon, however, another story emerged which supported the first. Hart and Donna had sailed in the previous March to the island of Bimini with another couple, also consisting of a married man and a single woman. The reported purpose of the trip was to inspect a damaged boat which was being repaired in the Bahamas. Hart counter-ed critics by asserting that, despite having made the trip together and staying overnight in Bimini, he and Donna had stayed on separate boats. The four people involved swore that nothing improper had occurred.

Soon after the incident, Donna went into temporary seclusion and Hart resigned from the presidential race in May, 1987. In December, he re-entered the race and told the media that he would let the people decide. He found that his popularity had plunged.

Donna Rice found her notoriety provided a needed career boost when she was hired as spokesmodel for "No Excuses" jeans, a company whose logo seemed custom-designed to capitalize on the affair. After the presidential race was run, the candidate's mistress no longer had commercial appeal and her name faded from the public's mind and eye.

Roberts, Kiki (1909–) Born Marion Strasmick in Boston, Kiki was beautiful and shapely, with big brown eyes, red hair, and a foul mouth.

Renamed Kiki Roberts, she met Jack "Legs" Diamond (born Jack Nolan in 1895 in an Irish tenement house in Philadelphia) in 1927 at a nightclub celebration of another Broadway show opening. She was a Ziegfeld Follies showgirl, having appeared in "Whoopee," "Simple Simon," and "Scandals." Diamond, the best dressed and most flamboyant gangster of his times, spent lavish amounts on Kiki's wardrobe and apartment furniture. He also opened charge accounts for Kiki in several exclusive New York City stores. Life for the notorious lovers was like the script for *Guys and Dolls*, as they moved from one uptown eatery to another, dropping into nightclubs and mixing with the glamorous and bawdy Broadway crowd.

Diamond kept both his wife, Alice, and his mistress in the mansion in Acra, New York, until Alice threatened to tear Kiki apart. So he moved Kiki to a nearby inn. Unknown to both women, however, Diamond had yet another secret girlfriend.

Kiki's face and description landed on a wanted poster in 1931, and she was charged with being an accomplice to Diamond's illegal activities. Two weeks after Diamond was killed in December 1931, Kiki exploited her connection by opening an act at the Manhattan Academy of Music as "Kiki – the Gangster's Girl." Although her star rose for a short while, she eventually faded into obscurity.

Rodin, Augustine (1840–1917) See **Claudel, Camille.**

Roosevelt, Franklin Delano (1882–1945) See **Mercer, Lucy; Suckley, Margaret.**

Rossellini, Roberto (1906–1977) See **Bergman, Ingrid.**

Rothschild, Baron James (1792–1868) See **Oldini, Virginia.**

Rouseau, Jean-Jacques (1712–1778) See **Levasseur, Therésè;
Warens, Louise Eleonore.**

Russell, Lillian (1861–1922) Helen Louise Leonard was born in
Clinton, Iowa, the youngest of five daughters of an easygoing
newspaperman father and a high-spirited, social reformer mother.
Called Nellie by her family, she exhibited special vocal talent at an
early age, and her mother decided to take the future "toast of
Broadway" to New York City to study voice. The seventeen-year-old
Nellie refused to be trained for grand opera, despite her unusual
ability to hit eight high C notes in one performance, and chose light
comic opera instead. A year later she used her hourglass figure,
creamy complexion, and blonde-haired, blue-eyed beauty to land
her first stage role in *H.M.S. Pinafore.* Within weeks, men waited by
her stage door, showered her with flowers and expensive gifts, and
begged for her attention. Wealthy men surrounded her, taking her to
exclusive restaurants, as they basked in her smile.

Lillian married four times, against her mother's wishes the first time
when she was eighteen, to musical conductor Harry Braham, leader of
the pit orchestra of *Pinafore.* When their child died as the result of
negligence by a nursemaid, the marriage ended. After the breakup of
her marriage in 1881, Lillian was spotted by vaudeville impressario
Tony Pastor, the starmaker of his day and the "father of vaudeville."
He heard her sing at the home of a friend and offered her a contract
for seventy-five dollars per week to sing at his variety theater, the
Casino. Still called Nellie, the young woman protested that her
mother would object to her appearing in an unrefined music hall, so
Pastor suggested that she change her name. He supplied her with a
list of names, from which she chose "Lillian Russell" because she liked
all of the l's in it. Renamed, she became "the English Ballad Singer."
Mrs. Leonard learned of Lillian's new act when a newspaperman who
lived in the same Brooklyn boardinghouse told her that the new
singer at Pastor's Casino looked a lot like Nellie and that she might
want to ask her daughter where she went each evening.

Lillian waited a few years before marrying another conductor,

Edward Solomon, who did not tell her until after their daughter Dorothy was born that he was still married to his former wife. Soon after, she met a handsome, vain tenor named Giovanni Perugini, born Jack Chatterton in Michigan, who was more interested in career advancement than in Lillian. The marriage only lasted two months, ending when Lillian left after he nearly threw her out of a seventh-story window. Her fourth and last husband, Alexander P. Moore, offered respectability if not excitement, at a time when Lillian saw stability as desirable.

Her reputation as an entertainer grew and, as she moved from one husband to the next, so did her reputation as a scarlet woman, as rumors of orgies and lovers abounded. For fourteen years, from 1892 through 1906, she was the mistress of Jesse Lewisohn, heir to a Colorado copper fortune who also served as her poker partner. They often joined wealthy railway car salesman "Diamond Jim" Brady and his mistress Edna McCauley, who posed as his niece for twelve years, for four-handed poker.

Born James Buchanan Brady in New York City in 1856, "Diamond Jim" began selling railway equipment for New York Central in 1879 and made a fortune which he invested in diamonds. He learned early in his selling career that appearing successful increased sales, so he spent his first paycheck on a glittering diamond pinky ring which he flaunted with clients. His taste for expensive jewelry earned him his nickname, and diamond rings covered his fingers while his cane held a three-carat diamond. Much of his incredible jewelry collection was amassed by shrewd bargaining with pawnbrokers, and "Diamond Jim" swore that he owned half of the old diamonds of European royalty. He also used his diamonds in making big sales by inviting a client and his wife to dinner, dazzling the lady with his sparkling gems, then offering her a token which cost him much less than the commission he stood to make.

When doctors advised Lewisohn in 1906 to get rest and to stay away from rich food, late nights, and women, after he had consulted them due to severe weight loss and trembling, "Diamond Jim" suggested that he retire to the farm he shared with Edna who could nurse him while Lillian was on the road. A few weeks later, Lewisohn and Edna announced that they were going to marry, leaving

"Diamond Jim" and Lillian to discover their shared interest in good living and enthusiastic eating.

The two-hundred-fifty-pound Brady often said that the increasingly corpulent Lillian was the only woman who could ever keep up with him at the table. This may have been an exaggeration because "Diamond Jim" consumed massive amounts of food at one sitting. He usually began his dinner with five or six dozen oysters and two or more tureens of turtle soup. These were followed by several huge steaks smothered with lamb chops, a pheasant or roast chicken, and several courses. He washed down his food with a gallon of orange juice, and ended most dinners by consuming a five-pound box of chocolates. While Lillian likely did not match him course for course, the two fleshy and flashy celebrities often competed in eating. Waist size was no impediment because the Edwardian era encouraged hearty appetites, and heft was popularized by the style-setter of the era, the corpulent Edward VII of England.

They seemed to have a lot more in common, and "Diamond Jim" proposed numerous times to Lillian, who refused with the excuse that marriage might ruin their beautiful friendship. To cool his ardor, she sometimes dated other men and took "Diamond Jim" along on her dates.

Lillian supported the women's suffrage movement in the last years of her life, enthusiastically marching in the great suffrage parade of 1915. She and "Diamond Jim" drifted apart as he continued his opulent lifestyle, dying in 1917 after suffering for some months from gastric ulcers. Lillian lived on for five more years, campaigning for Warren G. Harding and earning a presidential appointment in 1921 as Special Commissioner of Immigration after his election. She was sent to Europe to study the immigration problem despite the raised eyebrows of Congressmen who questioned her qualifications.

In May 1922 while returning by ship from Europe, Lillian slipped and fell, suffering internal injuries which she ignored. She died a month later of complications. President Harding ordered her buried with full military honors.

S

Sand, George (1804–1876) Women writers in the nineteenth century rarely received the respect for their writing which men enjoyed, a fact which Amandine Aurore Lucie Dupine recognized early in life. Thus, when she ran off to Paris to write after her first marriage crumpled, she took George Sand as her masculine-sounding pen name and enjoyed immediate success with her novel *Indiana*. Her work strongly influenced young nineteenth-century writers, but the novels were little read until their rediscovery by feminist critics which has revived interest in her work.

Born on her family's country estate one hundred-fifty miles south of Paris, her father died when she was five and her mother left her in the care of her cold and remote grandmother who gave no expressions of love to the lonely child. To fill the void, Aurore created a companion named Corambe to whom she attributed her early creativity, claiming that Corambe composed the stories which she merely recorded. She had only two years of formal education at a convent school in Paris, then married at eighteen to Casimir

Dudevant, former soldier, then country squire, who required that she play the role of the obedient, submissive wife. Two years after her son's birth in 1824, she fell in love with Aurelien de Seze, a young lawyer, with whom she carried on a passionate correspondence for six years until he discontinued the unconsummated relationship.

After nine years of marriage, twenty-seven-year-old Aurore left her husband and moved to Paris to write. She became the mistress of French novelist Jules Sandeau with whom she collaborated on two novels published under the name of Jules Sand, and in 1832 published her first novel *Indiana* under her new name of George Sand. Distressed by Sandeau's infidelity, she left him and began to write in earnest. Despite her limited formal education, her novels remain masterpieces which reflect her changing sensibility.

For the most part, the novels of her early period, such as *Valentine* (1832) and *Lelia* (1833), are intelligent romances in which the heroine might begin the novel trapped in an unhappy marriage, but fate often frees her to pursue her own life. In her second period, George became concerned with socialistic and humanistic ideals, expressed fully in *Consuelo* (1842). She retired to her country home after the Revolution of 1848 and began writing novels of her third period which focused on peasant life, among them *François le Champi* (1848) and *La Petite Fadette* (1849). In her last novels, George returned to far-ranging social concerns and the novels of this period, *Le Marquis de Villemer* (1861) and *Mlle de Quintinie* (1863), are viewed as her best. However, her irregular life and many love affairs which shocked Parisian society probably stimulated more interest at the time than did her novels.

In her own life, George was involved in a series of affairs with men who were younger than she and usually blond and frail in contrast to her swarthy, heavy features and dark eyes. After Sandeau, she moved on to writer Prosper Mérimée, the French novelist and historian whose numerous writings include *Carmen* (1846) which Georges Bizet made into the popular opera. A more intense relationship developed with poet-playwright Alfred de Musset in 1833 when the two were contributors to the magazine *Revue des Deux Mondes* (*Review of Two Worlds*). He moved in with George a week after they met and they later traveled to Italy before quarreling and parting. The young poet received guidance and support from George who had already enjoyed success with her first two novels. She was also briefly the mistress of painter Charles Marchal and literary critic Gustave Planche.

The most famous man to whom she was mistress was Polish composer Frederic Chopin. When they met in 1837, he was six years younger than George and noted as a piano virtuoso. At first, the sensual and passionate George complained in her journal that Chopin was like an old woman in bed, inhibited and uninterested in sex. When they parted, the thirty-five-year-old composer complained that his forty-one-year-old mistress no longer evidenced sexual desire.

A year after they met, Chopin began to suffer from tuberculosis. George nursed him at Majorca in the Balearic Islands and later in France. After nine very productive years together, the two became estranged and they parted in 1847. Soon after, George returned to her childhood home where she would live and write until the end of her life, beginning the most socially conscious phase of her writing. Chopin was devastated by the loss of his love who had tended him and encouraged him, and he composed no more music. He limited his activity to giving a few concerts and died in 1849 of tuberculosis. George lived twenty-seven years longer, and she explored their love in variations told in several later novels. She died in 1876, notorious even in old age.

Sandeau, Jules (1811–1883) See **Sand, George.**

Sanger, Margaret (1883–1966) Born in Corning, New York, of a devout Catholic mother and a free-thinking Irish father, Margaret Sanger began her life in an exceedingly large, poor family. Her mother was tubercular, and she was weakened substantially by her eighteen pregnancies, of which only eleven children survived. She died when Margaret was sixteen.

Margaret became a maternity nurse and saw firsthand the pain and suffering which many women endured because of repeated and debilitating pregnancies, and botched, self-induced abortions. The result of her experiences was twofold: she vowed to take control of her own sexual life and to promote causes which would help all women to do the same.

When Margaret married her first husband, William Sanger, she informed him at the outset that her involvement in disseminating birth control information demanded that she be permitted sexual freedom to make love to other men. After the marriage ended, she remarried a rich Dutch businessman from South Africa who happily agreed to her demand for sexual freedom as well as for a separate private apartment within their large home.

Throughout both marriages, and after her second husband died in 1941, Margaret had numerous lovers and became mistress to a few. The list is long and varied and includes novelist Hugh de Selincourt, chemical engineer Herbert Simonds, architect Angus MacDonald, and author H. G. Wells. She had a close, intimate relationship with sexologist Havelock Ellis, also an advocate of free love, but it is unknown if they made love, for Ellis experienced severe bouts of impotence as he grew older.

Margaret was forty-two when she met the fifty-three-year-old H. G. Wells. He developed passionate interests in both the birth control cause and in its premier advocate. After nights of intense passion, the substantially experienced Wells often sent notes to Margaret that seemed almost boyish in their content, thanking her or raving about his pleasure. He sometimes joined her on the dais at conferences, and she wrote that after one especially pleasurable night together, Wells could not resist whispering memories of the night before into her ear as she sat waiting to speak.

She died in Tucson, Arizona, in 1966, having vastly changed the way the United States and people all over the world thought about birth control.

Sarfatti, Margherita (1880–1961) Born to an influential Jewish family in Venice, Italy, Sarfatti was a renowned art critic and writer on art and literature, in addition to being the mistress of Benito Mussolini from 1911 to 1938. Highly educated, Sarfatti spoke several languages and combined an artistic temperament with a political conscience, characteristics that drew Mussolini to her, despite her relatively advanced age of 31 when they first met. Her first published piece was a review of the Venice Biennale of 1901. She solidified her reputation as an art critic in 1905 with her review of the Milano great art exhibit, which showed that she could write with equal skill and understanding about those who worked with wax, as well as the more traditional work of bronze and marble sculptors.

During World War I, she took the unpopular position of supporting the involvement of Italy in the war, which led to her expulsion from the Fascist Party. After the war, she joined her political imagination with Mussolini's to create a Fascist Party that spoke to the needs of both the nationalists and socialists, a possibility created by the mass unemployment and extensive public unrest occurring in Italy. After nearly two decades of a long-distance affair, Sarfatti moved to Rome in the early 1930s to be nearer to Mussolini. She became the editor of *Gerarchia*, a monthly political magazine, which Mussolini also edited. Sarfatti also became a proponent of the Novecento art movement, which came under bitter attack from both political and cultural critics.

As Italy headed towards another war, Mussolini began to exhibit a growing anti-Semitism that reflected the political feelings in Germany. Sarfatti found that, as her affair with the dictator waned, she lost political power and her influence in the art world was vastly weakened. Frightened by the increasingly dangerous political climate for Jews in Italy, Sarfatti packed two suitcases full of jewels and art and escaped to Argentina. She later used these hastily taken items and her native intelligence to establish herself as one of the most important art collectors of the mid-twentieth century. Sarfatti returned to Italy in the 1950s and died there in 1961.

Shaw, George Bernard (1856–1950) See **Tompkins, Mary Arthur.**

Shelley, Mary Godwin (1797–1851) The daughter of British philosopher William Godwin and British feminist Mary Wollstonecraft, who died at a few days after her birth, Mary Godwin Shelley was privately educated and surrounded by many of the best-known intellectuals of the period. Mary was independent and defiant. When she met the poet Percy Bysshe Shelley in 1814 she was only sixteen. He worshipped her father and often sat for hours discussing philosophy with Godwin.

When Shelley first declared his love to Mary, he had nothing to offer her. He was still married to Harriet Westbrook, and divorce was impossible. Although her father had espoused great ideas of freedom, he was not about to have his daughter live them out, and he forbade the couple to see each other. Mary hysterically fought with her father. Shelley suggested that they both take overdoses of laudanum and die together, then took the overdose himself when she refused. He was fortunate that a friend found him and revived him. After tears and confrontation, she ran off with Shelley to tour Europe. Mary was shunned by her family and her friends for having run off and for cohabiting openly with a married man. Shelley's wife hired a lawyer who worked to ruin Godwin's name as revenge for the romance.

Mary gave birth to a child about a year after they eloped, but the infant boy lived for only eleven days before dying of convulsions. The pair claimed not to believe in marriage because of its limitations and exclusiveness, yet three weeks after Shelley's first wife committed suicide by drowning herself in a lake in a London park, they married. Money was always short during their life together, but Mary thrived in the relationship. During their eight years together, Mary passionately admired Shelley and gladly lived the bohemian life which he chose. She did not agree with his requests to engage in a ménage à trois with her stepsister Claire Clairmont, who was later to bear a child fathered by Lord Byron.

Although she wrote four other novels, books of travel sketches, and tales and verse, Mary is best known for *Frankenstein*, written when she was twenty. While it contains a strongly philosophical discussion of the nature of creation and the extent of human knowledge, the novel has become a popular "horror" story upon which movies and plays have been based. She continued to write after Shelley's drowning death in Italy in 1822. At first devastated by her loss, Mary later began to live again, first for her son Percy and later for her writing. She died of a brain tumor at the age of fifty-three, having spent all of her widowhood mourning her husband and writing material which added to his legend.

Shelley, Percy Bysshe (1792–1822) See **Shelley, Mary Godwin.**

Sickles, Teresa Bagioli (1836–1867) Teresa Bagioli was only sixteen and rumored to have been seduced when she married thirty-three-year-old Daniel Sickles who was elected to Congress in 1856 as a supporter of President Buchanan. She met her future lover Philip Barton Key, son of composer Francis Scott Key, at Buchanan's inaugural ball where the two danced for much of the night. Key may have initially courted Teresa as a means of getting at her husband Daniel, whose influence he sought in securing the appointment of United States Attorney. When approached, Sickles agreed to help Key and to mention him favorably.

Soon after the initial meeting, and with her husband's blessing, Key began to escort Teresa every Thursday to the dances at the Willard Hotel and each Saturday to.dances held on the south terrace of the White House. Although he adored his young wife and bought her jewels and clothes in the latest fashion, Sickles was too busy to enjoy a social life, and nothing was made of it because many wives of lawmakers often accepted substitute escorts for social functions. Key was considered by many Washington women to be the best "catch" in the city, and the handsomest man around. A widower whose wife had died five years earlier, he was financially comfortable, socially adept, and charming.

He became a regular visitor to their Lafayette Square mansion, and his presence increased the Sickles' popularity in Washington because he brought with him many other socially prominent people.

Rumors ran rampant by 1859 when numerous servants had observed the pair meeting "accidentally" at the homes of various acquaintances, in parks, or while on walks. When Sickles was away on business, the two would lock themselves in the downstairs library, leaving the servants to gossip and surmise.

Finally sensitive to the need for greater discretion, Key rented a small house in a working class section of the city where Teresa met him several times weekly for an hour or two. News of this arrangement reached Sickles, who furiously confronted Teresa. Tearfully, Teresa confessed to everything and she fearfully agreed to write and to sign a confession which detailed her "improper interviews" and "intimacy of an improper kind."

While meeting with friends the net day, Sickles caught sight of the unsuspecting Key walking across the street from the Lafayette Square mansion and waving his handkerchief as a signal for a tryst with Teresa. The infuriated Sickles grabbed his pistol, rushed out into the street, and fatally shot the unarmed lover. Despite the fact that Sickles had shot an unarmed man without warning, he was acquitted of murder.

After the acquittal, Sickles rushed to New York City, where Teresa had returned in disgrace, and a reconciliation of sorts resulted. However, Teresa remained in New York City even when her husband returned to Washington to finish his term of office. Daniel Sickles gradually regained both his respectability and his political clout, but Teresa remained in the background for the remainder of her life, knowing that her indiscretion would keep her a social outcast.

She died in 1867, at the age of thirty-one, of a cold which had gradually worsened. Her death ended eight years of penance, and many people who had not spoken to her since the tragedy had occurred came to mourn.

Simpson, Wallis Warfield (1896–1986) The future Duchess of Windsor was born Bessie Wallis Warfield at a summer resort in Blue Ridge Summit, Pennsylvania, near the Maryland border. Her parents, Teackle Wallis Warfield and Alice Montague Warfield, had hoped for a son, so they had only planned on the name Wallis which they preceded by Bessie in honor of Alice's sister. Both families were prominent in Baltimore society.

Sick with tuberculosis when he married, Wallis' father died when she was four months old. The widow and infant moved in with Alice's mother-in-law and her eldest and most successful son, Solomon, the youngest postmaster in Baltimore history and the organizer of the Seaboard Air Line Railway. He would later serve as the president of the Continental Trust Company, consolidate the gas and electric companies of Baltimore, and become instrumental in connecting the east and west coasts of Florida. He also fell deeply in love with Wallis' mother and the awkward nature of the situation forced Alice and Wallis to find their own lodgings and to begin making their own living.

When Wallis was five, her mother began to work, sewing clothes for the Women's Exchange, then starting a boardinghouse where twelve-year-old Wallis would serve the guests. There was not much money for fun, but Wallis was sent to the Arundell School in

Mrs. Wallis Simpson (BETTMANN ARCHIVE)

Baltimore, a highly disciplined private school. Soon after, Alice remarried and Wallis had to learn to share her mother. She also had to make an odd decision early in her life. Her now extremely wealthy uncle Solomon, angered by her mother's rejection of him and remarriage to another man, asked Wallis to live with him and Grandma Warfield. She would not only have everything she wanted, but she would be his heir. There was only one condition – that she never again enter her mother's house. The sixteen-year-old flatly refused, despite the devious schemes cooked up by a friend, who suggested that she should agree, then sneak around to see her mother.

After her stepfather died in 1913, money was again a problem for Wallis and her mother, so much so that when she was to be presented at the Bachelor's Cotillion she was unable to buy her gown at the expensive shop where all of the debutantes shopped. The beautiful white satin gown trimmed in white beads was homesewn.

As with many girls of the time, her fantasy lover was the Prince of Wales, then a lieutenant in the Grenadier Guards in France, and she had a newspaper photo of him in her diary. Reality, however, demanded that she look closer to home and Wallis was practical. When she was sent after Grandma Warfield's death to visit a friend's sister at the Pensacola Naval Air Station in Florida, she found herself surrounded by adoring naval officers. Handsome, virile, and domineering, twenty-seven-year-old pilot Lieutenant (Junior Grade) Earl Winfield Spencer, Jr. captured nineteen-year-old Wallis' heart. Although her mother worried that Wallis might find navy life difficult, and the penny-pinching impossible, Wallis was adamant. She was in love and wanted to marry Winfield.

Wallis found life as a navy wife exciting, especially as her husband was first transferred from Pensacola to Boston to San Diego in a short time. While at San Diego in 1920, the Winfields attended a ball given for the Prince of Wales by the navy when the HMS *Renown* put into port. At the time they merely looked at him from the fringes of the crowd.

The marriage deteriorated as Wallis became more flirtatious and her husband began to resent her while he drank increasingly. She stayed behind while he went on several temporary duty assignments, joining him only when he was reassigned to Washington, D.C. The promised new beginning failed, and Wallis left Winfield to move in with her mother who had moved to Washington and was working as a hostess at the Chevy Chase Country Club. While Winfield left for Far East duty, Wallis became involved with thirty-five-year-old Don Felipe A. Espil, first secretary of the Argentine Embassy. Infatuated with him, she aimed to impress him and began to read the newspapers voraciously to keep current on world events. The affair ended when Espil broke off with the marriage-minded Wallis, who was still married to Winfield.

She decided to give her marriage another try, and met Winfield in China but the old difficulties arose. Separating from him again, she stayed with friends in Shanghai, then returned home after a year to formally end her marriage.

Wallis met her second husband in New York City, while visiting Mary Kirk Raffray, a friend who lived on Washington Square. Mr. and Mrs. Ernest Simpson were also dinner guests, and Wallis' vivacity and laughter captured Simpson's attention. In the three years following, he sent her flowers, took her to the theater, and sued his wife for divorce. He returned to London to run his family shipping firm and cabled for Wallis to go to London to marry him. To Wallis, Simpson represented security and stability, and they were married in the city Registry in 1928.

After purchasing their own home in Grosvenor Square they became acquainted with the famous Morgan sisters, Consuelo, Thelma, and Gloria, American royalty. Thelma Furness was currently the mistress of the Prince of Wales and she arranged for Ernest and Wallis to attend a weekend party which the Prince would also attend. The two couples got along well, and they met socially many other times. In 1931 Thelma asked the Prince to use his influence to permit the American divorcee Wallis Simpson to be presented at court. He did.

When Thelma returned to the United States for a family visit in 1934 she asked Wallis to take care of the prince and "See that he does not get into any mischief." By the time she returned, the two were in love.

By 1933 the Prince was deeply in love with Wallis. He told her that she was the only woman who had ever been interested in his job and the only one who had listened to him. They laughed and talked familiarly, and she fussed around the man whom she called David, his given name. Ernest quietly bowed out of the picture, declining invitations from the Prince while Wallis accepted, and the public soon learned of the growing romance. When King George V died in 1936, the Prince of Wales was crowned King Edward VIII. Wallis hurriedly completed plans for her divorce from Simpson, and the king told friends that he intended to have her crowned queen on his coronation date, 12 May 1937.

Britain buzzed with the gossip about the American divorcee and their new king, and high-ranking government officials met in closed advisory sessions to decide how to handle the crisis. Prime Minister Stanley Baldwin told the king that the cabinet would not approve a marriage to Wallis and the king said that he was ready to abdicate, which he was forced to do. On 11 December 1936, he broadcast a message on the BBC to explain his move. He said simply that he could not have handled the responsibilities of office without the support of the woman he loved.

After abdicating, the former Edward VIII received the title of Duke of Windsor and he married Wallis in June 1937. They lived outside of England for the next thirty-six years, maintaining a residence in Paris and living in the Bahama Islands where the Duke was governor from 1940 to 1945. After the war they moved freely between Britain and the United States. The Windsors briefly returned to Britain in 1952 where the Duke took part in a British royal ceremony for the first time since the abdication, but Wallis was shunned by the royal family. Although Wallis became the epitome of the sophisticated woman to whom designers flocked and whose fashion choices made news, she lived an essentially rootless life with the Duke. She was quoted often as having said "One can never be too rich or too thin," and her lifestyle seemed designed around that view.

When the Duke died in 1972, the Duchess of Windsor and the royal family finally spoke after all those years. In her remaining fourteen years alone, she became a recluse as ill health made leaving her home difficult.

Sorel, Agnes (1422–1450) Agnes Sorel was born in 1422, the year that King Charles VII of France ascended, into a family of lesser nobility in Touraine. At an early age she entered the service of Isabel of Lorraine, the queen of Sicily, who was married to René of Anjou, the king's blother-in-law. Agnes was the first official mistress of a French king and she is sometimes known as "Dame de Beaute" because of the estate which he gave her, named "Beaute-sur-Marne."

Agnes captivated the king at his court celebration during the festivals in 1444, and he fell instantly in love with her. He was to remain faithful to her until her death six years later. At Charles' behest, she was accorded the honor and respect of a queen, and despite the extensive disapproval, he gave her enormous wealth, several castles, and great parcels of land to make her a woman of substance. Such public recognition of a mistress shocked French subjects and members of the court and incited jealousy and intrigue. They were even more disturbed over the power wielded by Agnes who made her mark on the politics of the day as a sounding board to the king.

Discontentment remained in the court throughout her six years as mistress and Agnes died suddenly from dysentery soon after the birth of her fourth child with Charles. Poison was rumored, and the story persisted. Various nobles and even the dauphin, later Louis XI, were named as the perpetrators, but no proof exists for such charges.

Stael, Mme. Germaine de (1766–1817) Born Anne Louise Germaine Necker to a Swiss father who was also one of the richest men in Europe, she was raised in an intellectually charged atmosphere. Her parents regularly took her with them to Paris, and Mme. de Stael joined in political discussions even as a young woman.

She was not physically attractive and acquaintances described her as having the air of a chambermaid. Married at twenty to the Baron de Stael-Holstein, seventeen years her senior, she was an unenthusiastic wife but a highy enthusiastic mistress which made up for her lack of physical attractiveness. She was, at different times, the mistress of French statesman and diplomat Charles de Talleyrand, the Duc de Montmorency, and the Comte de Narbonne. Disguised as a male soldier, Germaine made several forays onto the military field to visit Narbonne, an army officer on active duty and the illegitimate son of King Louis XV of France. Over several years, she bore two sons to Narbonne.

She also had a long liaison with Benjamin Constant, a tall, redheaded, and awkward Oxford University graduate who later became famous in France as a writer and politician. Although Mme. de Stael claimed to have been repulsed by his looks when they first met, she became Constant's mistress for fifteen years. He often complained of being emotionally and intellectually drained by his mistress. When her husband died, Constant asked her to marry him to permit him at least to go to bed early, but Germaine refused. Soon after, he left her and married a less challenging German wife.

Crushed, Mme. de Stael threatened to sue Constant for money which she claimed that he owed her father, but she didn't act on that threat. Instead, she became the mistress of a twenty-three-year-old Italian army officer named Albert Jean Michel Rocca, with whom she had a daughter when she was forty-five and whom she later married.

While playing the role of mistress to various men, the wealthy Germaine continued to write novels and political pieces. She also attempted to attract the attention of General Napoleon Bonaparte. When writing letters proved fruitless, she managed to obtain an introduction through her husband's diplomatic connections and reported that she became both breathless and speechless when she first met the general. When they met a second time, she tried to discuss politics, but Napoleon's eyes glazed over so she switched her approach to one of seductive and feminine behavior.

Both tactics failed, so the aggressive woman tried the more direct approach. Without an invitation, she entered Napoleon's home and searched through it until she had cornered him in the bathroom. At his roar of protest, she left in indignation and later wrote tracts and books attacking his policies. For this, both Constant and Mme. de Stael were exiled from Paris, ordered to move at least forty leagues from the city. She returned alone to Paris after Waterloo and set up a lively salon which lasted until her death in 1817.

Stuart, Charles Edward ("Bonnie Prince Charlie") (1720–1788)
See **Walkinshaw, Clementine.**

Suckley, Margaret (1892–1991) Known as "Daisy" to her friends, Suckley was ten years younger than and the sixth cousin to Franklin

Delano Roosevelt, the only four-term United States President. While Lucy MERCER was FDR's mistress before he was stricken by polio, Suckley was the woman who became his "closest companion" in the decades afterward. They first met in 1922, the year after polio struck the formerly vital 39-year-old man, and she remained a constant physical presence in his life from his first inauguration as president in 1933 through to his death in 1945. Suckley never married, but descriptions in her carefully kept diary and the intimacies expressed to her by FDR in the handwritten letters that she preserved until her death show that she filled the role of loving wife on emotional and intellectual levels. Social propriety and her upbringing demanded that the extent of their physical intimacy would not be revealed, but biographers debate that she filled this role as well because many of the letters and diary entries contain crossed-out material and she destroyed other documents that might have proved embarrassing to FDR's family.

By his side when he travelled on his secret wartime cross-country inspection trips by train and at the White House, Suckley often served as a substitute hostess and tended to FDR's personal needs, making certain that he took his medication, making him comfortable during frequent lonely evenings when his wife Eleanor was away championing her own causes, and serving as buffer when Eleanor was present. Historian Geoffrey C. Ward writes that by 1935 FDR and Suckley had formed so strong a relationship that they selected a secluded area on his Hyde Park estate, which they called "our hill", and spoke of building a cottage there.

To provide Suckley with an official role at the White House, where she was already living in 1935, FDR arranged for her to be hired as a part-time employee on the presidential library payroll at an annual salary of $1,000. She came to know Lucy Mercer, widowed by then, and to like her, although the lengthy romantic relationship between FDR and Mercer remained a secret from her as from the world. So close was Suckley to FDR that she took one of only two photographs of him sitting in a wheelchair. He also trusted her in international matters, and among her letters are several long missives that FDR wrote in 1941 from the Churchill conference in which he provided her with extensive – secret – details of the proceedings. With Mercer, another FDR cousin, and an artist painting FDR's portrait, Suckley was present in the room at Warm Springs on the afternoon in 1945 when FDR began to experience the pain in his head that would shortly end in his death. His last words were directed to her, the woman of whom historian Ward has written, "No one ever loved Franklin Roosevelt more than Daisy Suckley did."

Summersby, Kay (1908–1975) Born Kathleen McCarthy-Morrogh, Kay had come from a monied family who owned an estate in County Cork, Ireland. She had been brought up with all of the accoutrements of the rich: governesses, lawn tennis, riding to the hounds, servants, and the enjoyment of tea poured from crested silver that had been in the family for hundreds of years. Tall, stately, and haughty-looking, she had worked for a time as a Worth mannequin in Paris and later as a runway model. An early marriage and divorce from Gordon Summersby had left her with a new surname.

Kay was thirty-four and about to remarry when she met Dwight David "Ike" Eisenhower. A volunteer for the war effort, she was assigned as a civilian driver of the Army motor transport corps in London. She was initially disappointed to learn that her assignment, Eisenhower, was only a Major General, a two-star general; she had hoped for three stars.

During their three years together, the two carried on a discreet affair during which they often met at the hideaway called Telegraph Cottage, a lovely home situated on ten acres adjacent to a golf course. Ike bought Kay a black Scotch terrier which they named Telek, a combination of Telegraph Cottage and Kay, as a secret gift which they led everyone else to believe was Ike's dog. Kay drove for Ike in London and he also arranged for her to travel with him to North Africa and Algiers.

Ike appeared to have every intention of marrying Kay. His letters home to Mamie abound in veiled denials and explanations. He pulled strings with the Roosevelt administration to arrange for her to be a WAC officer, so she could become his official aide, not just his driver. He also arranged for Kay to become an American citizen so that she could serve on his personal staff as an aide in the Pentagon when they left as planned in November 1945.

Kay Summersby (BETTMANN ARCHIVE)

Ike wrote to General George Marshall of his intentions to divorce Mamie and marry Kay after the war. Marshall recommended against it, pointing out it would be a dangerous example for American soldiers, plus a death blow to Ike's political ambitions. Ike gave up his job as Commander of Supreme Headquarters Allied Expeditionary Forces and left Germany for Washington on 10 November 1945. Kay was supposed to join him in Washington, but a telex arrived from the States a few days later ordering that her name be dropped from the list of personnel scheduled to leave for Washington. There was no explanation .

Kay worked for a while for General Lucius Clay, deputy military governor of Germany in Berlin, and then received a typed letter from Ike telling her that it was impossible for her to join his staff in the U.S. She tried to contact Ike by telephone and letter, but he didn't answer so Kay traveled to the Pentagon. Ike made it clear that their love affair was over.

A short while later, she resigned from the army and went to New York City to live. When Ike became president of Columbia University, she walked around the campus, hoping to meet him. Once when she managed to see him, he seemed to be annoyed and he told her bluntly that there could never be anything more between them.

Still, Kay persisted. In 1949, when she had returned to London and Ike and Mamie were in town, she sent them a note, asking them to stop by for a drink. Ike never responded, but Kay received a visitor a few days later. A young major told her that the general had asked him to escort her out for an evening. Over drinks, the man told Kay that Ike was "on a tight leash" and "not his own master."

In the years that followed, Kay returned to the U.S. and married Reginald Morgan. She died of cancer in 1975, months before her book *Past Forgetting* about her time as mistress to Ike was published.

Swanson, Gloria (1897–1983) Gloria Josephine Mae Swenson was born in Chicago and her beginning in films is the classic "discovery" story. She was sixteen and working as a clerk in a Chicago department store when her aunt invited her to tour the local Essanay Studios. A casting assistant thought she was photogenic and asked if she would like to work as an extra, and the long and successful career began. By eighteen, Gloria had earned the first of many film credits for *The Fable of Elvira* and *Farina and the Meal Ticket*. She worked with Wallace Beery, her first of six husbands, in several films, then moved on to work in ten films for Mack Sennett and six for Cecil B. DeMille, which earned her star status.

Gloria achieved most of her success in silent films, earning Oscar nominations for *Sadie Thompson* (1928) and her first "talkie" *The Trespasser* in 1929 in which she sang "Love, Your Magic Spell is Everywhere." Her popularity waned afterward, and her 1934 film *Music in the Air* was seen as her farewell film performance. Gloria pursued stage work throughout much of the 1930s, returning to the screen with the unsuccessful *Father Takes a Wife* in 1941. Nine years later, at fifty-three, she played the role of Norma Desmond in *Sunset Boulevard* for which she won an Oscar nomination. The part was her most famous role, but it failed to revive her career.

Of the many husbands, lovers, and admirers who shared the life and limelight of Gloria Swanson, her most notorious relationship was with Joseph Kennedy, father of American president John F. Kennedy and patriarch of America's royal family. Her two years as Kennedy's mistress began in 1926, when the twenty-nine-year-old film actress, one of the greatest of the silent screen stars, ran into financial difficulties with her newly formed film company, Gloria Productions, Incorporated. She was over-budget for her latest film and running into problems in maintaining expenses. When a friend suggested that she appeal to Joseph Kennedy, who had gotten into the movie industry by first buying a string of small New England theaters, she immediately invited him to lunch.

The two found that they had more than the movies in common. Kennedy agreed to help Gloria reorganize her business and the two formed a new company under which Kennedy provided the financial backing and production input for a movie idea which Gloria hoped to film. To cement their relationship, Kennedy invited Gloria and her third husband, an impoverished French nobleman named Marquis Henri de la Falaise de la Coudraye, to his Palm Beach home where he offered the marquis a job in his Paris office. While Henri fished off the Florida coast that weekend, Gloria and Kennedy became lovers. From that point, Gloria shared her time discreetly, often spending rapturous hours with Kennedy in his rented home on Rodeo Drive in California.

Early in 1929 Gloria received a call from a Kennedy employee who said that she had an appointment with an individual named O'Connell. Presuming that Kennedy had arranged the meeting, she went to meet the man who turned out to be William Cardinal O'Connell, a longtime friend of the Kennedy family who happened to be the archbishop of Boston. He told her that Kennedy had asked him for the sanction of the Catholic Church to set up a separate household with Gloria because his religion made divorce impossible. The cardinal then remonstrated with Gloria, telling her that each time Kennedy was with her, she became "an occasion for sin" for the forty-one-year-old father and husband. He also told her that the proposed arrangement was impossible and that Kennedy was creating a scandal by being seen in public with Gloria. The outraged actress told the cardinal that he was talking to the wrong person and that it was Kennedy with whom he should speak.

Although she never learned who had encouraged Cardinal O'Connell to speak with her, Gloria's role as Kennedy's mistress changed from that point. Her husband soon informed her that he was divorcing her. She also began to question Kennedy's actions regarding her finances rather than merely accepting his actions. This infuriated him more than ever and, after she questioned him about a move made regarding her personal checking account, he became angry. He left his home on Rodeo Drive the next day without a goodbye, and soon after liquidated all of his movie holdings. Their affair was over.

Gloria went on to marry three more times, to embark on a stage career, and to immortalize the character of the faded movie queen, Norma Desmond. In her late seventies, she began to sculpt and exhibited her works in a London gallery in 1979. She died four years later.

Talleyrand, Charles de (1754–1838) See Stael, Madame Germaine de.

Tarnower, Herman (1909–1980) See Harris, Jean.

Tenepal, Malinali (?1505–1540) Malinali Tenepal was born in the Oluta area of the Isthmus of Tehuantepec, a region of Mexico whose women were known to be stately, beautiful, and independent even at the time that explorer Hernan Cortes was beginning his conquests. She met Cortes when she was between the ages of fourteen and nineteen and he had her christened Marina and gave her the courtesy title of *dona* when he took her as his mistress. The natives, however, renamed her Malinche, adding the suffix -che as a sign of respect. That name, Malinche, has taken on a new meaning throughout the centuries, and it remains in Mexican slang as a terrn given to people who betray their heritage.

The daughter of a chief, Malinali's father had died when she was young and her mother remarried. A son was born of this second marriage and her mother feared that Malinali would interfere with the son inheriting the role of chief, so she sold Malinali as a slave to traders. To disguise this horrible act, her mother had a slave girl killed and displayed the body as that of her daughter.

When Cortes first captured Malinali, he presented her to one of his captains as a favor. Soon, however, he overheard her speaking with natives whom they encountered on a journey to Veracruz, and he realized that Malinali's bilingualism was valuable. She could translate from Nahuatl into Mayan, which another member of his crew could then translate into Spanish. Soon, she also learned Spanish, and she taught her captors important Indian expressions, gestures, and attitudes, saving them from death. Her beauty, teamed with her skills, appealed to Cortes, who took her as his mistress and with whom she gave birth to a son, whom Cortes named Martin.

In 1524 Cortes sought to free himself in order to contract a socially and financially desirable marriage. He therefore arranged a marriage between Malinali and a member of his entourage, Juan de Jaramillo, who was drunk during the ceremony. Even after marriage, Malinali continued for several years as interpreter.

Little is known of Malinali's life after the forced marriage, except that she gave birth to a daughter. The woman who had helped the conquistadors in so many ways, and whose memory was to inspire hatred among later Indians who despised her for having "sold out," died in obscurity in 1540.

Ternan, Ellen (1839–1914) The daughter of a failed Victorian actor and a spunky mother who carried on alone with her three young daughters after her husband had a mental breakdown, Ellen Ternan was around the stage from infancy. She made her stage debut at the age of three, but roles were scarce and her mother often scrambled to obtain acting jobs for herself and Ellen's two sisters.

Not until 1857 when she was eighteen, did Ellen make her adult stage debut. Charles Dickens was in the audience, and the forty-five-year-old author fell instantly in love with Ellen, whose role as Hippomenes in an extravagant stage play, *Atalanta*, required that she wear only skimpy clothing. Once he had arranged an introduction,

Ellen became his sole romantic interest until he died after suffering a stroke thirteen years later. Nothing, not his ten children, disgruntled wife, nor rumored affair with his sister-in-law, prevented him from providing for and striving to spend time with the woman who had captured his romantic imagination and his heart.

When Ellen's family first met Dickens, they were impressed because he was already a famous novelist. Further, since he was already accustomed to acting the role of father and family provider, he assumed this same role with Ellen and her family, to the point that he later placed property in her name which provided income for all of her life. Further, by 1859, only two years after the two met, Ellen played her last stage role and she never again worked while Dickens was alive. At the same time, her mother had no visible income, and it is probable that the already overburdened Dickens supported them, as well as his large brood.

Ellen was comfortable in her role as mistress to the great novelist who had bought her a home which remained in her mother's name until Ellen turned twenty-one. There, Dickens visited each evening, singing and playing games with the family, with Mrs. Ternan providing a dubious air of respectability.

Dickens' wife Catherine was very aware of his obsession and raged whenever he returned home. The duality of Victorian England permitted Dickens his mistress, but it also required that he maintain a semblance of respectability if he expected to remain a popular author and lecturer. Therefore, he tried to strike a balance between mistress and home. He had his large marital bedroom renovated and turned into two bedrooms, so that he would no longer have to sleep in the same room as his wife, but he continued to live with her.

Ellen provided Dickens with the romance, excitement, and vitality which he had thought had left his life forever. Everyone, except Dickens' wife, was happy with the arrangement. Catherine finally moved out, leaving the children, servants, and Dickens to go their own ways. Her vindictive husband felt the need to appear the victim so he issued a public denial that he was involved in any improprieties, then told as many people as would listen about Catherine's faults as a wife and mother.

For thirteen years, Ellen was Charles Dickens' mistress. His daughter Katie informed her of his fatal stroke and took Ellen with her for a final goodbye. She lived comfortably forty-four more years.

Thaw, Evelyn Nesbit (1884–1966) She was born Florence Evelyn Nesbit on Christmas Day in 1884 in the small village of Tarentum, Pennsylvania, about twenty-four miles from Pittsburgh. Her father, a Pittsburgh lawyer, died when she was eight and her widowed mother took Evelyn and her younger brother Howard to Pittsburgh and opened a roominghouse where she cooked, washed, ironed, and cleaned for boarders. The venture failed, and Mrs. Nesbit was forced to sell their furniture and then to move because they were unable to pay the rent on the roominghouse. Moving closer to the mill side of Pittsburgh, Mrs. Nesbit opened another roominghouse near the tenements which teemed with immigrant families. As they struggled, Evelyn helped her mother with the cooking and cleaning, and she dreamed of running away with the circus or a dancing troupe to escape the dirty mill world.

When Evelyn was fourteen, her mother moved the family to Philadelphia where they all found jobs at Wanamaker's department store. Mrs. Nesbit was a saleswoman, Howard became a cashboy, and Evelyn was a stockgirl. Howard became ill and was sent to a relative's farm while Evelyn and her mother moved into a cheaper boardinghouse. An elderly woman in their boardinghouse introduced Evelyn to her brother, artist John Storm, who paid her to pose for him. This led to another assignment to pose for stained glass windows for Violet Oakley, a designer of church windows. Garbed in long white robes, barefoot, and with her long curls tumbling around her face, Evelyn was immortalized in stained glass.

Evelyn met other famous artists and illustrators at Oakley's studio, and her face soon began to appear in magazines, books, and newspaper supplements. Encouraged by the attention, fourteen-year-old Evelyn and her mother moved to New York City. She was a success there, and soon had offers to pose for many of the leading illustrators of the day, including Frederick S. Church, James Carroll Beckwith, J. Wells Champney, Carl Blenner, George Grey Barnard, and Charles Dana Gibson. Barnard's sculpture of her as *Innocence* went to the Metropolitan Museum of Art, and Gibson's sketch of her in profile in the shape of a question mark became *The Eternal Question*. She also posed frequently for the fashion pages, just beginning to use live models, and made the grand sum of five dollars for a sitting.

Theatrical agent Ted Marks contacted the Nesbits and arranged for Evelyn to meet the producers of *Floradora*, and with great reluctance Mrs. Nesbit gave approval for Evelyn to join the show as a chorus girl. At sixteen Evelyn exuded an innocent charm and she was called "the kid" or "the baby" by the other girls when she danced in her first Broadway show. Mrs. Nesbit waited for her daughter every night to escort her home, and Evelyn was forced by her mother to refuse the candy, flowers, cards with fifty-dollar bills attached, and jewelry that male admirers had begun to send backstage to her. Her pouting lips, mass of copper-colored curls, slim body, and attractive legs also brought her invitations to after-theater parties, and finally an invitation for her and her mother to cruise upon the Hudson River in the yacht of the wealthy Mr. James A. Garland. The elderly millionaire took mother and daughter to dinner at the posh restaurants and escorted them to the Weber and Fields Music Hall to see the brightest show business names on stage. Evelyn was dazzled by Lillian Russell, Mazie Follette, and May MacKenzie. She also began to notice that men stared at her and flirted openly wherever she went, and she began to exploit her attractiveness.

Edna Goodrich, another chorus girl in *Floradora*, invited Evelyn to lunch with some "society people" she knew, but the host was Stanford White, who greeted them in the building called the Tower, which housed his studio. Known as a successful and innovative architect, White designed the original Madison Square Garden as well as most of the opulent mansions owned by the Vanderbilts, Astors, Choates, and other style-setters at the turn of the century. At forty-eight, he was tall and powerful in appearance, and Evelyn thought him very handsome. After lunch, the girls joined him in his special room at the top of the building which contained a studio at least two floors high. The walls were covered with paintings and etchings of nudes, and busts were all around the room. At the far end of the room was a red velvet swing suspended from the ceiling by red velvet ropes. Evelyn was invited to try the swing and White encouraged her to swing fiercely and high.

After that initial meeting, White contacted Mrs. Nesbit to arrange that Evelyn visit his dentist to correct her one flaw, a misaligned front tooth. Soon, he began to send flowers daily to both women and to provide gifts of expensive clothing. He even arranged for Howard to attend Chester Military School at Mrs. Nesbit's request. When she suggested that she would like visit her son to see how he was faring, White offered to take good care of sixteen-year-old Evelyn and Mrs. Nesbit heartily agreed. By that point, an arrangement had been entered into between Mrs. Nesbit and White. Evelyn frequently visited White's loft to dress in the expensive kimonos he provided, to drink champagne, to swing on the red velvet swing, and to make love with "Stanny" in his huge four-poster bed with its lush velvet drapes, mirrored headboard, and lighted canopy which was set next to a mirrored wall. Each night White would send a Union Club cab for her and they would meet at the Tower where celebrities might join them for a late supper, after which White might ignore Evelyn completely as he sketched and designed until morning.

By Christmas 1901, for which White gave Evelyn two solitaire diamond rings, a large pearl hung on a platinum chain, a ruby and diamond ring, and a set of white fox furs, Mrs. Nesbit and Evelyn were moved by White to an apartment in The Wellington, a new hotel on Seventh Avenue. Furnished mainly in white, the apartment featured white satin walls, thick red wool carpets, and a canopy bed covered in white satin. A white piano was included with the promise of lessons so that Evelyn could learn to play Beethoven for White.

Amid all of this opulence, Evelyn still pouted because White spent his weekends with his family on Long Island, and he took his wife whenever he traveled on business or met with clients. She decided that he had been taking her for granted by spending too much time with his family, and she decided to make him jealous. She began to accept dinner invitations from men who interested her and she received proposals from at least half a dozen millionaires when she was seventeen.

When *Floradora* closed in 1902, she worked in *The Wild Rose* which had a new comic star, Eddie Foy. At a party given by White, Evelyn met twenty-two-year-old John Barrymore, then a cartoonist on the *Evening Journal*, who wrote her phone number and address on his shirt cuff, then sent her violets later that night. While White went to Canada that summer on his annual salmon-fishing trip, Barrymore met Evelyn nightly at the stage door and escorted her to dinner at Rector's so frequently that the *Morning Telegraph* gossip column featured them.

Evelyn stayed over at Barrymore's apartment, an ugly firetrap, only one night, but her mother and White were waiting for her when she returned home. Both were white-lipped and upset. With Mrs. Nesbit's consent, White then took Evelyn to the offices of Dr. Nathaniel Bowditch Potter where she was questioned, examined, and tested. Afterward, White took her home and told her that her mother was furious with her and afraid that Evelyn might be pregnant. Evelyn retorted that she would happily marry Barrymore if she were pregnant. Barrymore was summoned and the two told White that, if Evelyn became pregnant, they would marry and live on love. White stormed out of the room, made a call, and with Mrs. Nesbit's approval shipped Evelyn to The DeMille School, an all-girls school in Pompton Lakes, New Jersey.

In April 1903, Harry Thaw, thirty-two and worth forty million dollars inherited from his father, a Pittsburgh industrialist, showed up at The DeMille School. He had been sending Evelyn gifts backstage at *Floradora* under the name of "Mr. Monroe" and he had tried to see her at The Wellington, but she had always refused him. When she mysteriously disappeared from New York City, he tracked her down. He bombarded Mrs. DeMille with candy, flowers, and gifts until the matron called Evelyn aside and suggested that she talk with the wealthy young man who was "madly in love" with her. A few days later, Evelyn experienced severe abdominal cramps and the school called her mother. Mrs. Nesbit called both White and Thaw, and they rushed by train to Pompton Lakes with two doctors. Although biographers suggest that a child was born, the official word sworn to by all involved was that eighteen-year-old Evelyn suffered a case of acute appendicitis.

Both White and Thaw visited Evelyn as she recuperated in a private sanatorium, luckily never meeting. When she was well enough, Evelyn and Mrs. Nesbit went to Europe with Thaw, who paid all expenses, but White saw them off and gave Evelyn a bon voyage gift of a letter of credit for five hundred dollars drawn on Cook's Bank.

Thaw entertained mother and daughter extravagantly in Europe, but his wild mood swings soon drove Mrs. Nesbit to make Evelyn choose between her and Thaw. Evelyn chose Thaw and moved in with him, then proceeded to travel with him. She became terrified of his mood swings and his violence. He often flew into rages in which he tied her up and then whipped her. She learned that he was addicted to morphine and that his mood swings coincided with his drug use.

Evelyn happily returned to New York City, and she tried to resume her relationship with White but his ardor had cooled. Thus, when Thaw began to court her again with gifts and flowers, she succumbed and they left for Europe in June 1904 for another lavish vacation. When they returned, in early 1905, Evelyn was again confined to a private hospital with another case of "acute appendicitis," from which she took six weeks to recuperate. Afterward, Thaw's mother visited her and told her that she wished that Evelyn would marry her son because he was very much in love. On 5 April 1905 Evelyn married Thaw in Pittsburgh. His jealous rages escalated, until Evelyn couldn't speak to another man. Thaw frequently spoke of her affair with White, his eyes glaring with jealous anger as he did so.

On 25 June 1906 Thaw shot White to death at the Roof Garden Theater and Restaurant of Madison Garden where both had been eating dinner with separate parties. The sensational revelations of the trial titillated New Yorkers for weeks. When it was over, Thaw was committed for life to the New York Asylum for the Criminally Insane at Matteawan, New York. He escaped once, was recommitted, then was released in 1922. He died in 1947 at the age of seventy-six.

Evelyn was promised a generous settlement by Thaw's mother for help in having him declared insane, and Evelyn trustingly took her word and ignored the advice of a lawyer that she receive the promise in writing. Once the jury had declared him insane, Evelyn was no longer needed and Mrs. Thaw ignored reminders of the promise. Because he was insane, she could not file for divorce because he was legally of unsound mind and not able to contract any settlement. His mother controlled the estate, and she gave Evelyn only $30,000 as insurance against further hearings. Evelyn was forced to sell her jewelry. In 1909 she gave birth to a baby boy named Russell whom she argued had been conceived with Thaw during a conjugal visit. She began to dance again and she was touring Europe when she learned that Thaw had been declared sane and she was served with divorce papers. In 1924 she began to receive paynents from Thaw and she used the money to open a nightclub, El Prinkipo, in Atlantic City.

After losing her club, she entertained in numerous speakeasies, then opened her own in New York, Chez Evelyn, which failed. When she was singing in a seedy roadhouse in Biloxi, Mississippi, the proprietor of The Kelly Ritz, a well-known whorehouse in Panama City, Panama, approached forty-five-year-old Evelyn and asked her to appear there for Mardi Gras week. Evelyn agreed. In 1934 she published her life story, then disappeared from public view until 1955 when the Technicolor movie *The Girl in the Red Velvet Swing* appeared and interest in her briefly emerged.

In her later years, Evelyn lived in a Hollywood boardinghouse after World War II, supported by Russell. She died in 1966, at the age of eighty-one.

Tilton, Elizabeth Richards (1836–1897) Henry Ward Beecher was proclaimed by his contemporaries as the greatest preacher that the world had ever known. Pastor of Plymouth Church in Brooklyn, New York, and confidant of presidents, Beecher had envisioned himself one day holding that high office. Brother to author Harriet Beecher Stowe, he was a leading voice in the anti-slavery movement, women's suffrage movement, and an early proponent of evolutionary theory.

In 1868 when she first became Beecher's mistress, Elizabeth Richards Tilton, who had been married for ten years, was a thirty-two-year-old Sunday school teacher and the mother of five children. Beecher had performed her marriage to husband Theodore and he was her pastoral confidant. The affair was actually encouraged by her mother who viewed her son-in-law as a loser who had thrown away many opportunities and who had no future, despite his success as the editor-in-chief of one magazine and involvement with another, his popularity as a speaker, and his success as a novelist and poet. She was dazzled by Beecher who was a powerful man with a lot of money and a direct line to the White House.

By 1870 a conscience-stricken Elizabeth had tearfully confessed to

Elizabeth Richards Tilton (LIBRARY OF CONGRESS)

her husband that she had been Beecher's mistress for two years, a confession likely motivated by her having recently miscarried a baby which was probably fathered by Beecher. Elizabeth had been particularly naive for she claimed to have been totally convinced by Beecher that their love was pure; therefore, any expression of that love including sex was also pure and could not even remotely be viewed as adultery.

The outraged husband sued, and the case of Tilton versus Beecher came to court trial in City Court, Brooklyn, before Chief Justice Joseph Neilson on 11 January 1875. The trial ended 112 days later, with a disagreement of the jury. For most of that time, the courtroom had been packed and vendors sold sandwiches, soft drinks, and souvenirs outside of the building. Foreign ambassadors, future presidents, congressmen, senators, judges, millionaires, and politicians packed the city court.

In the pre-trial period, Beecher had written numerous letters about the affair, but he denied everything once on the stand. Elizabeth was not allowed to testify.

At the start of the trial, Elizabeth had left her husband and children and supported herself on the interest from a $10,000 trust fund which had been established for her by some of Beecher's friends. She opened a small private school and leaders of the Plymouth Church promised to send their children there, but they reneged and the school failed. Beecher, while his political aspirations were squelched, became only more popular as a preacher.

Over the next twenty years, Elizabeth became a recluse. She died in 1897 and was buried in the same cemetery as Beecher.

Tompkins, Mary Arthur (1897–1956) Among the many women who pursued playwright George Bernard Shaw, and the many whose attentions he sought, Mary "Molly" Tompkins was the one woman whose passion and ardor frightened him. Admittedly the aggressor, Molly, whose stage experience to that point consisted of twelve weeks in a walk-on part in the Ziegfeld Follies, and her sculptor husband left the United States and arrived in London with their two-year-old son in 1921. They hoped to find Shaw and to arrange to found a Shavian theater in Georgia.

Once they met him, the sixty-five-year-old Shaw made twenty-four-year-old Mary his cause, and took on the role of Professor Higgins to his American Eliza. Shaw renamed her "Molly," a name which he decided had more character. Like his famous character, Professor Higgins in *My Fair Lady*, Shaw gave Molly diction lessons and critiqued the way she talked, walked, dressed, and put on makeup. Upset with what he called her "Sarah of Red Gulch" manner, he provided her with advice on etiquette and courtesy. In the process of remaking Molly, he also began to fall in love with her.

Due to Shaw's influence, Molly acquired several stage roles in the three years after they first met, before finally becoming tired of the stage and protesting that she now wanted to experience life. She first tried to coerce Shaw into letting her play Eliza, but he refused and told her that she had at least five long years of training and preparation before she would be ready. The impatient Molly then insisted that her husband join her in traveling to Italy, for she was "sick and tired" of London. The long-suffering Mr. Tompkins, who had just established his sculpting studio agreed without a fight, and they went to live on an island in the middle of Lake Maggiore.

At age seventy, Shaw accepted Molly's invitation to visit, his wife in tow. Shaw and Molly took long walks, swam in the ocean, and had picnics while Charlotte stiffly looked the other way. After returning to their hotel one afternoon, Shaw found a pair of powerful binoculars on the terrace outside his suite, a sharp reminder that his wife was watching. Molly flaunted Shaw's interest in her whenever his wife was around, and that finally ended the affair.

After two years Shaw ended this last love affair of his life, telling Molly that he was through with everyone and had nothing left but his "eternal genius." Almost twenty years later, forty-eight-year-old Molly contacted Shaw after she had lived a precarious life searching for love but never quite finding what she desired, and asked to visit him. His wife had died two years before, and Shaw was now eighty-nine years old. He adamantly refused to see his former mistress, and he protested that he wouldn't give up his peace of mind to live with anyone on earth.

Tz'u Hsi (1835–1908) Born Yehonala in Peking in 1835, the woman known to Western history as the Empress Dowager, Tz'u

Hsi, was the concubine of Chinese Celestial Emperor Hsien Feng. She entered his court in 1850, when she was only fifteen years old. Although Hsien Feng had other concubines, Tz'u Hsi must have exerted a special influence over the Emperor because he recognized their son T'ung Chih as his own, a rare move which established him as heir to the Celestial Throne although his parents never married.

When Emperor Hsien Feng died in 1861, six-year-old T'ung Chih ascended the throne, and his mother assumed power over China as regent. For the next fourteen years Tz'u Hsi ruled China through her son, then organized government and popular support for her handpicked successor to the throne, her nephew Kuang Hsu, whom she felt she could control. Tz'u Hsi continued to rule China through Kuang Hsu until 1898 when he decided to oust her from court and to take over the throne for himself. In his zeal for reform, Kuang Hsu rushed to introduce western technology and a range of reforms. His "Hundred Days' Reform" angered the tradition-oriented nobility and government. Tz'u Hsi took advantage of his unpopular move, effecting a bloodless coup and resuming her power, backed strongly by the tradition-minded nobles.

The new period of rule taxed Tz'u Hsi's political acumen as she faced the issue of foreign encroachment. As before, the Empress surrounded herself with experienced advisers to aid her in achieving her ambitions. In 1899, faced with widespread concern regarding territorial encroachment by foreign powers, Tz'u Hsi secretly engineered and supported the Chinese nationalist uprising against all representatives of alien powers, other foreigners, and Chinese Christians. The crafty Empress officially denounced the Boxers, a secret society which began its campaign of terror against Christian missionaries, then openly stormed the foreign legations in Peking. In secret, the ruler, with numerous other Chinese nobles, supported the Boxer Rebellion which fought back against the economic and political exploitation suffered at the hands of Japan and various Western powers and the humiliating military defeats of the earlier Opium War with Great Britain in 1840–1842.

After the Boxer Rebellion was put down in 1900, T'zu Hsi set her mind to creating a modern China. She put aside her former conservatism and encouraged many of the reforms begun earlier by Kuang Hsu and which she had formerly condemned. She also promised to grant China a constitutional government by 1916. She died before she could keep that promise.

V

Vanderbilt, Cornelius (1843–1899) See **Claflin, Tennessee.**

Velez, Lupe (1908–1944) Maria Guadalupe Velez de Villalabos was born in the village of San Luis Potosi, Mexico. After several years of convent education, she went to Mexico City to work and to study dance. By the age of sixteen, she had earned a role in *The Gaucho* which starred Douglas Fairbanks, Sr.

In her sixteen years in Hollywood, she was determined to shock. Her uninhibited public behavior, which included throwing her dress up to reveal her bare bottom, created scandal. Her tempestuous love affairs and violent temper made people approach her with caution. John Gilbert was her first Hollywood lover, followed soon after by Gary Cooper. She was Cooper's mistress for several months, during which she kept him on an emotional rollercoaster. After she moved on, Cooper reportedly had a nervous breakdown.

She married former Olympic swimming champion and Tarzan of the silver screen, Johnny Weissmuller, in 1933 but their marriage was filled with constant separations then reconciliations, as well as public fights. They divorced in 1938, at a time when Lupe's career had begun to fail. As she obtained fewer roles, Lupe began a mad succession of indiscriminate brief affairs with literally any man who would come to her bed. She spent money carelessly and soon was heavily in debt.

Her final lover was Harold Ramand, who in 1944 was twenty-seven to Lupe's thirty-six. The affair followed the usual course, and the couple fought constantly, living together only briefly in a wild and tantrum-filled relationship. When Lupe discovered that she was three months pregnant, she demanded that Ramand marry her, for she was a devout Catholic and didn't believe in abortion. He agreed, as long as she would sign a legal document which stated that she knew that marriage was only to give the baby a name. Ramand reneged on the agreement when Lupe continued her volatile abusive behavior toward him, and she became desperate and saw death as the better alternative to having an illegitimate child or an abortion.

Resolved to commit suicide, she filled her North Rodeo Drive home with gardenias and tuberoses, then had dinner with two close friends who shared her love of spicy food. After they left, she decorously dressed in blue silk pajamas, wrote her suicide note, swallowed seventy-five Seconal tablets, and lay down on her bed to die.

She was discovered the next morning by her maid. The pills made her nauseous before they could take their effect, and Lupe went to the bathroom to vomit. There, she slipped on the floor, and plunged headfirst into the toilet bowl where she drowned.

Victor Emmanuel II, King of Italy (1820–1878) See **Oldini, Virginia**.

Victoria, Queen (1819–1901) As England's longest-ruling monarch, she gave her name to an age which is viewed as stuffy, straitlaced, and repressed. Pictures of her usually depict the weighty widow, dressed and draped in black, with a stern frown on her large and chinless face. Yet, earlier, Alexandrina Victoria had been an attractive, very thin woman. She ascended the throne of England in 1837, married her cousin Prince Albert, became widowed at the age of forty-two, then lived unmarried for forty years. After Albert's death, she commissioned a large number of statues of the Prince Consort and attempted to create an "Albertropolis."

She also took as her "personal indoors" servant a man named John Brown, a Scot five years her junior, who became so intimate with the queen that her daughters referred disparagingly to him as "Mama's lover." Others called him "the Queen's stallion." Although much of the uproar may have been only gossip, her relationship with Brown led to the servants nicknaming him "the Great court Favorite" while disgruntled nobles and even scandal sheets of the day called him "the Shadow Behind the Throne" and "The Master of the Queen." Certainly the freedoms which Victoria permitted Brown to take encouraged such speculation that she may have taken him as a lover. In 1868, a pamphlet circulated throughout London which purported to tell the story of "Mrs. Brown," the English synonym for the queen, and which claimed that the two had been morganatically married in a secret ceremony.

Palace insiders further wondered when the Queen began to add framed photos of Brown to the tables already cluttered with photos of Albert. They were horrified when, in the mid 1870s, she sought to have privately printed a book entitled *Leaves from Our Life in the Highlands*. The book made a hero of Brown and it details how Brown slept, what he ate, and how he felt about life. Her already-miffed children, who were forced to go through Brown to get to their mother, protested her intentions and the book was put aside.

Victoria makes numerous references to John Brown in her journal before Albert's death, for Brown was her favorite Highland servant who would guide the royal couple, lift the queen onto her horse, and hike with them when Victoria visited her estates at Balmoral to escape the rigors of rule. Later, however, her children became aware of Brown's true importance when she ordered a bronze statue of him erected on the estate. Prince Albert was not the only man whom she honored and mourned in this manner.

Others in her court also recognized the good effect which Brown had on the widowed Victoria, who for the rest of her life wore black dresses cut in the fashion of 1861, the year in which Albert died.

He was brought from Balmoral to Windsor during the winter of

1864–1865 to attend her whenever she went riding or walking outdoors. Her journal praises him, calling him intelligent, and "so unlike any ordinary servant." Observers noted that the queen demurred to whatever Brown suggested, and she trusted him completely. In 1867 when alerted while at Balmoral that Irish radicals had threatened to kidnap and assassinate her, she continued to insist that Brown alone accompany her as they drove and walked around the estates without added guards. More than one biographer has described Brown as having "looked good in a kilt," and suggested that might be more likely what Victoria appreciated about the man, rather than his homey wit and outspoken comments. By 1865 Victoria had made Brown her personal "indoors" servant. He freely entered her bedroom without knocking, enjoyed lavish public and private praise from his queen, and appears frequently in her journals. By mid-1865, palace gossip referred to Victoria as "Mrs. Brown" and government officials wondered how long the story could be kept from the newspapers. Brown often voiced his desire, to both servants and the queen's children, to stay with Victoria and take care of her till the end of his life. Such complete loyalty and devotion earned him power, and other servants and many courtiers knew that Brown's recommendation could mean a job or promotion and that his disapproval could end their chances.

Once the press noticed Brown, cartoons and quips appeared which poked fun at "Mrs. Brown" and her coarse Highlander. She had remained secluded from the public for several years during which, the papers joked, her Highlander directed government for the invisible sovereign. Whatever the truth, Victoria finally began to attend official functions but demanded that Brown always be at her side during military reviews and other outdoor appearances. While Brown was alive, Victoria made only rare trips abroad because Brown hated such travel.

For eighteen-and-a-half years, Brown attended the queen daily. He died in 1883, after insisting that he be allowed to attend Victoria although he was weak with fever from a streptoccocal inflammation. Victoria was distraught, crying that she had lost her "dearest best friend" and she ordered that a nearly column-long obituary be placed in *The Times*. Her lamenting words for Brown echoed much of the same sentiment which she had expressed for Albert, twenty-two years earlier. Soon after the funeral, Victoria commissioned Sir Joseph Boehm to create a statue of Brown at Balmoral, and Lord Tennyson was asked to create the inscription. Further, she ordered that Brown's room at Windsor be kept forever as it had been while he was alive and that the maid place a flower on his pillow each day.

Villiers, Barbara, Lady Castlemaine, Duchess of Cleveland (1640–1709) Barbara Villiers' amorous career began in Cromwell's Puritan England when she was sixteen and passionately in love with Lord Chesterfield. Defying convention, she frequently visited Chesterfield at his lodgings in Lincoln's Inn Fields. The affair continued with no hint of marriage, so Barbara Villiers looked in a more promising direction to Cavalier Roger Palmer, whom she married at the age of eighteen. She remained officially married until his death forty-six years later, but her affairs with Chesterfield and others progressed.

Plots to restore Charles II abounded among the Royalist Cavaliers, and Barbara was in the thick of the excitement. When her cousin, a high-ranking Cavalier named Sir Allan Broderick, needed a reliable messenger to go to the exiled king's Brussels court, he asked Barbara because her husband was badly needed in England. Not only did she deliver the message, but she also delivered her considerable charms to the king. Charles II was so pleased with her that he summoned Barbara to his bed in Whitehall on the first night of his Restoration to the throne, with no thought to how her husband might react. On that night, or one soon after, Barbara became pregnant for the first time.

The king guaranteed the future of all of his children by Barbara by making her titular husband Roger Palmer an Irish earl, but the true beneficiaries were revealed when Charles stated that succession to the title was restricted to children borne by Barbara. The title was granted for the earldom of Castlemaine, and Barbara Villiers became Lady Castlemaine. He gave her seven children the surname of Fitzroy.

Despite his fascination with Barbara, Charles contracted a political marriage with the Infanta Catherine of Braganza in 1662. Pregnant with the king's second child who would be named Charles, and aware of her unofficial role in the king's life, Barbara chose to

Barbara Villiers (NATIONAL PORTRAIT GALLERY)

celebrate the royal wedding in her own way. She ordered that her vast number of underclothes be washed and hung out to dry on the palace grounds in full view.

Charles also wanted to bring Barbara into the palace in an official capacity, as the second most important lady in waiting, the Lady of the Bedchamber. Catherine vehemently refused, gossip abounded, and Roger Palmer legally separated from Barbara and declared himself no longer responsible for her debts. Barbara continued to welcome Charles into her bed and to satisfy his sexual desires. After months of threats and bullying, Charles prevailed and the queen was forced to welcome into her home and coach her husband's mistress. The "Royal Whore," as Barbara was openly known, seems to have been sexually insatiable.

Lady Castlemaine's apartments in Hampton Court served as a salon in which intelligent men discussed politics, affairs of state, culture, and personalities with their king. Although pregnant yearly from 1661 through 1665, Lady Castlemaine exerted great influence on the king and court politics. In the autumn of 1663 she converted to Catholicism, slyly indicating that this was the only way in which she could remain the king's mistress in title. She was the means by which many courtiers gained the ear of the king.

When Barbara saw that she had begun to lose her grip on Charles, she worked to guarantee her future by manuevering to have a close friend, Baptist May, appointed as Keeper of the Privy Purse. May routed funds and grants to Lady Castlemaine and her wealth accrued.

As the palace coffers emptied so that England could not even afford to send its navy to sea, King Charles II spent thirty thousand pounds to clear Lady Castlemaine's gambling debts and to cover her random purchases of jewels.

The king's attention to Lady Castlemaine waned as a number of rivals, particularly Moll Davis and Nell Gwyn, came on the scene. But Lady Castlemaine maintained her political influences and France's Louis XIV courted her opinion when attempting to forge an alliance with England.

While Lady Castlemaine enjoyed affairs with numerous men while she held the king enthralled, she sought to keep him ignorant of her dalliances. Her secret was almost exposed when twenty-seven-year-old civil servant John Ellis could not resist boasting openly of having been served like a king by the royal whore. Lady Castlemaine retaliated swiftly and directly. She hired several men to waylay Ellis and to castrate him.

As she became older, she paid for men's favors. Among her later lovers were an actor, a rope dancer, and a charming young lover who bilked her of one hundred thousand pounds and then left her. She was forty-four when she took up with a thirty-four-year-old part-time actor and highwayman/robber, Cardonell Goodmen, whose acquaintances called him "Scum." Their relationship lasted six years, during which she gave birth to a son. This relationship soon died.

When Roger Palmer died in 1705, sixty-four-year-old Lady Castlemaine declared herself finally free, then promptly began an association with "Beau" Fielding, an adventurer and opportunist who was ten years her junior. Her new husband beat her to obtain money from her and he tried to kill her when he learned that she had told her sons and grandsons about her ill treatment. The one-time mistress of a king was reduced to screaming "Murder!" out of an open window as Feilding aimed a blunderbuss at her, then shot randomly at passersby. Barbara's sons obtained legal intervention and the marriage was anulled and Feilding thrown into Newgate Prison.

As she neared the end of her life, the once beautiful and powerful woman developed dropsy which made her body swell hideously. Lady Castlemaine died in 1709 at her grandson's home with only memories of her royal paramour.

Voltaire (François Marie Arouet) (1694–1778) See **Chatelet, Emilie Du.**

Walewska, Maria (1789–1817) Born Maria Laczinska in Poland of impoverished nobility, she was married at sixteen to a wealthy sixty-eight-year-old landowner Count Anastasio Colonna Walewski, who owned a great castle and who had already been a widower twice. The unhappy young woman sacrificed her youth to save her five brothers and sisters and widowed mother from starvation, and the generous yet morose nobleman not only paid the family debts but he also restored the family estate and provided her brother with an education in France.

A year after her marriage, Maria met the man who was to be the liberator of her beloved Poland and conqueror of her heart. Napoleon Bonaparte arrived in Warsaw to gather his forces in readiness to fight the Russians and the Austrians. During his triumphal march through the city, he spotted Maria in the crowd and handed her a bouquet. Later, after driving back the Russians, he returned to Warsaw and made inquiries to learn Maria's identity and to pursue her.

After a formal ball given by Polish patriots during which

Countess Marie Walewska (BETTMANN ARCHIVE)

Napoleon tried to attract Maria's attention, he sent her notes professing his ardor, but Maria refused to answer him. When this didn't work, he hinted broadly that she could influence the extent to which he would defend and work for a liberated Poland, and he let his views be known to all the members of Poland's provisional government. Maria was confronted by government representatives who told her that the lives and freedom of twenty million Poles depended upon her. When Maria challenged them that they were asking her to break her marriage vows, she was told that there were sacrifices to be made, however painful they might be.

Maria submitted to the demand and met with Napoleon, who declared his love and spoke of his plans to make Poland independent. Although she escaped from this first meeting untouched, Maria received a bouquet of diamonds the next morning with a more strongly worded message that demanded her appearance at dinner. She did not answer the note, but she unhappily attended his dinner. Afterward, Napoleon took her to his private quarters and raped her, then apologetically asked her to spend the night. The night turned into months, during which time Maria became pregnant but miscarried. In 1810, however, she gave birth to a son by Napoleon, whom she named Alexandre Walewski. In her time with Napoleon, she grew to admire and to love him, despite the brutal beginning of their relationship. She willingly stayed with him as his mistress, caring for their child.

In the following four years Maria reconciled with her husband and returned to her home. She had become famous as Napoleon's Polish wife, and as the woman who had saved her homeland through her sacrifice. She met Napoleon only twice in the years which followed. After her husband's death, she married a distant cousin of Napoleon's, a French officer named General d'Ornano. During her year of marriage, Maria gave birth to a son before dying in 1817 at the age of twenty-eight. Reportedly, she called for Napoleon with her last breath.

Walkinshaw, Clementina (1719–1802) Born the youngest of ten daughters of her father's third marriage, Clementina Walkinshaw was named after Bonnie Prince Charles' mother because her family had long been supporters of the Stuart cause. Fate brought the Pretender to the throne of England and Clementine together first in Glasgow, Scotland, during Charles' unsuccessful military campaign, then in Bannockburn where Clementina was chosen to be his hostess and his nurse through a bout of influenza. She was a plain-looking virgin at twenty-six, one year older than Charles. After he recuperated and left Bannockburn, he extracted from Clementina a promise that she would come to him should he ever send word that he needed her.

Clementina entered a convent and become a canoness due to family influence. She had been there six years when Charles sent for her to meet him in Paris in 1752. His letters warned that they were to be reunited secretly and that she must keep her secret or risk his eternal displeasure. Clementina agreed readily, and they finally consummated their relationship and set up housekeeping as man and wife. A year later, when Clementina was thirty-three, their daughter Charlotte was born and registered in Liège under fictitious parentage. From that point, the relationship was rocky. Money was scarce for the Pretender to the throne and Clementina nagged constantly regarding her needs. They fought publicly, shouting loudly and drawing attention to their noisy rows. Acquaintances tried not to notice Clementina's bruises and the public ill treatment.

Less than a month after their child was born, Charles tried to evict Clementina, but she fought back and declared that he would have to keep her if he wanted to keep their child. Charles relented, but the brawling continued.

Clementina endured this ill treatment for eight years, then appealed to Charles' father James for help. The older man arranged for Clementina and Charlotte to escape by coach to a convent at Meaux, France, and James supported her. Charles' older brother Henry continued the support after James' death.

When Charlotte was nearly twenty Clementina arrived in Rome, only weeks after Charles' marriage to Princess Louise of Stolberg, with the aim of obtaining a dowry for Charlotte whose future was dim as an illegitimate girl with no money and future prospects. Charles told intermediaries that he could offer Charlotte a place in his household but her mother was to be sent away. Clementina returned with Charlotte to Paris.

Clementina lived to the age of eighty-three on the small pension, never increased, which had been established many years before by her brother-in-law. She died of malnutrition after a difficult and pain-filled life, but she always spoke with respect and affection of her one-time love.

Walter, Lucy (1630–1658) Welsh by birth, Lucy Walter had been brought to the Hague as the fourteen-year-old mistress of a colonel in Cromwell's New Army, who later gave her to his brother Robert, the groom of the bedchamber to young Charles. At eighteen she met the future King Charles II of England, who was the same age, when he was visiting his sister and brother-in-law at the Hague in 1648 while finalizing plans for a joint Scot and English assault to regain the English throne. Charles requisitioned her for himself and she became his public mistress and known as Mrs. Barlow. Their son, James, was born the following April.

Unlike Charles' later mistresses, Lucy had a strong and violent personality, and she had no intention of being discarded. She extracted a verbal promise from Charles that he would marry her and legitimize their son, although he remained preoccupied with winning back the throne. Although Charles asked Lucy to remain behind while he went about the business of building support to reclaim his throne, she secretly followed him and monitored his activities. When she joined him at Ghent, the Spanish Governor refused to allow him to stay at the official residence because of Lucy's presence. The Scots were equally prudish about the presence of "Mrs. Barlow" and Charles pushed her far into the background.

By 1757 Charles had tired of Lucy and used intermediaries to arrange a pension and to negotiate custody of his son. Lucy had neglected the boy's education and was the mistress of several men who contributed to her support at the same time that Charles was also supporting his son. When Lucy set foot in England, Charles vindictively had her and her entourage detained. Lucy was imprisoned for a short while in the Tower before being exiled.

She continued to move in and out of Charles' life, always dangling their son as the temptation which led Charles to meet with her. In 1657, Charles learned of Lucy's involvement in a new scandal. Estranged from her earlier lover Colonel Howard, Lucy had become the mistress of a young Welsh cousin whom she encouraged to challenge Howard when he reappeared on the scene. The colonel refused to fight over Lucy and the young lover stabbed him, then escaped.

Friends of Charles decided to end his embarrassment and they worked to have Lucy imprisoned for debt and her son taken away from her. When the constable appeared, however, Lucy ran screaming into the street and passersby and neighbors tried to help her. He suffered further embarrassment when she threatened to produce certain letters which would prove that they had been married and that James was his legitimate son. Charles reacted even more harshly and had James forcibly removed from Lucy, who continued to try to find him. Finally, she followed the trail to Paris where she died of a venereal disease in 1658.

Warens, Louise Eleonore de (1700–1762) Madame Louise Eleonore de Warens was born in Vevey, Switzerland, and married the Baron de Warens at a young age. She converted from Protestantism to Catholicism after her marriage. She later fled Switzerland with her gardener's son, Claude Anet, after stripping her husband of all his money and as much jewelry as she could carry. Once in Savoy she acted as an unofficial Catholic missionary with the goal of converting young Protestant males. This ambition was fueled in part by the encouragement of King Victor of Savoy, whose protection she had acquired and who engaged her in political espionage against Protestant forces. One of her most famous converts was the French philosopher Jean-Jacques Rousseau, raised a Calvinist in Geneva, whom she provided with the education and training which developed him into a philosopher, a man of letters, and a musician. She was twelve years his senior and his benefactress, and they lived together for ten years.

The fifteen-year-old Rousseau began living with her in 1728 after he had escaped from his apprenticeship with a clockmaker. When Rousseau arrived at Mme. Warens' door, he was uneducated and penniless. She took him in and hired him as her steward, and she also began his education. His benefactress was an intelligent and energetic woman who was also familiar with the business world, although her silk stocking factory failed. She was well-read and possessed a keenly analytic mind. Five years after she had been like a mother to him, the two became lovers Before she became the young man's mistress, Mme. Warens gave him eight days to decide if he was willing to accept her conditions. She made it clear to the twenty-year-old lover that he would have to share her with the garden man/man of affairs, Claude Anet, who was already her lover. At the suggestion, so says Rousseau in *Confessions*, he feared that she was suggesting a ménage à trois, but his mind was soon set at ease. She just wanted to be mistress to both men – on her own schedule.

The arrangement worked well for ten years, during which time she supported Rousseau and his wild spending. She also formed the thinking of this philosopher, who would later rival Voltaire in prominence. She may have provided him the inspiration for his belief in man's natural goodness through her experiences as a student of the Protestant Pietists who taught her their sentimental views of human purity when she was a child in Bern.

He called her "Maman" out of respect, and perhaps as a substitute for his own mother who died in childbirth, and notes in his *Confessions* that he often felt as if he was committing incest. Finally, the garden man passed away, and Mme. Warens acquired a younger, more virile replacement whom she decided also eliminated her need for Rousseau, but she continued to remain his advisor and friend until her death.

Washington, George (1732–1799) See **Fairfax, Sally Cary.**

Weekly, Frieda von Richthofen (1879–1956) Frieda von Richthofen was born in Metz, Germany, the sister of Martin von Richthofen, "The Red Baron," the legendary World War I pilot. She was married to Ernest Weekly and had three children by him when she met D.H. Lawrence. She was thirty-six, six years older than the starving poet and writer. She soon left her husband and children – whom she sorely missed – and was Lawrence's mistress for two years before they married.

Frieda satisfied Lawrence's dual need for a passionate and lustful physical relationship combined with a moderate form of the nurturing adoration which he had received from his mother, whose smothering attentions came under heavy fire in most of his work. For

Frieda, Lawrence provided the promise of the unexpected, an existence directly opposite to the staid and respectable upper-middle-class life which she had always lived. Together they attempted to live out Lawrence's philosophy that sex was a motivating force in life which produced a state of being that was almost religious in nature. During their years together, Lawrence produced such novels as *Sons and Lovers* and *Lady Chatterley's Lover*.

In reality, however, their sexual life was less than perfect, especially in later years. Although Frieda continued to play the role of nurturer, by 1926 when they were living in Taos, New Mexico, on a ranch owned by American heiress Mabel Dodge Luhan, both Frieda and Lawrence were having not-so-discreet affairs with members of the informal writers' colony which had formed there. Frieda may have begun a casual affair in 1926 or 1928 with Angelo Ravagli, who became her husband after Lawrence died, although she continued to support his work.

When tuberculosis finally took the life of D.H. Lawrence in 1930, Frieda mourned him deeply, and she became the executor of his estate. She remarried a few years later, but her memoir, *Not I But the Wind* spills over with respect, admiration, and love for the man whose passion she could not resist and for whom she gave up everything.

Wells, H. G. (1866–1946) See **Sanger, Margaret; West, Rebecca.**

Wesley, John (1703–1791) See **Hopkey, Sophia Christiana.**

West, Rebecca (1892–1983) Born Cicily Isabel Fairfield Andrews, this English novelist, critic, and journalist took her pseudonym from Henrik Ibsen's play *Rosmersholm.* An ardent feminist and Fabian socialist, Rebecca began writing while in her twenties and later achieved literary recognition for her novels as well as for her nonfiction.

At the age of twenty Rebecca became the mistress of writer H.G. Wells who claimed that he had finally found his ideal woman, someone who would stimulate him both sexually and intellectually. He was still married to the woman whom he married the year in which Rebecca was born, and he remained married long after

Rebecca was no longer his mistress. Rebecca, then on the staff of a small feminist magazine, met Wells after she wrote an unfavorable review of his book *Marriage*. They moved in together, and their son Anthony was born two years later.

Rebecca was Wells' equal in intelligence, wit, and imagination, and her youthful ardor more than matched that of the forty-six-year-old Wells. Passionately in love with Rebecca, Wells said that no other woman had ever captured his attention and desire so completely. He often placed sketches of a panther and a jaguar at the top of the letters, signifying their equal strength in the relationship. Rebecca enjoyed the traditional aspects of mistresshood, but she also learned substantially from Wells who became a mentor to her fledgling writing career. Despite Rebecca's fidelity, Wells continued to have outside relationships.

Rebecca tolerated Wells' marriage, and she accepted his wife's occasional visits to their home. What she couldn't accept was to have her name dragged through the newspapers when another of Wells' lovers, Hedwig Gatternigg, tried to kill herself in the flat which Rebecca shared with Wells. She wasn't home at the time of the incident, but Wells' wife found the woman and had her taken to a hospital.

This incident was the death knell to the relationship which had been slowly dying as Rebecca garnered more attention as a writer. His own career flagging, Wells showed indifference to her success. They parted in 1922, and Rebecca never married. An ardent feminist, her works are devoid of sexual prejudice and range over fiction, reportage, and literary criticism and include *The Judge* (1922), *St. Augustin* (1933), *The Thinking Reed* (1936), *Black Lamb and Grey Falcon* (1942), *The Meaning of Treason* (1947), *A Train of Powder* (1955), *The Court and the Castle* (1958), and *The Birds Fall Down* (1966). She became a Dame Commander of the British Empire in 1959.

White, Stanford (1853–1906) See **Thaw, Evelyn Nesbit.**

Wilhelm, Crown Prince of Germany (1859–1941) See **Mata Hari.**

William IV, King of England (1765–1837) See **Jordan, Dorothea.**

Wolff, Toni (1888–1953) Toni Wolff first approached Carl Jung, the creator of analytical psychology, as a patient in 1910, then later stayed with him as mistress and professional equal for forty-three years.

Elegant and aristocratic in appearance, she offered a distinct contrast to Jung's wife, Emma, whom he had married in 1903. Toni was thirteen years younger than her mentor, and Jung struggled to find a way in which he could create a peaceful triangle in which he could maintain his marriage and still have Toni in his life. Despite his wife's objections, Jung insisted that Toni become a friend of the family and she became a regular guest at the family Sunday dinners.

Emma remained jealous of the arrangement, but Jung continued his relationship with Toni, spending long hours at her apartment then returning to his wife to talk about where he had been. He later developed professional theories which were intended to justify his triangular living arrangement, depicting himself as a "many-faceted gem" who had to look outside of marriage to attain satisfaction when the "simple cube," which he viewed his wife to be, was inadequate.

When Jung nearly had a breakdown in 1913 (which he later called a "confrontation with his consciousness" in his writings) which took several years to work through, Toni was present and provided valuable assistance in helping Jung to get in touch with feelings and she aided him in searching out and understanding his female nature (*anima*). He later spoke of her as his inspiration, while Emma remained the steady rock in his life.

Toni, Emma, and Jung remained in this triangle for nearly forty years, during which both women became practicing analysts. Toni went on to develop sound original theories related to female functioning.

In the late 1940s Toni demanded that Jung divorce his wife and finally legalize their union. She moved out of Carl's home and into her own apartment which Jung criticized as being all cold marble with the study of a dictator. He refused to leave Emma and asked that Toni return to the old arrangement. She declined.

Despite her success as an analyst, Toni Wolff found life alone to be unbearable. She began to drink and smoke heavily, and she remained heartbroken over her lost lover. In 1953 she died alone at the age of sixty-four.

Wollstonecraft, Mary (1759–1797) Author of the feminist tract *A Vindication of the Rights of Women*, Mary Wollstonecraft decided early in life that she wanted no part of marriage, which she called "legalized prostitution," nor did she ever want to be dependent upon someone else. She had been forced as a child to tolerate her father's drunken rages, and she often protected her mother from her father's blows. Her beloved sister Eliza was locked into an unhappy marriage, and Mary helped her to escape by providing financial assistance.

In her writings, she advocated full social and sexual equality for women with men, as well as full educational rights, views which shocked people of her time. Physically attractive, she was slender and tall, with long eyelashes, auburn hair, and seductive hazel eyes. She was also intellectually sharp and engaging. At the age of thirty-three she met American frontiersman and writer Captain Gilbert Imlay in Paris. Tall, lean, and confident, he was Mary's first lover and she passionately gave herself to him. They lived together for a year before their daughter Fanny was born, during which time Imlay often traveled and Mary wrote long, rhapsodizing love letters which gushed with her love. After the baby came, Mary learned that Imlay was having an affair with an actress in London, and she attempted suicide by jumping from a bridge over the Thames.

Two years later in April 1796 she had recovered her self-esteem and decided to meet with radical philosopher William Godwin, whom she had met five years previously. She soon became his mistress, and both denounced marriage as being confining and enslaving. Although they maintained separate residences, they met frequently and sent notes to each other constantly.

Mary bloomed in this new romance, and wrote that she saw a physical change in her features because of her new-found pleasure. Seven months after she became his mistress, Mary learned that she was pregnant. Despite their ideals, the two were married in March 1797, but they continued to live apart. Their daughter, the future Mary Shelley, wife of the poet and author of *Frankenstein*, was born five months later. The birth was mishandled, and Mary developed puerperal fever. She died at the age of thirty-eight, ten days after her daughter's birth.

Wu Ze Tian (623–705) The first woman ever to rule China, Wu Ze Tian began her life in the Chinese court as the favored concubine of Emperor Tai-tsung. She was known as a highly cultured woman of good family whose charm overpowered the emperor's defenses, but her later political actions prove her to have also been a ruthless and cruel woman.

Astute in her realization that the emperor would not replace his wife with her, Wu Ze Tian singled out for her favors his son Tai Zong, the successor to the throne, and bewitched him with her beauty. The two were married, and Tai Zong reluctantly ascended the throne in 650. Wu was enthusiastic in her role as wife to a very weak ruler who suffered from ill health and who more than willingly turned over his power to her. She ran the government until his death in 683, then she had her son Chung-tsung made Imperial Emperor and she continued her reign. When Chung appeared unsuitable for the role of imperial front for Wu, she ousted him and replaced him with a second son, Jui-tsung.

A few years later, in 690, Wu abandoned the role of directing power from behind the scenes as she removed her son from the throne and had herself declared the Emperor Sheng Shen. There was no vocabulary to describe or name an empress because there had never before been a female ruler of China.

Wu's rule angered the nobles, because she doled out bureaucratic positions according to performance on government examinations rather than upon royal connections. Despite numerous attempts on her life, Wu managed to rule successfully for fifteen years with the protection of assasination squads and an extensive spy network which helped to eliminate potential trouble. Her rule ended in 705 when a palace coup removed her from the throne and her eldest son Chung-tsung returned.

The former concubine had enjoyed nearly fifty-five years as Imperial ruler.

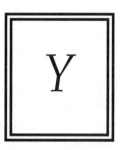

Y

Yezierska, Anzia (1880–1970) Anzia Yezierska was born in Russia of Jewish parents and came to America at the age of thirteen to begin her free life in New York City's Lower East Side. There the family found tenement slums and hard labor rather than streets paved with gold. To escape persecution, Anzia's older brother changed the family surname to Mayer and anglicized his first name to better fit in. Thus, Anzia Yezierska became "Hattie Mayer" for the next twenty years.

Anzia was physically striking, with flame-red hair, violet-blue eyes, and creamy white skin which drew attention to her. An emotionally volatile woman of thirty-seven when she first met John Dewey, she contrasted sharply with the gray-haired and bespectacled appearance of the fifty-nine-year-old educator who was the prototype of the New England establishment intellectual. The two fell deeply in love upon first meeting, and the two years of their affair opened new worlds for both. As mistress to John Dewey, Anzia entered the world of mainstream America, pushing aside the barriers of ethnicity, class, and education. She had finally arrived and joined the world of native-born Americans.

For Dewey, life with Anzia meant not only a life of passionate intensity but he was also introduced to the immigrant world to which he had so long been only an outsider. He wrote love poetry to Anzia, as well as the poetry of regrets, which was hidden throughout his office and not published until years after his death in 1952. His marriage and children weighed heavily on his mind, and terms of imprisonment and shackles recur throughout the poems. Although Anzia confided in friends the possibility that Dewey might leave his wife, there doesn't seem to have been much possibility of that.

Despite her feelings of inadequacy due to her lack of formal education, Anzia later forged a successful career as a writer of fiction and achieved fame on her own after breaking with Dewey. Dewey was a coward in ending the affair, and he simply withdrew from his mistress with no explanation and only the request that she return his letters. In 1919, Dewey sailed for Japan with his wife and did not return until 1921, when Anzia had achieved fame for her writing. Although Dewey avoided all contact and mention of the relationship, Anzia remained obsessed with the affair for the rest of her life, creating thinly veiled characters, obsessively recreating the affair in novels, and arranging assignments which permitted her to review his books.

As a writer Anzia was hailed as the "queen of the ghetto" and a "sweatshop Cinderella." After a stint in Hollywood as a scenario writer, Anzia returned to New York to teach writing at night and to take any writing job offered. An early book, *Red Ribbon on a White Horse* was resurrected for publication in 1950, with an introduction by poet W.H. Auden. The success of the book gave her new-found respect, and she was a steady reviewer of books for *The New York Times* throughout the 1950s. Anzia's health failed in the 1960s, and she died outside of Los Angeles in 1970.

Z

Zoe (?–1050) Of royal pedigree, Zoe used her considerable powers of attraction to eventually become a powerful Byzantine ruler despite the tradition of male rulers for centuries before. As the daughter of Byzantine Emperor Constantine VIII, Zoe could not ascend the throne alone because she was female, so her father found her a suitable husband to rule jointly with her at his death. With the help of a lover, she captured the throne for herself.

Romanus III and Zoe became joint Emperor when Constantine died in 1028, but Zoe was extremely unhappy in her marriage. She took a lover named Michael Paphlagonian at the outset, and he was so enthralled with his royal mistress that he was willing to chance anything for her. In 1034, Zoe and her lover poisoned Romanus and the empress made her lover the new emperor, renaming him Michael IV. Zoe exerted the major power as she ruled from Constantinople while Michael led military campaigns. At her second husband's death in 1041, Zoe made his young nephew, also named Michael, the Emperor Michael V.

The young man was not as manipulable as his uncle, most likely because he was not susceptible to Zoe's sexual wiles, and he immediately put a stop to her attempts to direct his rule. Michael V ordered his soldiers to arrest Zoe and she was incarcerated in a convent on the island of Prinkipo. The maneuver gained him the throne, but he could do little to influence Zoe's many popular friends.

After less than a year, rebellion among the people seemed imminent and the court officials recalled Zoe to calm the populous, and Michael V was mysteriously strangled. Zoe created a triumvirate government by enthroning her sister Theodora as joint empress and through her marriage to an aging adventurer named Constantine. The three ruled the Byzantine empire for eight years, until Zoe's death in 1050.

Born the daughter of an emperor, Zoe desired power which could only be gained through sexual conquest and manipulation, despite her lineage.

References

Andrews, Allen. *The Royal Whore: Barbara Villiers, Countess of Castlemain:* New York: Chilton Book Company, 1970.

Ashdown, Dulcie. *Royal Paramours.* New York: Dorset Press, 1979.

Ashley, Maurice. *Charles II: The Man and the Statesman.* New York: Praeger Publishers, 1971.

Astor, Mary. *A Life on Film.* New York: Delacorte Press, 1967.

Ayling, Stanley. *John Wesley.* Nashville, TN: Abingdon Press, 1979.

Babcock, Bernie. *The Heart of George Washington.* Philadelphia: J.B. Lippincott Co., 193.

Bagland, Eileen. *Mary Shelley.* New York: Appleton-Century Crofts, Inc., 1959.

Bair, Deirdre. *Simone De Beauvoir.* New York: Summit Books, 1990.

Baldwin, Charles C. *Stanford White.* New York: Dodd, Mead and Co., 1931.

Bellamy, Francis Rufus. *The Private Life of George Washington.* New York: Thomas Y. Crowell Co., 1951.

Bernier, Oliver. *Louis the Beloved: The Life of Louis XV.* New York: Doubleday and Co., 1984.

Bishop, John. *Nero: The Man and the Legend.* New York: A.S. Barnes and Co., 1964.

Blair, Fredrika. *Isadora: Portrait of the Artist as a Woman.* New York: McGraw-Hill Book Co., 1986.

Blunden, Margaret. *The Countess of Warwick: A Biography.* London: Cassell, 1967.

Brombert, Beth Archer. *Cristina: Portrait of a Princess.* New York: Alfred A. Knopf, 1977.

Brough, James. *The Prince and the Lily.* New York: Coward, McCann, and Geoghan, Inc., 1975.

Burke, John. *Duet in Diamonds: The Flamboyant Saga of Lillian Russell and Diamond Jim Brady in*

America's Gilded Age. New York: G.P. Putnam's Sons, 1972.

Cannistraro, Philip, and Brian R. Sullivan. *Il Duce's Other Woman*. New York: William Morrow and Company, 1993.

Caro, Robert. *The Years of Lyndon Johnson: The Path to Power*. New York: Alfred A. Knopf, 1982.

Cary, Wilson Miles. *Sally Cary: A Long Hidden Romance of George Washington's Life*. New York: The De Vinne Press, 1919.

Casanova, Giacomo. *History of My Life*. New York: Harcourt Brace Jovanovich Inc., 1967.

Chapman, Hester W. *The Tragedy of Charles II in the Years 1630–1660*. Boston: Little, Brown and Co., 1964.

Cheetham, Nicholas. *Keepers of the Keys: A History of the Popes St. Peter to John Paul II*. New York: Charles Scribner's Sons, 1982.

Collier, Peter, and David Horowitz. *The Fords: An American Epic*. New York: Summit Books, 1987.

Cowles, Virginia. *Gay Monarch: The Life and Pleasures of Edward VII*. New York: Harper and Bros., Publishers, 1956.

Cronin, Vincent. *Louis XIV*. Boston: Houghton-Mifflin Co., 1965.

Crow, Duncan. *The Edwardian Woman*. New York: St. Martin's Press, 1978.

Crow, Duncan. *The Victorian Woman*. New York: Stein and Day, 1972.

Dahlinger, John Cote. *The Secret Life of Henry Ford*. New York: The Bobbs-Merrill Co., Inc., 1978.

Dalby, Liza Crihfield. *Geisha*. Los Angeles: University of California Press, 1983.

Danilova, Alexandra. *Choura: The Memoirs of Alexandra Danilova*. New York: Alfred A. Knopf, 1986.

Darling, Amanda. *Lola Montez*. New York: Stein and Day, Publishers, 1972.

Davies, Marion. *The Times We Had: Life with William Randolph Hearst*. New York: The Bobbs-Merrill Company, Inc., 1975.

Dearbom, Mary V. *Love in the Promised Land: The Story of Anzia Yezierska and John Dewey*. New York: The Free Press, 1988.

De Barbin, Lucy, and Dary Matera. *Are You Lonesome Tonight?* New York: Villard Books, 1987.

Delderfield, R.F. *Napoleon in Love*. New York: Simon and Schuster, 1959.

DeRosa, Peter. *Vicars of Christ: The Dark Side of the Papacy*. New York: Crown Publishers, Inc., 1988.

Ditzion, Sidney. *Marriage, Morals and Sex in America*. New York: Octagon Books, 1969.

Edwards, Samuel. *The Divine Mistress: A Biography of Emilie Du Chatelet*. New York: David McKay Co., Inc., 1970.

Emboden, William. *Sarah Bernhardt*. New York: Macmillan Publishing Co., Inc., 1975.

Erickson, Carolly. *To the Scaffold: The Life of Marie Antoinette*. New York: William Morrow and Co., Inc., 1991.

Erlanger, Rachel. *Lucrezia Borgia*. New York: Hawthorn Books, Inc., 1978.

Ethridge, Willie Snow. *Strange Fires: The True Story of John Wesley's Love Affair in Georgia*. New York: Vanguard Press, Inc., 1971.

Evans, Peter. *Ari: The Life and Times of Aristotle Socrates Onassis*. New York: Summit Books, 1986.

Exner, Judith. *My Story*. New York: Grove Press, 1977.

References

Falkus, Christopher. *The Life and Times of Charles II*. New York: Doubleday & Co., 1972.

Fallon, Ivan. *Billionaire: The Life and Times of Sir James Goldsmith*. Boston: Little, Brown & Company, 1991.

Fay, Bernard. *Franklin the Apostle of Modern Times*. Boston: Little, Brown and Co., 1929.

Forster, Margaret. *The Rash Adventurer: The Rise and Fall of Bonnie Prince Charlie*. New York: Stein and Day, 1973.

Fraser, Antonia. *Royal Charles: Charles II and the Restoration*. New York: Alfred A. Knopf, 1979.

Fraser, Flora. *Emma, Lady Hamilton*. New York: Alfred A. Knopf, 1987.

Fuller, Robert, Jr. *Jubilee Jim The Life of Colonel James Fisk, Jr.* New York: The Macmillan Co., 198.

Gavoty, Bernard. *Frederick Chopin*. Trans. by Martin Sokolinsky. New York: Charles Scribner's Sons, 1977.

Gilot, Françoise. *Life with Picasso*. New York: McGraw Hill Publishers, 1964.

Graham, Sheilah. *Beloved Infidel*. New York: Holt, Rinehart & Co., 1958.

Grant, Michael. *Nero Emperor in Revolt*. New York: American Heritage Press, 1970.

Gray, Madeline. *Margaret Sanger*. New York: Richard Marek Publishing, 1979.

Guiles, Fred Laurence. *Marion Davies*. New York: McGraw-Hill Book Company, 1972.

Gun, Nerin E. *Eva Braun: Hitler's Mistress*. New York: Meredith Press, 1968.

Haldane, Charlotte. *The Last Great Empress of China*. New York: Bobbs Merrill Inc., 1965.

Hallam, Elizabeth, ed. *The Plantagenet Chronicles*. London: Weidenfeld and Nicolson, 1986.

Hamilton, Elizabeth. *The Illustrious Lady Barbara Villiers, Countess of Castlemaine, Duchess of Cleveland*. North Pomfret, VT: Hamish Hamilton, 1980.

Haney, Lynn. *Naked at the Feast: A Biography of Josephine Baker*. New York: Dodd Mead and Co., 1981.

Harris, Jean. *Stranger in Two Worlds*. New York: Macmillan Publishing Co., 1986.

Hecht, Marie B. *Odd Destiny: The Life of Alexander Hamilton*. New York: Macmillan Co., Inc., 1982.

Hemmings, F.W.J. *Alexander Dumas: The King of Romance*. New York: Charles Scribner's Sons, 1979.

Herold, Christopher J. *Mistress to an Age*. New York: Time, Inc., 1958.

Hibben, Paxton. *Henry Ward Beecher: An American Portrait*. New York: The Press of the Readers Club, 1942.

Hibbert, Christopher. *Il Duce: The Life of Benito Mussolini*. Boston: Little, Brown and Co., 1962.

Hogrefe, Pearl. *Tudor Women: Commoners and Queens*. Ames, IA: University of Iowa Press, 1975.

Holmes, George, ed. *The Oxford History of Medieval Europe*. Cambridge: Oxford University Press, 1988.

Holroyd, Michael. *Bernard Shaw: The Pursuit of Power*. New York: Random House, 1989.

Howe, Russell Warren. *Mata Hari: The True Story*. New York: Dodd Mead and Co., 1986.

Huizinga, J.H. *Rousseau: The Self-Made Saint*. New York: Grossman Publishers, 1976.

Hunt, Irma. *Dearest Madame: The Presidents' Mistresses*. New York: McGraw-Hill Book Company, 1978.

Infield, Glenn. *Eva and Adolf*. New York: Grosset and Dunlap, Publishers, 1974

Jackson, Joseph C. *Louise Colet et ses amis litteraires*. New Haven: Yale University Press, 1937.

References

Jackson, Stanley. *Caruso*. New York: Stein and Day, 1972.

Jacob, E.F. *The 5th Century*. Cambridge: Oxford University Press, 1987.

Jenner, Heather. *Royal Wives*. New York: St. Martin's Press, 1967.

Johnson, Stephen. *Later Roman Britain*. London: Routledge and Kegan Paul, 1980.

Johnson, William Weber. *Cortes: Conquering the New World*. Boston: Little Brown & Co., 1975.

Jullian, Philippe, and John Phillips. *The Other Woman: A Life of Violet Trefusis*. Boston: Houghton Mifflin, 1976.

Kaplan, Fred. *Dickens: A Biography*. New York: William Morrow & Co., 1988.

Kelen, Betty. *The Mistresses: Domestic Scandals of the Nineteenth-Century Monarchs*. New York: Random House, 1966.

Klein, Carole. *Aline*. New York: Harper & Row Publishers, 1979.

Knightley, Phillip, and Caroline Kennedy. *An Affair of State*. New York: Atheneum, 1987.

Lacey, Robert. *Ford: The Man and the Machine*. Boston: Little, Brown & Co., 1986.

Lague, David, and Mark Riley. 'True Romance: The Mistress and Her Mogul'. *The Sydney Morning Herald*, April 30, 1999.

Lawner, Lynne. *Lives of the Courtesans*. New York: Rizzoli International Publishing, 1987.

Leamer, Lawrence. *As Time Goes By: The Life of Ingrid Bergman*. New York: Harper & Row, Publishers, 1986.

Le Comte, Edward. *The Notorious Lady Essex*. New York: The Dial Press, 1969.

Levaillant, Maurice. *The Passionate Exiles: Madame de Stael and Madame Recamier*. Trans. by Malcolm Barnes. New York: Farrar, Strauss & Company, 1958.

Levine, Gary. *Anatomy of a Gangster Jack "Legs" Diamond*. New York: A.S. Barnes and Co., Inc., 1979.

Linakis, Stephen. *Diva: The Life and Death of Maria Callas*. Englewood Cliffs, NJ: Prentice-Hall Inc., 1980.

Longstreet, Stephen and Ethel. *Yoshiwara: City of the Senses*. New York: David McKay Company, 1970.

Loomis, Stanley. *The Fatal Friendship*. New York: Richardson & Stierman, 1986.

Lopez, Claude-Anne. *Mon Cher Papa Franklin and the Ladies of Paris*. New Haven: Yale University Press, 1966.

Lorenz, Marita, and Ted Schwarz. *Marita: A Woman's Extraordinary Tale of Love and Espionage from Castro to Kennedy*. New York: Thunder's Mouth Press, 1993.

Lot, Ferdinand. *The End of the Ancient World*. London: Routledge and Kegan Paul, 1966.

Lottman, Herbert. *Flaubert: A Biography*. Boston: Little, Brown and Co., 1989.

Maddox, Brenda. *Nora: The Real Life of Molly Bloom*. Boston: Houghton Mifflin, 1988.

Martin, Ralph G. *Jennie: The Life of Lady Randolph Churchill*. 2 vols. Englewood Cliffs, NJ: Prentice-Hall, Inc., 1969.

Martin, Ralph G., *The Woman He Loved*. New York: Simon and Schuster, 1973.

Masson, Georgina. *Courtesans of the Italian Renaissance*. New York: St. Martin's Press, 1975.

Masters, John. *Casanova*. New York: Bernard Geis Associates, 1969.

Mavor, Elizabeth. *The Virgin Mistress: A Study in Survival*. New York: Doubleday & Company, Inc., 1964.

Mee, Charles L. *The Ohio Gang: The World of Warren G. Harding*. New York: M. Evans and Co., Inc., 1981.

Mitford, Nancy. *Madame de Pompadour*. New York: Random House, 1953.

Monti, Carlotta, with Cy Rice. *W.C. Fields and Me*. Englewood Cliffs, NJ: Prentice-Hall, 1971.

Mooney, Michael MacDonald. *Evelyn Nesbit and Stanford White: Love and Death in the Gilded Age*. New York: William Morrow and Co., 1976.

Moore, George. *Héloïse and Abélard*. New York: Liveright Publishing Corp., 1921.

Morgan, Michael. *Lenin*. London: Edward Arnold Publishing Ltd., 1971.

Morgan, Kay Summersby. *Past Forgetting: My Love Affair with Dwight D. Eisenhower*. New York: Simon and Schuster, 1976.

Morrell, Parker. *Lillian Russell: The Era of Plush*. New York: Random House, 1940.

Nevins, Allan. *Grover Cleveland: A Study in Courage*. New York: Dodd, Mead, and Co., 1932.

Nordham, George W. *George Washington's Women: Mary, Martha, Sally and 146 Others*. Philadelphia: Dorrance and Co., 1977.

Origo, Iris. *The Last Attachment*. New York: Charles Scribner's Sons, 1971.

Ostrovsky, Eric. *Eye of Dawn: The Rise and Fall of Mata Hari*. New York: Macmillan and Co., Inc., 1978.

Pang, May, and Henry Edwards. *Loving John: The Untold Story*. New York: Warner Books, 1983.

Papich, Stephen. *Remembering Josephine*. New York: The Bobbs-Merrill Co.,1976.

Paris, Reine-Marie. *Camille: The Life of Camille Claudel, Rodin's Muse and Mistress*. Trans. by Lillian Tuck. New York: Henry Holt and Co., 1984.

Parker, John. *King of Fools*. New York: St. Martin's Press, 1988.

Payne, Robert. *The Life and Death of Lenin*. New York: Simon & Schuster, 1964.

Pearson, Hesketh. *Merry Monarch: The Life and Likeness of Charles II*. New York: Harper & Bros., 1960.

Peters, Margot. *Bernard Shaw and the Actresses: A Biography*. New York: Doubleday and Co., 1980.

Pomeroy, Sarah. *Goddesses, Whores, Wives, and Slaves Women in Classical Antiquity*. New York: Schocken, 1975.

Richardson, Joanna. *The Courtesans: The Demimonde in Nineteenth-Century France*. New York: The World Publishing Co., 1967.

Richardson, Joanna. *Sarah Bernhardt and Her World*. New York: G.P. Putnam's Sons, 1977.

Robins, Sally Nelson. *Love Stories of Famous Virginians*. Richmond, VA: Press of the Dietz Printing Co., 1923.

Ross, Josephine. *Suitors to the Queen: The Men in the Life of Elizabeth I of England*. New York: Coward, McCann & Geoghan, Inc., 1975.

Sanger, Margaret. *Women and the New Race*. New York: Truth PublishingCo., 1920.

Schachner, Nathan. *Alexander Hamilton*. New York: Appleton-Century Crofts Co., Inc., 1946.

Sears, Hal D. *The Sex Radicals: Free Love in High Victorian America*. Lawrence, KS: The Regents Press of Kansas, 1977.

Seward, Desmond. *Napoleon's Family*. New York: Viking Press, 1986.

Shaplen, Robert. *Free Love and Heavenly Sinners*. New York: Alfred A. Knopf, 1954.

Skinner, Cornelia Otis. *Madame Sarah*. Boston: Houghton-Mifflin, 1966.

Slatzer, Robert. *The Life and Curious Death of Marilyn Monroe*. New York: Pinnacle Books, 1974.

Stassinopoulos, Arianna. *Maria Callas: The Woman Behind the Legend*. New York: Simon and Schuster, 1981.

Stearns, Monroe. *Goya and His Times*. New York: Franklin Watts, Inc., 1 966.

Stock, Noel. *The Life of Ezra Pound*. New York: Random House Inc., 1970.

Summers, Anthony. *Goddess: The Secret Lives of Marilyn Monroe*. New York: Macmillan Publishing Co., 1985.

Sunstein, Emily W. *Mary Shelley: Romance and Reality*. Boston: Little, Brown & Co., 1989.

Swanberg, W.A. *Jim Fisk: The Career of an Improbable Rascal*. New York: Charles Scribner's Sons, 1959.

Swanberg, W. A. *Sickles: The Incredible*. New York: Charles Schribner's Sons, 1956.

Sykes, Christopher Simon. *Black Sheep*. New York: The Viking Press, 1982.

Taper, Bernard. *Balanchine: A Biography*. New York: Times Books, 1984.

Thompson, Roger. *Women in Stuart England and America: A Comparative Study*. Boston: Routledge & Kegan Paul, 1974.

Tisdall, E.E.P. *Queen Victoria's Private Life (1837–1901)*. New York: The John Day Co., 1961.

Tompkins, Peter. *Shaw and Molly Tompkins*. New York: Clarkson N. Potter, 1961.

Waller, Altina L. *Reverend Beecher and Mrs. Tilton*. Amherst: University of Massachusetts Press, 1982.

Ward, Geoffrey C., ed. *Closest Companion: The Unknown Story of the Intimate Friendship Between Franklin Roosevelt and Margaret Suckley*. Boston, MA: Houghton Mifflin Company, 1995.

Weintraub, Stanley. *Victoria: An Intimate Biography*. New York: E.P. Dutton, 1987.

West, Rebecca. *Family Memories: An Autobiographical Journey*. Edited and introduced by Faith Evans. New York: Viking Penguin Inc., 1988.

Wexler, Alice. *Emma Goldman: An Intimate Life*. New York: Pantheon Books, 1984.

Wheatley, Dennis. *'Old Rowley': A Private life of Charles II*. London: Hutchinson and Co., 1933.

Whittle, Peter. *One Afternoon in Mezzegra*. Englewood Cliffs, NJ: Prentice-Hall, 1969.

Wilde, Meta Carpenter, and Orin Borsten. *A Loving Gentleman: The Love Story of William Faulkner and Meta Carpenter*. New York: Simon & Schuster, 1976.

Wilson, John Harold. *Nell Gwyn, Royal Mistress*. New York: Pellegrini and Cudahy, 1952.

Ybarra, T.R. *Caruso: The Man of Naples and the Voice of Gold*. New York: Harcourt, Brace and Company, 1953.

Zamoyski, Adam. *Chopin*. New York: Doubleday and Co., Inc., 1980.